Hemingway on Politics and Rebellion

Routledge Studies in Social and Political Thought

For a full list of titles in this series, please visit www.routledge.com

29. Post-Marxism
An Intellectual History
Stuart Sim

30. The Intellectual as Stranger
Studies in Spokespersonship
Dick Pels

31. Hermeneutic Dialogue and Social Science
A Critique of Gadamer and Habermas
Austin Harrington

32. Methodological Individualism
Background, History and Meaning
Lars Udehn

33. John Stuart Mill and Freedom of Expression
The Genesis of a Theory
K.C. O'Rourke

34. The Politics of Atrocity and Reconciliation
From Terror to Trauma
Michael Humphrey

35. Marx and Wittgenstein
Knowledge, Morality, Politics
Edited by Gavin Kitching and Nigel Pleasants

36. The Genesis of Modernity
Arpad Szakolczai

37. Ignorance and Liberty
Lorenzo Infantino

38. Deleuze, Marx and Politics
Nicholas Thoburn

39. The Structure of Social Theory
Anthony King

40. Adorno, Habermas and the Search for a Rational Society
Deborah Cook

41. Tocqueville's Moral and Political Thought
New Liberalism
M.R.R. Ossewaarde

42. Adam Smith's Political Philosophy
The Invisible Hand and Spontaneous Order
Craig Smith

43. Social and Political Ideas of Mahatma Gandi
Bidyut Chakrabarty

44. Counter-Enlightenments
From the Eighteenth Century to the Present
Graeme Garrard

45. The Social and Political Thought of George Orwell
A Reassessment
Stephen Ingle

46. Habermas
Rescuing the Public Sphere
Pauline Johnson

47. **The Politics and Philosophy of Michael Oakeshott**
Stuart Isaacs

48. **Pareto and Political Theory**
Joseph Femia

49. **German Political Philosophy**
The Metaphysics of Law
Chris Thornhill

50. **The Sociology of Elites**
Michael Hartmann

51. **Deconstructing Habermas**
Lasse Thomassen

52. **Young Citizens and New Media**
Learning for Democractic Participation
Edited by Peter Dahlgren

53. **Gambling, Freedom and Democracy**
Peter J. Adams

54. **The Quest for Jewish Assimilation in Modern Social Science**
Amos Morris-Reich

55. **Frankfurt School Perspectives on Globalization, Democracy, and the Law**
William E. Scheuerman

56. **Hegemony**
Studies in Consensus and Coercion
Edited by Richard Howson and Kylie Smith

57. **Governmentality, Biopower, and Everyday Life**
Majia Holmer Nadesan

58. **Sustainability and Security within Liberal Societies**
Learning to Live with the Future
Edited by Stephen Gough and Andrew Stables

59. **The Mythological State and its Empire**
David Grant

60. **Globalizing Dissent**
Essays on Arundhat Roy
Edited by Ranjan Ghosh and Antonia Navarro-Tejero

61. **The Political Philosophy of Michel Foucault**
Mark G.E. Kelly

62. **Democratic Legitimacy**
Fabienne Peter

63. **Edward Said and the Literary, Social, and Political World**
Edited by Ranjan Ghosh

64. **Perspectives on Gramsci**
Politics, Culture and Social Theory
Edited by Joseph Francese

65. **Enlightenment Political Thought and Non-Western Societies**
Sultans and Savages
Frederick G. Whelan

66. **Liberalism, Neoliberalism, Social Democracy**
Thin Communitarian Perspectives on Political Philosophy and Education
Mark Olssen

67. **Oppositional Discourses and Democracies**
Edited by Michael Huspek

68. **The Contemporary Goffman**
Edited by Michael Hviid Jacobsen

69. **Hemingway on Politics and Rebellion**
Edited by Lauretta Conklin Frederking

Hemingway on Politics and Rebellion

Edited by
Lauretta Conklin Frederking

Routledge
Taylor & Francis Group
NEW YORK AND LONDON

First published 2010
by Routledge
711 Third Avenue, New York, NY 10017

Simultaneously published in the UK
by Routledge
2 Park Square, Milton Park, Abingdon, Oxfordshire OX14 4RN

First issued in paperback 2014

Routledge is an imprint of the Taylor & Francis Group, an informa business

© 2010 Taylor & Francis

The right of Lauretta Conklin Frederking to be identified as author of this work has been asserted by her in accordance with sections 77 and 78 of the Copyright, Designs and Patents Act 1988.

Typeset in Sabon by IBT Global.

All rights reserved. No part of this book may be reprinted or reproduced or utilised in any form or by any electronic, mechanical, or other means, now known or hereafter invented, including photocopying and recording, or in any information storage or retrieval system, without permission in writing from the publishers.

Trademark Notice: Product or corporate names may be trademarks or registered trademarks, and are used only for identification and explanation without intent to infringe.

Library of Congress Cataloging-in-Publication Data

Hemingway on politics and rebellion / edited by Lauretta Conklin Frederking.
   p. cm.
   Includes bibliographical references and index.
   1. Hemingway, Ernest, 1899-1961—Political and social views. 2. Hemingway, Erneset, 1899–1961—Criticism and interpretation. 3. Politics in literature. 4. Politics and culture. 5. Civil war. I. Frederking, Lauretta Conklin, 1969–
   PS3515.E37H46 2010
   813'.52—dc22

ISBN 13: 978-0-415-87222-5 (hbk)
ISBN 13: 978-1-138-83329-6 (pbk)

*To my Mum, who taught me when to rebel
And to my Dad, who taught me when not to rebel
And to Clete, my Hemingway hero,
who does both so very, very well*

Contents

PART I
Introduction

1 The Rebel: Hemingway and the Struggle Against Politics   3
 LAURETTA CONKLIN FREDERKING

PART II
Hemingway in Liberal Times

2 Hemingway on Being in Our Time   19
 CATHERINE ZUCKERT

3 Hemingway, Hopelessness, and Liberalism   50
 WILLIAM CURTIS

PART III
The Politics of Morality, Manliness, and God

4 Ethics Without Theodicy in Ernest Hemingway's
 A Farewell to Arms   75
 SAYRES RUDY

5 Manly Assertion   91
 HARVEY MANSFIELD

6 Hemingway, Religion, and Masculine Virtue   104
 JOSEPH PRUD'HOMME

PART IV
The Impossibility of Politics

7 Hemingway's *For Whom the Bell Tolls*: Rebellion and
   the Meaning of Politics in the Spanish Civil War   133
   KERSTIN HAMANN

8 "The Revolutionist"   151
   DAVID WINSTON CONKLIN

9 *To Have and Have Not*: Hemingway Through the
   Lens of Theodor Adorno   171
   LAURETTA CONKLIN FREDERKING

Contributors   197
Index   199

Part I
Introduction

1 The Rebel
Hemingway and the Struggle Against Politics

Lauretta Conklin Frederking

Likely every American has read a novel or short story by Hemingway at some point in their formal education. Also likely, anyone reading this book has been driven to move beyond the required reading texts and immerse themselves a little longer with this great American writer. Hemingway captures the struggle of our lives, both the quotidian and the tragic, and nurtures a reader response that is quietly fierce. His stories do not necessarily foist the reader to battle but they do stir passion for resistance. While pondering what we might oppose, the reader participates in an intoxicating process of self-scrutiny; we want to wallow around inside ourselves hoping to find the truth, a better truth, of ourselves. Often Hemingway's protagonists are at the center of political conflict but the deeply personal unfolding of his characters immediately suggests an overriding emphasis on the private realm. Within these private realm revelations, the reader continually confronts an outsider who, through war or resistance or isolation, rebels. It may be rebellion in a national battle but just as likely it may be rebellion in sport or a marriage. However, it is precisely when the individual confronts the collective, when the private and public intersect, that Hemingway's probing insights into individual souls becomes profoundly political.

As political scientists we place politics at the center of our study. We look at politics, and more usually political institutions, as the cause of particular phenomena or alternatively we focus on politics as the outcome under investigation. Always, the collective is central to analysis. Even within a rational choice paradigm, which places the individual as the central unit of analysis, the goal is to assume the strategies of one in order to make sense of the collective. So while we study regimes in terms of the freedoms and rights they permit its citizens, we rarely consider politics as the grist or process for individual liberation. And very rarely do we move beyond the realm of what is transparently oriented toward political outcomes or behavior within a set of political institutions to locate politics *emerging*. From this perspective, Hemingway is an unusual place to focus the attention of political scientists.

As academics, we are drawn to understand change and as political scientists we scrutinize the cause and effect of politics. But to the extent that we succumb to the territorial integrity of our discipline we often miss the other places and the other ways that politics is being expressed. The 1970s feminist movement announced that the personal is political but increasingly, perhaps, we have relegated many aspects of this sentiment to historical epitaph. Studying Hemingway as an author relevant for our discipline proposes that we reconsider the meaningful boundaries of political action. On the one hand, this collection of chapters suggests that we circumscribe a much wider space of what may be politically relevant but also that we define a much more limited space of what we value as individuals from the political process.

To be clear, by Hemingway's oeuvre, Aristotle's statement is turned on its head: Rather than reinforcing man is by nature political, we find that politics is important but only as grist for an individual to discover his or her natural or authentic self. From this very different perspective, it is no longer most concerning that bowling alone suggests a decline in political participation, but it becomes most interesting that politics has driven Americans to find pleasure—no longer from competitive bowling leagues, but instead through more autonomous play independent of team uniforms, power trips, and competition. There is another point to resurrecting Putnam's (2000) well traveled analysis: New politics may not look like politics at all. As much as a decline in political participation, for example, the evidence reminds us that the places to study political change are not the transparent institutions of politics. More generally, instead of looking within new parties or interest group coalitions for political change, perhaps one needs to look under the rocks of literature or in the more isolated alleys of play to find the latent tremors pulsing toward political change. Similarly, our central figures of politics more and more frequently may not be participating in the political field at all.

The authors of this volume push forward the study of politics in unexpected places in order to present the rebel and politics emerging. Within Hemingway's work, we gain insight into what an emerging rebel is and what an emerging rebel is not. We experience the types of processes propelling the individual toward rebellion and we glean specific examples of outcomes. From *The Old Man and the Sea* (1952) we learn that the rebel fights alone. He or she embraces the battles of Nature and returns from the battle broken by conventional standards but embodying the vitality of reinforced "manliness". But while we accept the challenge of Nature, we also learn that Nature can be the escape from empty battles that occupy civil society. For Nick Adams, rebellion takes him back to nature (2003 [1972]). Throughout so many of Hemingway's novels and short stories, Nature is the noble opponent that never surrenders but offers an infinite font of wisdom about the character of the human confronting her. In these toughest moments, and often final moments, of life Hemingway's characters establish authentic identity and the characters themselves feel the importance of authenticity. Whether it is Harry Morgan in *To Have and Have Not* (1937) or the Colonel in *Across the River and Into the Trees* (1950), the dying process brings exquisite pain, a clarity of life that embraces its piquancy and respects its complexity. Similarly, to the extent that government and also society's conventions carry the rigidity of power, we suffer from exploitation but we benefit from the ripe opportunity to oppose. Regardless of regime type or ideology, we find our identity by the very act of confronting and opposing the strength and seduction of participation within these institutions. In *To Have and Have Not* (1937) and *For Whom the Bell Tolls* (1940) we realize the impossibilities of formal channels of participation in politics for our individual fulfillment.

Even if one carries a goal of reform or revolution, acquiescing participation in any of the rigid structures of exploitation including politics or economy or ideology, surrenders possibility to myth and ultimately the status quo. Hemingway's work is thick with cynicisms about government workers, the wealthy, and those who tie themselves to revolutionary ideals. However, the emerging rebel can come from these groups through any catalyst that brings awakening consciousness. Marriage, war, a bull—all of these can throttle the individual into consciousness, and awaken him or her to new possibilities of liberation. Liberation cannot be realized through a set of formal institutions but thrives from the ebb and flow between individual experience and reflection. The liberated individual is a perpetual rebel grinding against conventions and oppression to distinguish himself or herself. Liberation does not mean happiness but it does mean a rich journey of unpacking infinite potentialities.

Within this context, Hemingway affirms that politics can be a mere vehicle for discovering a better self. From this ancillary role, politics does not manifest human development as much as it propels it. Through Hemingway, we look at politics differently. Rebellion against political oppression, with consciousness, can drive people to discover more of themselves and better parts of themselves. Rebellion gains more importance not as the cause for collective political change but as an opportunity for individual realization. The complexity of experience and authenticity means that political action can fall apart or never begin. This personal and individual realization as a type of liberation cannot be imposed by a democratic constitution or a market economy; and in fact, as a regime type, democratic capitalism can be more oppressive than any other. Indeed, precisely because one is lulled into complacency rather than propelled to consciousness, democratic capitalism can be a dangerous set of political institutions. Ultimately, our authentic fulfillment cannot come through a particular political regime type, but rather, in our fight against it.

These claims that tie Hemingway's literature to the study of politics have been proposed in different ways by the scholars contributing to this volume. Each author emphasizes particular political thinkers and concepts with a specific novel or set of stories. Hemingway is understood in terms of nihilism, existentialism, Communism, liberalism, and religious ideologies. His contributions about the rebel and rebellion are framed by great political philosophers including Jean-Jacques Rousseau, Theodor Adorno, Heidegger, and Richard Rorty, as well as empirical theories of revolution. The collection of these analyses affirms Hemingway's complexity, his unique voice, and also his legitimate place at the table of political philosophy conversation.

I. HEMINGWAY: FITTING IN AND THINKING APART

Political perspectives on Hemingway and his writings include labels such as 'Communist sympathizer' (Kinnamon 1996); 'elitist' (Donaldson 1977), and 'rugged individualist' (Cooper 1987). As an American author, Hemingway's characters invite connections with "independence and manliness" (Emerson, CS No XXII in Roberson), and "man-making" (Roberson 128) as expressed by American political thinker Ralph Waldo Emerson. The emphasis on freedom, transformation, and self-reliance: That "what we are depends on what we do" (Emerson, CS No I: 211–212 in Roberson) and "our character is in our own hands" (Emerson, CS No I: 211–212 in Roberson) fits comfortably with many of Hemingway's protagonists. As Emerson's writings evolved they increasingly emphasized self-reliance as heroic (Emerson, CS No XXII in Roberson) and pushed away from society to recognize an ideal "man whose mind is poised on itself" and who "appeals to his own eye, and his own conscience" rather than to "the great names for truth"" (Emerson, CS No XXII in Roberson). In his later writings, Emerson riles against society's standards of morality that ensnare man from a genuine, liberated self. While he recommended democracy he settled on a critical view of its inevitable limitations relative to the individual: "But our institutions, though in coincidence with the spirit of the age, have not any exemption from the practical defects which have discredited other forms. Every actual State is corrupt. Good men must not obey the laws too well." (Emerson, CS No VII in Kazin 340) Similarly, he attacks political parties and the particular political parties of his time: "From neither party, when in power, has the world any benefit to expect in science, art, or humanity, at all commensurate with the resource of the nation" (Emerson, CS No VII in Kazin 341). And in sharp contrast to his criticisms of the state, he praises human nature which is undeniably capable of overcoming the inevitable corruptions of institutions. To the extent that Emerson's sermons and essays emphasize a self-development that "mirrors the political project of self-formation" (Roberson 1995, 109), his writings are a significant departure for Hemingway. Hemingway's protagonists are far removed from both the illusion and participation in the state as the place for individual fulfillment, limiting the potential importance of the politics of the state as an oppressive possibility that drives individuals into personal development.

Compared to Emerson, Hemingway's picture of politics is both bleaker in terms of oppression and therefore more promising as a catalyst for liberation. In order to reach the potentials described by Emerson, an individual can't just dwell on individual transformation but needs to confront society. Emerson's confidence rested primarily in an expectation of inner transformation combined with enlightened self-interest, but he avoids discussing the process or impact of the transformation itself. An individual necessarily confronts society's constraints and this is the place of fertile ground for Hemingway's literature. To some extent, Hemingway's characters provide vignettes of the possible manifestation of Emerson's prescriptive sermons. We see the consequences when one individual undergoes the type of transformation suggested by Emerson. Within a society of ubiquitous political and economic constraints these individuals become rebels.

While both Emerson and Hemingway convey this primary ideal trait of self-reliance, we need to look elsewhere to connect Hemingway's study of the individual's transformation, the rebellion, in order to reach and sustain self-reliance. Literary analysts who write about Hemingway and politics acknowledge the contradictions and often settle upon Hemingway's own declaration that his writing remained 'apolitical' (Kinnamon 1996). Surely it is not surprising then, that political scientists have not focused on his novels in spite of a strong and growing body of work on politics and literature. Theodor Adorno reminds us to be cautious in defining what is political:

> Art is political only when it refuses to be ideological: Not rejecting this or that ideology but the very force with which modern being becomes formed into ideology. Art's political relevance lies in its refusal to be political: "This is not a time for political works of art, but politics has migrated into autonomous works, and nowhere more so than where these seem politically dead" (Adorno 1977, quoted in Ziarek 2002, 318).

Hemingway as 'apolitical' can make sense in only a very dismissive way and in terms of the wide range of political positions held by his characters and supported by themes in his novels and short stories. However, the very complexity of political positions and apparent contradictions in supporting ideologies or themes in politics hardly suggests a lack of politics. Indeed, it is an unfortunate absence that scholars have accepted the complexity as a sign of political irrelevance and allowed Hemingway to remain unaddressed in terms of his contributions to political theory.

Compared with his contemporaries like Dos Passos for example, Hemingway's political advocacy is not consistent around a particular set of beliefs or institutions and his underlying emphasis on spontaneous pursuits of realizing the self seem poorly designed for political rigor. For example, as Jeffrey Meyers suggested "he portrayed authentic lower-class characters but did not (like most writers of the thirties) treat them from a left-wing, social-realist point of view" (Meyers 1985, 258). Yet other scholars acknowledge his writing as an advocacy of the Communist cause. Whatever ideological sympathies expressed, Hemingway's characters are individuals typically working through an ideology rather than surrendering to it. Always,

Hemingway uncover individual meaning and realization in response to the status quo which is fluid and multi-layered. Contrary to the absence of politics or irrelevance of politics, Hemingway's perspective includes statements about individuals' engagement with politics and ultimately, the place of politics in our lives.

Through emphasis on the theme of rebellion, the seeming contradictions fit comfortably and uncover a consistent ideology of politics and its role in our lives. There is no ambiguity that Hemingway's statement is political, but not in terms of a contemporary placard or responsive commentary to the politics of his time. Rather, his contribution to the understanding of politics lies in his ability to articulate the nuanced boundaries of the political domain in terms of the individual. Hemingway's characters seem to embody a nihilist drive but also the wariness about the potential oppression of nihilism just as much as other ideologies. Identity and meaning evolves from engagement through rebellion and not necessarily good citizenship, but rebellion cannot become the raison d'etre. Just as likely there can be decisions to cooperate with economic and political elites or isolate from potential comrades; either portrayal separates Hemingway from nihilism and the radical left associated with the Frankfurt school (Huhn 2004).

Whether it is in Fascist Spain, Communist Cuba, colonial Africa, U.S. hegemony, or within the matrimonial joust, Hemingway's characters discover their best and worst selves through the act of confrontation. Finding this authentic self connects so many of his character studies, and while the political grist is not the only engine for discovery, it offers a rich opportunity for transformation. The rebel emerges throughout his novels and short stories, and the acts of rebellion range from opposing current politics of very different regimes and ideologies, to romantic illusions for a past or future political arrangement, to violent confrontations focused on faith, Nature, and religion.

At the time of writing *Green Hills of Africa* in 1935, Hemingway was criticized for avoiding the political and social issues of the Depression but by 1937 he was named as the favorite non-Russian writer by a majority of leading Soviet authors (Mellow 1992, 478). In 1937, Hemingway published *To Have and Have Not* which sharply criticizes the corruption of bureaucracy, and Roosevelt's bureaucracy in particular, but also condemns the Communist cause at the same time. And even in one of his most explicitly political novels, *For Whom the Bell Tolls,* he focuses on the rebellion in individual terms of courage and bravery during battle. It is not enough to find one's place in society or to intellectually figure out the problems of one's social, economic, and political environment. These characters physically, intellectually, and spiritually become part of resisting current conditions and affirm the value of resistance, even destruction, regardless of political outcome. According to Camus, "rebellion, though apparently negative, since it creates nothing, is profoundly positive in that it reveals the part of man which must always be defended" (1991 [1956]). Like Camus,

Hemingway's writings reveal virtues within the process of rebellion. Much more than political nihilism, and closer to existentialism, rebellion allows man to realize the potentialities of his greatness as a leader, the realities of his solidarity as a comrade, and the simple sensations of everyday living.

Regardless of the particular political context in each of the novels, it is through the act of rebellion that we awaken to ourselves through feeling the possibility of our many potential selves—whether unrelenting leader wrapped in solidarity with others or corrupted individual left dying in isolation. As Zuckert points out in her essay, because humans "feel that life is good—he (Hemingway) saw—human beings try to preserve it. Failing that, they engage in violent killing—they hunt and they war—in rebellion against their inescapable fate" (Zuckert in this volume). But beyond rebellion as a reactionary coping mechanism, it is from rebellion that humans find the goodness of coming together, and affirm the goodness of life. It is through this lens of the rebel that the seeming contradictions in Hemingway's political teachings become much less problematic. For him, the political settings, whether Communist, Fascist, imperialist, or capitalist, are merely the context and ripe opportunities for the more righteous political act of rebellion. And the outcome of the rebellion is not necessarily, nor even likely, a better political world, but perhaps instead a less disillusioned, more authentic individual. In rebellion, we feel a self-defined meaning of life, and while it is transitory it gives man/woman his or her worth and becomes a worthy goal. For humans to find and define meaning it must be through rebellion against these realities rather than compliance with them. Rebellion becomes an important step in the authentication of self, and so it is precisely the discontent with politics that becomes a foundation for self-creation and self-realization.

This volume embraces the very complexity of political advocacy in Hemingway's novels and short stories in order to penetrate a very consistent perspective about politics—put simply, that the act of rebellion against our status quo defines the most important role of politics in our lives because it defines the relevance of politics for developing our authentic selves. The contributing authors resolve apparent complexity in the political meaning of Hemingway's writing with a focus on the underlying shared themes of political rebellion and individual identity formation. Rather than convergence around a set of particular political outcomes or a particular regime type, the cast of Hemingway's characters share pursuit of their individual identity and social meaning through confrontation with the status quo. Certainly, the political content of his novels including interstate war, civil war, Fascism, Communism, capitalism, gender identity, and nationalism makes Hemingway relevant within the study of politics. The inability to locate Hemingway's novels and characters consistently in terms of a political ideology or set of institutions perhaps explains why he has been unattended in political analysis.

In the process of articulating the relevance and boundaries of man in relation to the political world, Hemingway's writings convey a good deal of disillusionment with politics and cynicism about the possibilities from any political system. More generally, "it was not the sentimental view of civilization however, that Hemingway espoused in writing. Instead, his symbol was the image of a garbage scow, piled high and foul-smelling, dumping the refuse of society into deep waters" (Mellow, 458). Any truth of human meaning remains apart from politics, but often requires individuals to engage in politics precisely in order to confront disillusionment and desperation of life.

II. HEMINGWAY IN LIBERAL TIMES

Zuckert's chapter introduces many of the themes that are the foundation for this volume. For Hemingway, despite the fact that the goodness of life is found in Nature, Nature cannot be the basis for enduring community. Because humans are sensitive, the foundation of any social contract begins to erode and becomes empty if not oppressive. Similarly, however, government cannot resolve the tensions from a Hobbesian 'war of all against all'. Hemingway reveals disillusionment with politics: Politics most often becomes an institution that permits primitive feelings of hostility to be realized with impunity. Whether liberal or Communist, government cannot become the place where rights are found and secured, but nor is it the source of the problem.

As Zuckert points out, in terms of rights and community this conflict with both Nature and politics is problematic except that Hemingway teaches us that the truth about human life comes from confrontation (most especially with one's own death) and then finding some satisfaction in this life. While struggle with Nature cannot bind us, and while it cannot *endure* as truth for each one of us, it can provide temporary meaning. Retreat to Nature is not safe and peaceful, but it is less vicious, less disillusioning and despairing than political life. In this volume, Curtis extends the theme of a return to Nature drawing a connection between Jean-Jacques Rousseau and Hemingway's nostalgia for Nature and retreat from formal politics. He filters Hemingway through Richard Rorty's modern political project to establish liberal justice through deliberative institutions. Because art fosters identity, it can be a critical part of a political project, in this case liberalism. Curtis concludes that Hemingway's anti-intellectualism challenges speech and thought as a remedy for man's crisis with politics. In his study of Hemingway's critique of politics and its corrupting effects, he finds Rousseau a more comfortable ally for Hemingway's fiction. Hemingway's hopelessness about the political sphere of activities may not be compatible with liberalism but perhaps remains a relevant voice especially for today's reader.

III. THE POLITICS OF MORALITY, MANLINESS, AND GOD

Rudy explores the morality guiding an American rebel characterized in *Farewell to Arms* and concludes that Hemingway expresses a very human "politics of subjective striving". This chapter probes the legitimacy but also complexity of morality without ideology and without theodicy. The novel "condemns mass political, institutionalized behavior for destroying human speech, action, subjectivity, and meaning itself". Through his rawness and rejection of ideals as well as formal politics, Lieutenant Henry embodies a version of rebellion that resurrects interpersonal intimacies and innocence. Within the attack of these empty tales and promises, there is the possibility of re-humanization or the re-creation of an authentic self.

Mansfield and Prud'homme focus on Hemingway and his study of Man's struggle to conquer Nature and/or God, and the humanization and re-humanization as he fails. Nature and God tempt man to rebel, and in the process of unfolding defeat, Man realizes his vulnerabilities along with his virtues. From the earlier discussions of Hemingway it is clear that there is a tension between ideals and the actualization of ideals in terms of human fulfillment. If ideals could be realized successfully it would defeat the possibility of further development. Discontent and the pain from struggle is fundamental to the human condition but through rebellion, the subsequent identity formation is part of human triumph. From Mansfield "the manly man stubbornly insists on himself. Not only is he manly, but he also represents the need for manly men" (this volume, 97). Mansfield's study of Santiago in *The Old Man and the Sea* (1952) draws parallels between this type of non-political manly assertion and the political manifestation of manly assertion through the example of Achilles. Manliness means unconventional virtue, risk, and connecting oneself to the gods. Hemingway pushes our understanding of the ways that gods become necessary for manliness but also get in the way as their presence seems to demand supplication.

Prud'homme's chapter focuses more specifically on the relationship between manliness and man's relationship with a Christian God. Whereas Mansfield emphasized the conquest in order to fully develop 'manliness', Prud'homme addresses the extent to which his characters surrender to God and into 'manliness'. Prud'homme's argument unfolds in a way that reinforces the individual and human power, precisely when an individual subjects himself or herself to higher accountability. Prud'homme presents Hemingway's hero as a Christian ideal of manliness that is appropriate for the post-feminist world. This vision of masculinity challenges two other modern visions of religious manliness—Mel Gibson's violent Christ in *The Passion* and the Promise Keepers movement. This is a Christian perspective that elevates individualistic ruggedness and self-sacrifice in ways that are compatible with Catholic doctrine as well as the underlying theme of rebellion. *For Whom the Bell Tolls, The Old Man and the Sea,* and 'Today is Friday' frame this conceptualization of masculinity at the same time that they affirm Hemingway's profoundly Christian, specifically Catholic, sentiment. In this way, self-sacrifice is a form of rebelling against oneself, one's preservation and interests.

IV. THE IMPOSSIBILITY OF POLITICS

Hamann, Conklin, and Frederking address the role of political ideals and ideologies within Hemingway's novels and short stories. Hamman's chapter explores disillusionment in one of Hemingway's most explicitly political novels, For Whom the Bell Tolls. Ernest Hemingway began to write For Whom the Bell Tolls in 1939, towards the end of the Spanish civil war that had begun in 1936 between the supporters of the Republic and the Nationalist troops, led by Francisco Franco. Hemingway's text reveals the loss of individualism if one prioritizes ideology yet the camaraderie and love through the participation of politics and rebellion in particular. The novel raises questions about the political aftermath of a democracy when individualism is suppressed in the process of reaching it. This chapter reinforces the temporary status of any one rebellion and war as a source for individual meaning and collectively meaningful political development. There is no 'right' political outcome that can satisfy human meaning and there is no political solution to prevent human yearning. The virtues of rebellion contribute to an untenable political conclusion that at the very best, begins the cycle of rebellion once again.

Conklin raises the question of the rationality of the rebel. Hemingway defines boundaries about revolutionary behavior that extend beyond political science explanations. Within the social sciences we have seminal macro level theories that explain revolution in terms of economic and political conditions relative to capitalist production and conditions of relative deprivation. At the micro level, theories explain revolutions in terms of rational calculations, thresholds, and tipping points. None of these theories adequately address the individual who may be a key frontrunner for a wider rebellion, or the revolutionist as terrorist for example. Hemingway offers the essential insight about the individual rebel that is beyond existing theories, macro or micro, and Conklin argues that the matador, the solider, and revolutionist share this same characteristic of the will to fight. For some the will to fight is hard wired but for others, the "born-again warriors", it can emerge spontaneously like Francis in "The Short Happy Life of Francis Macomber". The potential ordinariness of this type of rebel carries through Hemingway's oeuvre. Conklin draws the relevance of these character insights about the rebel in terms of recent demographic analysis of suicide terrorists for example. Quite apart from rationality, these rebels push beyond calculations, in spite of defeat, and against existing politics much more than toward a new set of political possibilities. In an interesting shift away from the focus of existing theories on the causes of revolution, Conklin draws out Hemingway's emphasis on the importance of fighting as the cause of the personal realization of inequalities and oppression. This process of self-discovery awakens the emerging rebel into a more determined will to fight.

Frederking concludes the volume with an analysis of To Have and Have Not (2003 [1937]) through the lens of Theodor Adorno's political philosophy. Adorno writes about liberation in terms of individual autonomy, authenticity, and reflectivity. Liberation is not a political manifestation but confronting political rigidities and ideology can be the grist for its realization. *To Have and Have Not* conveys many of the problems described by Adorno and endemic to political and economic system regardless of regime type. Similarly, Hemingway conveys the insurmountable challenges of all political ideals and ideologies manifest in political institutions but also fought for through revolutions. The protagonist Harry Morgan embodies the challenges of these systems but also the qualities of autonomy, authenticity, and reflectivity. With autonomy, authenticity, and reflectivity an individual carves out a private space for liberation that is necessarily apart from politics. At the same time, the wrestle against politics, the rebellion, can be a critical step to reach the consciousness necessary for autonomy, authenticity, and reflectivity. The central character of Harry Morgan turns from fishing to smuggling between Cuba and Key West. His entrance into the world of illegal contraband that includes drugs, people, and stolen goods is juxtaposed with his family relationships—the picture presents the honest and loving family man turned criminal. Ultimately, Harry's fate becomes tied to the Cuban revolutionaries he is transporting. They too have fallen from the ideals of the revolution entering a criminal spiral of stealing and killing and their fate has similarly become tied to Harry, the American capitalist who is carrying them on his boat.

In a critique of capitalism, and the winners and losers that it produces, Hemingway visits a theme common to his writing. In *To Have and Have Not*, the story of desperation, corruption, and criminality within capitalism is paralleled by the story of desperation, corruption, and criminality of the Cuban revolutionaries. Ultimately, if government cannot nurture, and cannot even protect, then how does an individual find purpose and meaning? Ultimately, politics with all of its limits becomes a focus for man to discover his power and passion through rebellion. However, the rebellion offers only that: transitory, albeit temporarily satisfying emotions of passion and sometimes conquest, rather than realizing political ideals. In *To Have and Have Not* the rebellion is revealed in criminal acts and while the criminal acts are justified by the almost mythical political goals, the process takes the protagonists further away from the possibility of reaching those goals. Throughout the process of rebellion Harry Morgan affirms his autonomy and discovers new authentic dimensions of himself at the same time that ideals begin to slip away.

V. HEMINGWAY: A POLITICAL AUTHOR FOR OUR TIMES

These chapters present the importance of rebellion against politics, whether democracy, Communist, or Fascist, and collectively the essays draw attention to the limits of politics in realizing the ideals that drive rebellion. As

Hemingway's writings suggest, politics is not truthful and one cannot realize ideal beliefs and hopes through a political system. Politics cannot bring people together, nor can it bring meaning to life itself. Politics is about manipulation, contradiction, and frustration. Underlying the very critique of politics, however, is recognition that it can also be the source for finding authenticity—not through compliance, not through chance, but through the outright challenge. By fighting what is clearly false and vicious one can discover the emotional if not rational possibility for authenticity, solidarity, and virtue. And Hemingway seems to suggest that even if this is transitory and not Truth in some metaphysical sense, it feels valid to the individual and this may be good enough. Passions emerge from the fight and affirm the human-ness of relationships in contrast with the emptiness and falseness of political power. From Hemingway's writings, politics are the engine for human development not through the success of legislation and organization, but rather through confrontation against the system however it exists. In this way, politics can never be the solution for human development and government will never be the setting for the most purposeful realization of human potential and authenticity except through its invitation for rebellion and challenge.

One needs only to reflect on recent U.S. elections to realize the relevance of Hemingway's political perspective for our young people today. In the last decade millions of young voters picked up a political cause and defined themselves by this new dimension of political participation. Regardless of party politics, the sharply rising levels of different types of participation by the youth celebrated the possibilities of political citizenship. Then there was the reality that much of this mobilization was focused around the phenomenon of winning a particular election and the myth of ubiquitous change. Tough lessons follow from defeat. Just as quickly as students had jumped into political participation, they receded from the political process. Teaching on a college campus I hear again and again that students felt (or feel depending on party allegiance) emotionally and intellectually defeated and this defined their political participation—winners or losers in the political game. So many of Hemingway's stories include (political) defeats and his significant message comes through in the meaning of the battle for the individual realizing self. The loss may carry relevance in terms of new political outcomes on the macro level, but the macro level is significant only to the extent that it creates a different backdrop for individual exploration and development through struggle.

For Hemingway, the battle is within and politics remains grist for self-study and authentication. Any political loss may be victory for the self. For an apathetic generation Hemingway's work is a call to discover a necessary place for politics in self transformation and self-realization. Max Horkheimer's signed "Alright" as an apparent parody of American complacency" (Rubin 2002, 175). If we admit Hemingway's own declarative label as apolitical, we must understand that he does not mean 'Alright' and apolitical does not mean apathetic. Through his novels and short stories we understand the importance of political engagement without blind adherence to a particular set of outcomes. Hemingway's mother spoke of him: "When Ernest gets through this period he's going through of fighting himself and everybody else, and turns his energy toward something positive, he will be a fine man." (Mellow 1992, 123). Like the author, Hemingway's characters are a study of the rebel and the meaning of rebellion as a process for living—as a mode of being.

Finally, we are reminded that academe invites territorially defined boundaries around our subject. As political scientists we study politics. However, bringing Hemingway to the table of political philosophy reminds us that politics can be found in more interesting places and in more interesting ways than our traditional divisions of labor. Furthermore, this volume insists on a consideration of political rebellion and the emerging political rebel in the experiences outside of formal politics. It follows then that we cannot rely solely on our tools or ways of thinking about political science to understand politics. While art may not be wholly determinative it can open our eyes to new ways of seeing politics.

> Such art is neither political nor apolitical but, rather, political otherwise, otherwise than what society would like to define and "preserve" as the meaning of the political. In this phrase, "political otherwise", I want to capture the force with which art can capsize in its aesthetic space not just this or that political order but, rather, the very order of politics (Ziarek 2002, 349).

Rebellion is not a necessary evil on the path to goodness and a particular outcome. It is through Hemingway's characters we find purpose beyond specific political goals and outcomes. The type of political engagement can be a perpetual struggle against the status quo, whatever the status quo, and rebellion in order to find one's potential and perhaps realize a part of the human condition.

WORKS CITED

Adorno, Theodor. "Commitment." In *Aesthetics and Politics: Debates between Bloch, Lukacs, Brecht, Benjamin, Adorno*. Edited by Ronald Taylor, 177–195. London: New Left Books, 1977.

Camus, Albert. *The Rebel: An Essay on Man in Revolt*, New York: Vintage International, 1991 [1956].

Cooper, Stephen. *The Politics of Ernest Hemingway*. Ann Arbor, MI: UMI Research Press, 1987.

Donaldson, Scott. *By Force of Will: The Life and Art of Ernest Hemingway*. New York: Viking, 1977.

Emerson, Ralph Waldo. "Politics." In *Essays: Second Series*. Introduction by Alfred Kazin, 333–348. Cambridge: Harvard University Press, 1979.

———. *Selected Sermons*. Quoted in Susan L. Roberson. *Emerson in His Sermons A Man-Made Self*. Columbia: University of Columbia Press, 1995.

Hemingway, Ernest. *Green Hills of Africa*, New York: Charles Scribner's Sons, 1935.

Huhn, John. "Introduction: Thoughts Besides Themselves." In *The Cambridge Companion to Adorno*, edited by Tom Huhn, 1–18. Cambridge: Cambridge University Press, 2004.

———. *To Have and Have Not*, New York: P. F. Colliers and Son, 1937.

———. *For Whom the Bell Tolls*. New York: Charles Scribner's Sons, 2003 [1940].

———. *Across the River and Into the Trees*. New York: Charles Scribner's Sons, 1950.

———. *The Old Man and the Sea*. New York: Scribner, 1952.

———. *The Nick Adams Stories*. New York: Charles Scribner's Sons, 2003 [1972].

———. *A Farewell to Arms*. New York: Charles Scribner's Sons, 1929.

Kinnamon, Keith. "Hemingway and Politics," in *The Cambridge Companion to Hemingway*, edited by Scott Donaldson, 149–169. Cambridge: Cambridge University Press, 1996.

Mellow, J. R. *Hemingway: A Life Without Consequences*, Reading, MA: Perseus Books, 1992.

Meyers, J. *Hemingway: A Biography*, New York: Harper and Row, 1985.

Putnam, Robert. *Bowling Alone: The Collapse and Revival of American Community*. New York: Simon and Schuster, 2000.

Roberson, Susan L. *Emerson in His Sermons: A Man-Made Self*. Columbia and London: University Press, 1995.

Rubin, Andrew. "The Adorno Files." In *Adorno: A Critical Reader*. Edited by Nigel Gibson and Andrew Rubin, 172–190. Oxford: Blackwell Publishers, 2002.

Ziarek, Krzysztof. "Radical Art: Refelctions After Adorno and Heidegger." In *Adorno: A Critical Reader*, edited by Nigel Gibson and Andrew Rubin, 341–360. Oxford: Blackwell Publishers, 2002.

Zuckert, C. *Natural Right and the American Imagination: Political Philosophy in Novel Form*, Savage: Rowman and Littlefield, 1990.

Part II
Hemingway in Liberal Times

2 Hemingway on Being in Our Time

Catherine Zuckert

The United States began with a rebellion. The colonists thought it necessary to justify their actions with a Declaration of Independence, and in this declaration, the Americans famously announced:

> We hold these truths to be self-evident, that all men are created equal, that they are endowed by their Creator with certain unalienable Rights, that among these are Life, Liberty, and the pursuit of Happiness.—That to secure these rights, Governments are instituted among Men, deriving their just powers from the consent of the governed,—That whenever any Form of Government becomes destructive of these ends, it is the Right of the People to alter or to abolish it, and to institute new Government, laying its foundation on such principles and organizing its powers in such form, as to them shall seem most likely to effect their Safety and Happiness. All men are created equal; that they are endowed by their Creator with certain inalienable rights; that among these rights are life, liberty, and the pursuit of happiness.

Reflecting both the content and movement of this fundamental statement of American political principles, classic nineteenth century American novels like the Leatherstocking tales, *Moby Dick,* and *Adventures of Huckleberry Finn* depicted the withdrawal of their protagonists from civil society back to a "state of nature" when they felt their lives, liberties, and happiness threatened, as well as their attempts to find and reconstitute a better form of communal relations (Zuckert 1990).[1]

Like James Fenimore Cooper, Herman Melville, and Mark Twain, in his Nick Adams stories (1972) Ernest Hemingway showed that not only human relations outside the law, but the whole of nature constituted a Hobbesian "war of all against all" (Young 1966).[2] But in opposition to both the American literary tradition and the social contract theory inherent in the American founding, Hemingway denied that human beings can remove or protect themselves from this deadly combat by promising to obey a government, which would then act to secure their rights. Nor did Hemingway think that humans could find solace and support in private, through (male) companionship or marriage. The reason in all cases was the same. By nature, human beings are sensitive animals; and their natural feelings are essentially transitory. Any oath, commitment, or contract based on such natural feelings will, therefore, eventually find its source or foundation eroded; any institution, partnership, or compact based on perfectly natural desires and passions will inevitably become an empty, external, oppressive shell. There is no natural basis for any enduring form of human community—public or private—because we all live and die essentially alone.

In questioning both the basis and the conclusion of the classic American story (and thus the principles embedded in it), Hemingway made four fundamental changes in it. First, he reversed the direction of the movement or action. "Heroes" like Natty Bumppo, Ishmael, and Huck traveled from civil society to the state of nature; Hemingway's semi-autobiographical protagonist Nick Adams summers in the Michigan woods, runs away from home to join the war in Europe, and then returns home to find peace and satisfaction living all by himself in the state of nature (Baker 1969).[3] For Hemingway, that which is good in human life is to be found in nature. Characterized by a cycle of birth and death, nature is the beginning and the end.

Second, where the protagonists of Cooper, Melville, and Twain's classic novels were essentially solitary figures, Hemingway showed Nick maturing to become a husband and father. Like Twain (and Rousseau), Hemingway believed that human beings find pleasure and satisfaction simply in feeling alive—*le sentiment de son existence* or *amour de soi*, as Rousseau called it. But Hemingway also recognized that such pleasures are transitory. Human beings prefer company—especially the company of members of the opposite sex—to solitude (Hemingway 1927a, 110).[4] Like the sheer satisfaction in feeling alive, however, sexual attraction is also based on a transient sensation. It does not provide a firm foundation for lasting social relations. Sexual relations do result in the next generation of children. And most parents—unlike Pap—do love their children. But natural procreation does not enable human beings to overcome the essentially transitory character of life any more than marriage itself does. On the contrary, having children forces people to think about the future, and so reminds them of their own inescapable future as individuals—or their own inevitable deaths.

Third, where Natty, Ishmael, and Huck are shown to have experienced not only the liberty and equality but also the insecurity of human life in the state of nature in the forest or on the sea or river, Hemingway shows Nick discovering this fundamental truth about human life in war (Young 1966, 40).[5] Facing the immediate possibility of his own death for the first time, Nick realizes that human beings all live—because they all die—essentially alone. No one can truly die for another; no political organization can really secure anyone's right to life.

In light of the truth revealed in war, the promises involved in the social contract and the institutions erected on it appear to be fundamentally false. Hemingway thus introduced a fourth, generational difference into the classic American story. In earlier versions, the protagonist or narrator himself had withdrawn from civil society to live in the state of nature. But in Hemingway's Nick Adams stories, it is the hero's father—a doctor—who flees the Chicago suburbs to raise his son during the summer in the North Michigan woods. The hope that Americans can establish a better life for themselves by beginning anew in nature belongs to the past generation, Hemingway is suggesting, if not to the past century.

I. POSTWAR DISILLUSIONMENT

Hemingway's first collection of Nick Adams stories clearly reflects the disillusionment with the results of liberal political experiments that were prevalent following World War I. Like his protagonist, Hemingway himself left the United States to join the Red Cross as an ambulance driver in Europe, and he stayed there after its conclusion. Unlike most of the European artists with whom he associated, however, Hemingway did not let his political disillusionment degenerate into complete cynicism or nihilism. On the contrary, in the concluding story of his first collection, he affirmed that human life is in and by nature good.

Since he admitted that the goodness of immediate or natural sensation is transitory, Hemingway's stance was obviously problematic. To bring out both the merits and the difficulties involved in this affirmation of the goodness of nature in the face of an historical disillusionment with politics, in the concluding section of this chapter I will contrast Hemingway's position with that of the German philosopher Martin Heidegger.[6]

Like Hemingway, Heidegger was writing to a people who were disillusioned with liberal politics. Further like Hemingway, Heidegger argued that the truth about human life is revealed only through a direct confrontation with the possibility of one's own death. In light of that most fundamental of alienating experience—both American novelist and German philosopher agreed—ordinary social and political institutions appear empty and inauthentic. Whereas Hemingway returned to nature to find some satisfaction in life, Heidegger argued that human life is not merely a matter of transient sensations: It is essentially temporal and should be understood as such. Heidegger's insistence that human life be understood in terms of history rather than nature had even worse political implications than Hemingway's retreat into nature, however. The comparison between the American novelist and the German philosopher thus brings out the crisis of natural rights theory in the twentieth century in the opposition between nature and history.

22 *Catherine Zuckert*

II. ON THE DEATH OF GOD—*IN OUR TIME*

Hemingway wrote the disjunction between individual, personal experience or life (nature) and external, political events or history into the very organization of his first collection of short stories, which he entitled *In Our Time*.[7] There is no unified or unifying narrative. Instead, each story is introduced and separated from the others by an historical vignette (See also Kort 1980, 582).[8]

Despite the fractured and apparently disordered surface, the collection of stories does have a clear organization (Slabey 1983; Burhazns 1983; Benson 1983; Lee 1983; Hoffman and Hoffmann 1983, 99–114).[9] In the first half, each story of a boy's growing up in America is prefaced by a scene from World War I (Hagemann 1980, 255–261).[10] In the second half, each story of a young American's attempt to come to terms with the alienating truth learned in war is introduced by a bullfighting scene. As Hemingway later observed in *Death in the Afternoon*, bullfighting is the art of confronting death par excellence (Cooper 1987, 23).[11]

By introducing the story of a young boy's growing up in the hinterlands of the United States with scenes from the war in Europe, Hemingway clearly intends that his readers consider the relation between the two (Cooper 1987, 23).[12] Americans had fought World War I "to make the world safe for democracy." But, Hemingway suggests, their experiences in that war raised questions about the promise and foundations of American democracy itself. According to the Declaration of Independence, governments are instituted to secure their citizens' rights to life, liberty, and the pursuit of happiness. As the phenomenon of war illustrates so vividly, liberal governments do not and cannot actually achieve what they promise. On the contrary, they lead human beings to their deaths. Hemingway thus prefaces the last story in each half of the collection with a vignette describing not the war or bullfighting, but the operation of the American criminal justice system. Rather than secure life—he implies—the institution of government merely allows certain human beings to act out their hostility toward others with impunity (Hemingway 1932).[13]

In the Declaration Jefferson claims that America's government will be based on "the law of nature and nature's God." But Hemingway indicates in the title of his first collection that, for people in the twentieth century, God is dead. Like many of the titles that he would select for his later novels, *In Our Time* has not only a literary, but also a religious, source. "Give us peace in our time," the Book of Common Prayer beseeches. In light of its World War I setting, Hemingway's title is clearly ironic. There certainly was cause to seek assistance from on high; and in the seventh preface, Hemingway shows a soldier praying to Jesus while under bombardment at Fossalta. If Jesus would only save him, the soldier promises, he will serve as a witness; he will spread the gospel, "the good news" (Baker 1969, 115–116).[14] But when the soldier does survive, Hemingway reports, he goes straight to a whorehouse and says nothing to anybody about Jesus. People in our time do not really believe that there is a God with the power to bring peace.

If God is dead, as Nietzsche dramatically announced, establishing peace and order has become especially difficult in our time, because there is no transcendent or enduring foundation for politics or morality (Reynolds 1981, 163).[15] All life is transitory; and Hemingway's book reflects that transitoriness insofar as it depicts disjointed, although intense, incidents, sensations, and experiences (Johnston 1984, 28–34).[16]

III. NICK'S ADVENTURES IN THE STATE OF NATURE

In the stories that lead up to his protagonist's being wounded at Fossalta, Hemingway depicts the events or experiences that have caused Nick, like Ishmael at the beginning of *Moby Dick,* to question the value of life altogether. Like Ishmael, Nick thus withdraws from civil society. But, Hemingway shows, life in the state of nature where Nick grows up is not altogether humanly satisfying.

Just as the American troops marching to Champagne in the first vignette are about to be initiated into deadly battle without any real preparation, so in the first story Nick is unintentionally introduced to the mysterious interrelation between life and death (Wilson 1952, 123).[17] When the doctor takes his son along to the Indian camp where he is expecting to deliver a baby by caesarean section, he wants to show Nick the marvels of modern medicine. In fact, the doctor confronts his son with the ineradicable connection between birth and death.

While the squaws attempt to help the woman in the cabin, the men all move far enough away so that they will no longer hear her screams. When Nick asks if his father can give the woman something to stop her screaming, the doctor explains that he has no anesthetic. "Her screams are not important. I don't hear them because they are not important" (Hemingway 1925, 17).[18] Having washed his hands and boiled the instruments, the doctor proceeds to deliver the baby with a jackknife. "That's one for the medical journal," he tells his brother George, who is waiting in attendance. "Oh, you're a great man, all right," George sarcastically responds. The doctor is elated by his success and in a talkative mood until he decides that he "ought to have a look at the proud father," who has been lying—wounded in the leg—in the bunk above his birthing wife. "They're usually the worst sufferers in these little affairs," the doctor observes. "I must say he took it all pretty quietly" (20). Having slit his throat open with a razor, the father could not very well have made much noise.

The screams do matter to those who hold themselves responsible for the pain and even to those, without responsibility, who simply care about the suffering of a loved one. Medicine cannot cure all, perhaps not even the most important kinds of suffering, Hemingway suggests, because modern science cannot explain, much less prevent, human death.[19]

The doctor is now sorry that he brought his son along, and tries to reassure him.

> "Do many men kill themselves, Daddy?" Nick asked. "Is dying hard . . . ?"
> "No, I think it's pretty easy, Nick. It all depends."

Neither the conversation nor the incident seem to have much impact on Nick, however, for the story concludes: "Nick trailed his hand in the water. It felt warm in the sharp chill of the morning. In the early morning on the lake sitting in the stem of the boat with his father rowing, he felt quite sure that he would never die" (21).

The first and most fundamental lesson that Nick must learn has to do with the inevitability of his own death. He eventually learns this lesson in war; but going to war and learning this lesson do not happen immediately. Nick goes abroad in search of adventure only after he has become dissatisfied and disillusioned with life up in the Michigan woods. Unfortunately, Nick's father provides an all too good model of disillusionment.

The cabin in the upper peninsula of Michigan where Nick receives much of his formative education is on a lake not far from a lumber mill. Every year, in the process of being towed to the mill, some of the logs come loose from the "boom" and drift to the beach. The lumber companies do mark the logs in case they decide to come back and claim them, but it is not clear that it would actually pay to hire a crew for this purpose. Assuming that it would not and that the logs would simply become waterlogged and rot if nobody used them, the doctor hires Indians to come down from the camp and split them into firewood.

Spoilage constitutes a natural limitation on the right of acquisition or property, as John Locke argued; by nature, a man has a right only to what he can use, because he literally cannot keep or possess goods that are rotting (1952, ch. 5).[20] This natural limitation has been overcome, however, first, by the invention of money (which does not spoil) and, second, by the laws of property.

Taking advantage of the ambiguous relation between natural and conventional right in this situation of the lumber on the lakeshore, a half-breed named Dick Boulton reminds the doctor that, strictly speaking, the log he is working on belongs to the company of White and McNally.

> "Don't get huffy, Doc," the Indian taunted. "I don't care who you steal from."
> "If you think the logs are stolen," the doctor responded, "take your stuff and get out."

Unable to answer such a challenge to his moral authority, the doctor loses not only the wood, but also the labor that the Indian owes him in exchange for treating his squaw the previous winter. And then the doctor makes himself ridiculous by threatening to use physical force.

> "If you call me Doc once again, I'll knock your eye teeth down your throat."
> "Oh, no, you won't, Doc."
> Dick Boulton looked at the doctor. Dick was a big man. He knew how big a man he was. He liked to get into fights (28).

Where there is no appeal to law, Hemingway shows, appeals degenerate into contests of physical force.

Unwilling to concede that might makes right even if he can see no clear alternative, the doctor retreats. Returning to the cabin, he busies himself not with reading the stack of medical journals lying unopened on the floor, but rather with cleaning his gun. He could have used his technical knowledge or equipment "to even up the sides," readers are reminded. The doctor's refusal to fight does not stem so much from physical incapacity or fear as from principle. Should a doctor dedicated to relieving pain and preserving life threaten it in order to assert his own economic interest?

Unfortunately, the doctor no longer believes entirely in the validity of his vocation. He does not even demand that his wife recognize its value. Although she is in bed with a perpetual headache, she never looks to him for a cure. She is a Christian Scientist, and the doctor would apparently not have his wife act against her own beliefs any more than the doctor would have the half-breed chop wood that he thinks was stolen.

The doctor does not assert himself because he himself does not know what is right. Thinking that no one else does either, he sees only one way to prevent differences of opinion and interest from degenerating into conflict and injury: refusing to fight. He thus repeatedly retreats—from the Chicago suburbs where he had a private practice, from the rude Indian, from his wife—to hunt in the woods. He is indeed rather like Ishmael, who went to sea in order to avoid knocking off heads—his own included. The doctor is trying to escape his despairing sense that no life may be worth living—or worth saving—and that his science and vocation are therefore a bitter irony.

Finding his son reading in the woods, the doctor dutifully relates his wife's message: "Your mother wants you to come and see her." But Nick responds, "I want to go with you." At this point, the son gladly joins his father in running off. Whereas a boy can be thoroughly absorbed in the pleasure not only of the hunt itself but also of an escape from constraining authority, if only temporarily, a man cannot. The implicit question is whether the boy will continue to follow his father into the ultimate retreat (suicide) or whether Nick will find some way of affirming the value of life.

When Hemingway next presents Nick in "The End of Something," he is no longer an innocent boy.[21] He has experienced love and discovered that it does not last. He thus faces the unpleasant task of ending an affair with an absolutely unsuspecting girl named Marjorie, with whom (we learn in the following story) he had genuinely and generously discussed marriage. "It isn't fun any more," he tells her. "Not any of it" (40). "Isn't love any fun?" Marjorie asks. "No," Nick answers. Marjorie leaves with great dignity, and Nick is left to seek solace and support from his friend Bill.

But neither male camaraderie nor the assertion of masculine strength and independence suffice to assuage Nick's sense of emptiness and loss.[22] Ironically, he finds relief only when Bill worries that Nick "might get back into it again. Nick had not thought about that. It had seemed so absolute . . . . He felt happy now. There was not anything that was irrevocable" (59).

Just as his experience in the Indian camp involved an unexpected lesson that Nick did not want to learn, so, too, does the affair with Marge. All human passions are transitory; feelings die as absolutely as their authors. But if human attachments and commitments—and perhaps even contracts (recall the half-breed Boulton's breach of faith)—must be based on feelings in order to be genuine, true, and effective, then such commitments are fundamentally unreliable, whatever the present intentions of the parties, because feelings change and passions grow cold. The past is irrevocable; and the future, beyond planning and control.

In fact, Nick does not pick up the affair again. He had been planning to get a job and marry Marge, even though, as Bill reminds him, she comes from a distinctly lower class family. Disillusioned by his parents' empty marriage, Nick does not act on the basis of calculation or convention. He acts out of real feeling; but when that feeling evaporates, he does not know what to do. Having no direction in his life, Hemingway shows us in the subsequent story, Nick decides to bum around.

When Nick leaves home to travel abroad on his own, he quickly discovers that human beings do not hurt others merely from incapacity or indifference. Like the brakeman who knocks Nick off the train, they may enjoy inflicting pain. They may even inflict it out of affection, as Ad Frances's black companion Bugs does when he blackjacks the ex-fighter to prevent him from going crazy. In either case, there is a certain assertion of control and superiority. Caretaking itself (whether in the name of property rights of the railroad or in the name of friendship) often seems merely to provide a justification for violence.[23]

Camping in the woods to avoid towns, the little white boxer (who looks childlike in repose) with his big black companion cannot but remind readers of Huck and Jim. If these two friends that Nick meets are not currently fugitives from the law, then they are at least ex-convicts. But the life of these modern hobos is hardly pastoral or idyllic; and the things that

Nick learns from them about life outside the bounds of civil society are not pretty.

Like Jim in the previous century, the big black man preserves the external marks of the conventional inequality between the races by assiduously addressing both whites as "mister." Nevertheless, Bugs is clearly in control. Whereas Huck was the one who went into town to buy or "borrow" supplies for his friend on the river, Bugs does all the shopping. It is Bugs who invites Nick to join them for supper, and Bugs decides when Nick should go. The black apparently manages the money that Ad's ex-wife sends him; he most certainly manages the ex-fighter himself, with the blackjack.

Once again, Hemingway reminds his readers, force rules when people put themselves outside the range of legal protection. Unfortunately, he also shows, the law does not protect people's rights to life, liberty, and the pursuit of happiness very well in civil society, either. The law had, for example, allowed another manager to put Ad in so many fights that his brain became as mutilated as his face. According to Bugs, however, what really drove Ad crazy, caused him to be hitting everyone, and therefore got him expelled from society was not his beatings so much as the breakup of his marriage. Looking very much like Ad, his manager/wife had been written up in the newspapers as his sister. When they got married, there was a lot of ugliness about incest in the newspapers. And eventually she left.[24]

If force rules in Nature, conventional opinion rules in society; and neither genuine affection nor willingness to fight is sufficient to counteract its sway. Natural relations—even incest—might be truer and perhaps even kinder than purely legal or economic associations, but they too can be exploitative. Neither Bugs's nor the "sister's" apparently genuine affection for Ad prevented them from living off his misery in one way or another. Civil society does not end the "war of all against all, ceasing only in death." If anything, civil society only makes that war worse.

IV. HOW A CONFRONTATION WITH DEATH REVEALS THE FALSE FOUNDATIONS OF SOCIETY

Nick's travels away from home eventually take him altogether out of the United States and into the European war where, in the following vignette, we find him wounded. And confronting the immediate possibility of his own death for the first time, Nick self-consciously severs all ties to country and community. "Senta Rinaldi," he says to the man dying beside him. "You and me we've made a separate peace . . . . We're not patriots."

No individual can really die for another, Nick realizes (See also *For Whom the Bell Tolls* Hemingway 1940, 463).[25] No organization can actually guarantee anyone's right to life, liberty, and the pursuit of happiness. If he dies, Nick sees, he will no longer benefit from the collective that he has been defending. Nor will he enjoy any posthumous glory and honor. The people at home may never even hear of his "sacrifice." If Nick and all his fellows die, who will there be to tell the tale? As Hemingway subsequently shows in "Soldier's Home," the people a soldier has served do not like to be reminded of that fact for very long.

Leaving Nick wounded in Chapter 6 of *In Our Time*, Hemingway does not tell his readers anything more about him until Chapter 11, where the hero announces that he is returning to the states. Until he makes this decision to go home, Nick is still basically just running away. In the interim chapters, Hemingway indirectly presents the dilemma that Nick is facing by relating the experiences of other characters, because Nick himself is not yet willing or able to face his problem directly (Williams 1981, 36).[26]

Americans could not just return from the war and take up life where they left it. As Nick's experience demonstrates, the American regime is based on a series of falsehoods. With the story of the unnamed soldier that follows Nick's wounding, Hemingway reminds his readers that human promises are vacuous, because the thoughts and passions that give rise to the promises are transient (See also *A Farewell to Arms* 1929, 84–85).[27] And, he suggests in the subsequent vignette depicting the soldier who breaks his promise to Jesus, there does not appear to be any divine power that will force fallible human beings to live up to their word.

Divine love was once taken to be the ground not merely of human community, but of the entire cosmic order. But if war teaches human beings anything, Hemingway seems to be saying, it teaches them that God is dead. Under conditions of modern war, men do not live or die as a result of their individual courage and virtue. Why, for example, should Nick have been wounded by the shelling at Fossalta, and the whoring soldier saved (See also *Winner Take Nothing* 1927, 63–85; *Across the River and into the Trees* 1950, 17–18)?[28] It is a matter of chance. Evidence of divine justice appears to be just as difficult to find on earth as peace and goodwill among men (See also p. 98).[29]

Their experience in war thus set young American soldiers apart from their compatriots. In "Soldiers Home" Hemingway shows that Harold Krebs was not able to communicate his feelings to people who had not shared them.[30] And being unable to communicate, he himself lost them (See also p. 90).[31] He was left, as a consequence, with nothing at all.

Krebs was not even able to preserve the memory of his own manliness and courage in the company of other soldiers. Not everyone had been brave. A man could demonstrate his courage in action for others to see, but merely to talk about bravery would appear to be bragging. Thus

> when he occasionally met another man who had really been a soldier and they talked a few minutes in the dressing room at a dance he fell into the easy pose of the old soldier among other soldiers: that he had been badly, sickeningly frightened all the time. In this way he lost everything.

So "Krebs acquired the nausea in regard to experience that was the result of untruth or exaggeration" (91).[32]

The problem was not that Krebs is completely asocial. On the contrary, he "would like to have a girl." But the girls he watched walking down the street

> lived in such a complicated world of already defined alliances and shifting feuds that Krebs did not feel the energy or the courage to break into it . . . . He did not want to get into the intrigue and the politics. He did not want to have to do any courting. He did not want to tell any more lies (92–93).

In civil society, it is impossible to maintain and thus to act on the basis of pure, genuine feeling (See also p. 97).[33] All conventional social relations are based on lies.

American government represents an even bigger lie and hypocrisy, Hemingway indicates in the next vignette. That government was purportedly established to secure people's rights to life and liberty. In fact, it merely gives to some citizens the license to kill others—in peace, as well as in war. After a policeman in Kansas City shoots two Hungarian thieves in the back, Hemingway reports, his partner Boyle protests,

> "Hell, Jimmy, . . . you oughtn't to have done it. There's liable to be a hell of a lot of trouble."
> "They're crooks, ain't they? . . . They're wops, ain't they? Who the hell is going to make any trouble?" Drevitts responded.
> "That's all right maybe this time . . . but how did you know they were wops when you bumped them off?"
> "I can tell wops a mile off."

Even the immigrants who specifically came to the United States to escape Old World oppression and to begin anew as Americans have not proved able to overcome divisive ethnic prejudices and old nationalistic ties. Irishmen shoot Hungarians (mistaken for Italians) with official, even legal sanction in the United States just as well as in the war in Europe.

To believe that human beings can overcome the war of all against all by constructing a new political order requires that people—like the revolutionist of the next story—ignore their own experience as well as American history. But to believe that government is the source of the problem and that men would live in peace as brothers if only the state were abolished is equally naïve (See Republic 414b–415c).[34]

The communist alternative is no better than liberal democracy. At the center of the book, Hemingway thus takes himself and his protagonist out of the "cold war" debate that defined twentieth-century politics.[35] Government cannot secure any individual's life or liberty any more than it can bind that individual to others. Nor will government wither away. It is more apt, as Hemingway relates in the next story, to put the opposition in jail.

"The Revolutionist" is the story of a young Hungarian communist. (After the communists overthrew the Hungarian monarchy, Hemingway reminds his readers, Colonel Horthy displaced them and established a fascist regime.) "Horthy's men had done some bad things to him" so the revolutionist seeks asylum, first in Italy and then in Switzerland. He has no money, but out of sympathy for his sufferings his comrades take him in and feed him before they pass him on to their fellows at the next railroad station.

The youth "was delighted with Italy. It was a beautiful country, he said. The people were all kind." In a land of plenty, the young communist believes, people would live together in peace and harmony. Hearing that the movement is not going well in Italy, he thus assures his comrade: "It will go better . . . . You have everything here. It is the one country that everyone is sure of. It will be the starting point of everything."

The young communist does not understand the source and character of his own political movement any more than the young Americans understand theirs. He "had been in many towns, walked much, and seen many pictures," the narrator reports. "Giotto, Masaccio, and Piero della Francesca he bought reproductions of and carried them wrapped in a copy of *Avanti*. Mantegna he did not like" (105). As his dislike of Mantegna indicates, the youth refuses to countenance the role of martyrs and suffering in fostering the mutual sympathies that produce revolutions. Mantegna's painting of St. Sebastian is a reminder that human beings seek salvation out of suffering, not contentment, and that they often persecute agitators whom they hold to be responsible for disturbing their peace. Perceiving the youth's unwillingness to see his own situation and the world around him, the narrator does "not say anything." He merely states that "the last I heard of [the young communist] the Swiss had him in jail near Sion" (106).

The brotherhood of all mankind thus represents the dream of a naive youth who refuses to take account of his own experience, Hemingway is suggesting. Life in the twentieth century gives people no more reason to believe that they can achieve peace and goodwill on earth by instituting a new world order than it does to maintain faith in divine justice (Stephens 1968, 180–192).[36]

Disillusioned with both religion and politics, people in our time must come to terms with their mortality as no generation before them. They must live and die without hope either of saving themselves or of creating a better life for posterity. What they need above all is to find some satisfaction in this *life*, and Nick finds it, finally, at "the big two-hearted river." Death would not be so terrible if life in itself were not good, Hemingway recognizes. Because the pleasure merely in feeling alive is transient, however, nature does not provide a basis for a lasting or just community.

Unable to believe in either God or country, the postwar generation seems to have no alternative but to form small private societies of *cognosci*, who know that there is nothing to live for but the present moment. In the five stories leading up to Nick's return to the Michigan woods, Hemingway thus portrays the lives of a series of American émigrés (See also *The Sun Also Rises* 1926).[37]

All the émigrés depicted here are intellectuals, who live more according to ideas they have gotten from books than according to real feelings or experience. For example, in the third story the narrator observes that a "young gentleman" is amazed when his guide orders Marsala, because "that's what Max Beerbohm drinks" (127). The young gentlemen know the tastes and even the affectations of the literati, but they never notice the habits of the local populace.

These American émigrés are much less daring and unconventional and much more pretentious and uncomprehending than they themselves realize. Having arranged for an Italian ex-soldier to take him and his companion trout-fishing out of season, Hemingway reports, the young gentleman was relieved when the expedition failed. "He was no longer breaking the law" (133).

The intellectuals do not understand the source of their failure to form lasting communities, nor the price. They do not see that they are running away, at bottom, from the prospect of death (See also "Hills Like Elephants 1927, 39–44).[38]

Although political and nationalistic ties constitute illusions, Hemingway recognizes, human sexuality seems to indicate that society does have a natural foundation. All of the young American gentlemen whom he describes living in Europe have women, or "wives." These couples have difficulty conceiving and raising children, however.[39] Alienated not merely from their own particular nation but also from the natural generative cycle, their lives are empty and full of frustration.[40]

Procreation is the natural outcome of human sexuality. Noticing that their waitress is pregnant and without a wedding band, in the next story Nick explains to his friend George that men in the Swiss hinterland do not marry women until they have proved themselves able to bear children. The American émigrés are living in defiance of the natural cycle. But Hemingway indicates also that literally producing a new life by having a baby and assuming responsibility for its upbringing does not constitute an adequate or satisfying response to an individual's confrontation with death.

Like Krebs the ex-soldier, the young American émigrés are tempted to postpone, if not altogether to avoid, assuming their conventional adult responsibilities: settling down and having a family. "Didn't you wish we could just bum together?" George asks in "Cross-Country Ski." "[We could] take our skis and . . . repair kit and extra sweaters and pyjamas in our ruck-sacks and not give a damn about school or anything" (144). "Yes," Nick responds, "and go through the Schwartzwald . . . where [I] went fishing last summer" (145).

But, Hemingway indicates, it is not the desire to avoid responsibility and its associated constraints that fundamentally moves these young men. George does go back to school. Nick and his wife Helen return to the States, even though they do not want to, because she is pregnant. And when George observes sympathetically, "It's hell, isn't it," Nick responds, "No, not exactly." He might not be happy to be going home, but he is glad that Helen is having a baby.

Procreation constitutes the natural way of overcoming the prospective loss of individual life, through the perpetuation of the species. Men as well as women want to have children, Hemingway observes. They hope to live on, in a way, through their sons. The problem in our time is that men like Nick are not sure that they want to live on.

Once people have children, they must think about the future. But, Hemingway indicates, it is impossible to look toward the future without coming to terms with the past. In order to greet the birth of his son completely cheerfully, Nick must come to terms with his feelings about his own father; and he is not yet able to do this. In "My Old Man" Hemingway addresses Nick's problem indirectly by depicting the disillusionment of an émigré's young son at his father's death.[41]

V. THE GOODNESS OF LIFE MAKES DEATH EVEN HARDER

The fundamental problem or weakness that Nick's father had bequeathed to him was the doctor's inability to affirm that life is worth living. But at the end of the book, we see that Nick, in contrast to his father, concludes that life is good (See Nakajima 1979).[42] According to Hemingway's own later testimony, "Big Two-hearted River" is a "story about coming back from the war [although] there was no mention of the war in it (Baker 1976, 31–38)."[43] The boy who "felt quite sure that he would never die" now knows that he indubitably will. He returns, almost, to the locus of his childhood, with a new sensibility.[44]

Finding the town of Seney and the surrounding countryside burned to the ground, Nick is reminded that nature can be as destructive as war. He knows that it cannot all be burned, however; he has already seen the river and the trout swimming in it. Life goes on. He experiences the continuity in himself. "He felt all the old feeling . . . . He was happy" (179). Picking up a pack that he realizes is too heavy, Nick nevertheless feels a certain relief because he has "left everything behind, the need for thinking, the need to write, other needs" (179). So when he later makes camp—exhausted from the hard walk with the heavy pack—he is still happy.

> He had not been unhappy all day. This was different though. . . . It had been a hard trip. . . . He had made his camp. He was settled. Nothing

could touch him. It was a good place to camp. . . . He was in his home where he had made it. (187)⁴⁵

Nick is so much at home that he can allow himself to think, to recall a friend who went off after striking it rich, and to laugh when the coffee made according to that friend's recipe turns out to be bitter.

Nick's satisfaction will not last, however. Hemingway reminds his readers of the fundamental human problem in the vignette that divides the two halves of "Big Two-hearted River." "They hanged Sam Cardinella at six o'clock in the morning," the newspaper report reads. Is this the reality that Nick must wake up to?

"Be a man," a priest urges as they carry the prisoner onto the gallows. But "when they came toward him with the cap to go over his head Sam Cardinella lost control of his sphincter muscles. The guards who had been holding him . . . were both disgusted." Disgust does not keep the guards from hanging Cardinella, however, any more than compassion prevented the revolutionaries from shooting the minister too sick to stand up against the wall of the hospital in the vignette that introduced Chapter 5. In both cases, the executioners simply prop up their victim with a chair. Cardinella's gross, if natural reaction to the prospect of his own imminent death raises a serious question, however: Is the truth revealed in this death scene that "man" is no more than a dung-producing reflex? Hemingway is never quite sure.⁴⁶

In the second half of "Big Two-hearted River," Hemingway indicates the limits of Nick's recovery from his wartime experience, when he goes fishing the next day. Nick is emphatically alone. After he loses his first big trout, he feels shaky and wants to sit down. "The thrill had been too much. . . . He did not want to rush his sensations any" (204). After he catches two other large trout, he calls it a day. He does not want to try too much. In particular, he does not feel ready to enter the swamp, "to hook big trout in places impossible to land them. . . . In the swamp fishing was a tragic adventure."

In the swamp Nick would again have to confront his own limits directly. He would not be able to catch trout in the deep dark waters, and would then be reminded of the ultimate futility of all striving. When he kills a trout at the swamp's edge, he is reminded of his own death. Contemplating all that the swamp means, Nick wishes that "he had brought something to read" (211). He wants to use his mind and imagination to escape the prospect of inevitable physical decay.

VI. ART DOES NOT CONSTITUTE AN ADEQUATE ANSWER

Hemingway explored the possibility that human beings might come to terms with their inevitable demise indirectly through art. Because he was a writer, Nick could express and so preserve the "cool and clear" sense of his own existence that Krebs had lost.[47] In the draft of an alternative conclusion, Hemingway thus presented Nick as the author of all the stories. In "On Writing," Nick finally rushed back to camp to write down what was in his head (1972, 240–241).[48]

In nature, Nick had found a kind of truth. And Hemingway recognized that in truth there was a kind of individual, if not societal morality. "So far," he wrote in *Death in the Afternoon*, "about morals I know only that what is moral is what you feel good after and what is immoral is what you feel bad after" (4). One can lie about one's memory and about one's intentions; but one cannot deceive oneself about immediate feelings.

Above all, Hemingway strove to recapture those feelings in his own prose (Hemingway 1932, 2).[49] Because he found truth and hence a kind of morality in immediate sensation, he did not, like many of his Paris associates, embrace art for art's sake. For Hemingway, art was not the means by which human beings bring order out of a natural chaos and so give their lives a significance otherwise lacking. For Hemingway, writing remained a means of expression. Rather than stress the means of expression, Hemingway sought to communicate experience as directly and purely as possible. The artistry of his prose is therefore radically understated. Because he was trying to communicate what really happened, without any interpretative embroidery or exaggeration, his writing was intentionally rather flat and journalistic. He began his writing career as a reporter, and his fiction was always emphatically realistic. Nevertheless, he clearly distinguished the fiction to which he aspired from journalistic factuality.

> In writing for a newspaper you told what happened, and with one trick and another, you communicated the emotion aided by the element of timeliness which gives a certain emotion to any account of something that has happened on that day; but the real thing, the sequence of motion and fact which made the emotion and which would be as valid in a year or in ten years or, with luck and if you stated it purely enough, always, was beyond me and I was working very hard to get it (Hemingway 1932, 2).[50]

Journalism has an impact basically because of its timeliness, whereas Hemingway was seeking to capture the enduring core of the seemingly transitory, historical incidents or events in human life.

Nevertheless, he concluded that art is no better and no more enduring a response to the fact of individual death than politics or procreation. The self-reflective conclusion called "On Writing" detracted from the immediacy of the experience depicted in "Big Two-Hearted River," and so he deleted it. In the finished version of the story, Nick does not look back on the fellowship of his youth from the later vantage point of marriage. Hemingway does not make explicit Nick's stance toward his past or toward civil society. Nor does he indicate Nick's final stance toward death. For Hemingway, the problem is fundamentally insoluble.

Human beings kill in rebellion against their mortality, Hemingway later explained in *Death in the Afternoon* (1932, 232–233).[51] And in its final form, "Big Two-Hearted River" ends with the killing of the trout at the outer edge of the swamp. His solitary fishing trip had made Nick happy, temporarily, but it had not solved all his problems. It had simply postponed them. "There were plenty of days coming when he could fish the swamp" (212).

VII. THERE IS NO LASTING SOLUTION

Nick's problems were not merely personal, Hemingway reminded his readers in the last vignette by pointing to the connection between events in Europe and the now somewhat ambiguous meaning of the return to nature in America. In "L'Envoi," a reporter interviews the deposed Greek king in the palace gardens where the revolutionary committee has, in effect, been holding him prisoner. Pruning his roses, the king appears to be the image of an English country gentleman (Fenton 1954 quoted by Slabey; Meyers 1984, 25–36).[52] Not wanting to seem a bad sport or a sore loser, the king even praises his captor: "Plastiras is a very good man, . . . but frightfully difficult. I think he did right, though, shooting those chaps" (213). "Those chaps" are the six ministers whose execution was depicted in the preface to Chapter 5. In prosecuting an otherwise unnecessary war against Turkey, these ministers no doubt thought that they were loyally serving their king, furthering his interests by extending his empire. But, Hemingway indicates, loyalty is not rewarded in this world. Political order is not founded on tradition or consent so much as on force, even in constitutional democracies. "If Kerensky had shot a few men," the king reflects, "things might have been altogether different."

"Of course," the king then comments, "the great thing in this sort of an affair is not to be shot oneself." If the first lesson of politics is the need to use force, the second is the need to attend to one's own interests. The king may seem indifferent to his loss of power and status, but he is by no means oblivious to his personal safety. (That is the reason, we suspect, he praises his captors in an interview with a journalist who might be expected to report what the king has said.) For a man facing his own impending death, Hemingway consistently shows—politics, position, regime, and wealth become secondary considerations.

"It was very jolly," the reporter concludes. "We talked for a long time. Like all Greeks he wanted to go to America" (213). In the wake of imperialistic wars and revolutionary reaction, it is—ironically enough—the king who wishes the opportunity to begin anew in the New World, free from class prejudices.

America was the source of the revolutionary hope that human beings could secure liberty, equality, and fraternity by founding a new political order based on the right of nature. Unfortunately, Hemingway thinks, modern history has shown that this hope was as ill founded as the faith in king and church that preceded it. Human beings do not treat each other as equals, much less as brothers. Like all animals, they live in competition with one another, and hence in an essentially hostile relation.

In contrast to civil society, which attempts to justify the present sacrifices and burdens individuals make in war with promises of future glory or peace and prosperity for generations to come, nature reveals the fundamentally transitory character of all existence in a perpetual cycle of prey and predator, birth and death. Nature is not a "garden" any more than American government is a protector of life and liberty. On the contrary, as Nick discovered at the big two-hearted river, nature constitutes a war of all against all, in which grasshoppers, fish, and men alike struggle to live and then live only at each other's expense.

Nature does not, therefore, provide an adequate foundation for human life or society. Although a return to nature can remind one that life is good, it also gives proof that nothing endures beyond the cycle of birth and death. Nature is indeed two-hearted.

VIII. HEMINGWAY AND HEIDEGGER

Death remained an insuperable problem for Hemingway. It was death itself that was the problem, however, not fear. If Nick had simply feared death, he would not have voluntarily gone to war. He did not particularly seek honor; and he did not make his "separate peace" because he was afraid. He left the United States for the same reason that Ishmael shipped aboard the *Pequod*: He wanted to discover a reason to live. And, Hemingway showed, Nick was able to appreciate what is good in life itself in the state of nature only after he had directly confronted the possibility of his own death.

In emphasizing the confrontation with the immediate possibility of death as the definitive experience in the life of an individual, Hemingway anticipated the influential analysis of human existence that the postwar German philosopher Martin Heidegger offered in *Being and Time* only a few years later (1962 [1927]).[53] To fear death, Heidegger argued, is to treat it as an external phenomenon—something that might even be avoided (1962 [1927], div. 1, ch. 5, sect. 30).[54] Like Hemingway, he considered death to be the most personal, inalienable, "own-most" possibility that an individual human being ever faces (div. 2, ch. I, sects. 46–53).[55] Only direct confrontation with the ever-present possibility of death would show an individual the fundamental uncertainty and radical insecurity of human existence.

Few human beings can continually live in the face of such radical insecurity. So, Heidegger argued, they "fall" or turn away from contemplating the possibility of death into the comforting, although fundamentally illusory routines and opinions of everyday life. By dramatizing the courage that it takes even the lowliest sailor to live actually in the face of death, Melville thought that he was reminding his readers of the true grounds of democratic fellowship. Unfortunately, Hemingway and Heidegger agreed, confronting the ever-present possibility of one's own death does not, as Ishmael suggested, lead human beings to appreciate the essentially interdependent character of their existence or arouse a sense of compassion. Contemplating the possibility of their own demise leads them rather to perceive the essential emptiness of all social and political opinions and institutions (div. 1, ch. 5, sect. 38).[56]

If the truth of human life is found only in the prospect of death "authentically" contemplated as one's own, neither that truth nor that life can really be shared. Neither liberal democracy nor its communist alternative has a valid foundation, Hemingway and Heidegger both concluded. To promise to secure an individual's right to life is to deny the fundamental truth of human existence, by suggesting that his life can be preserved by institutional or other cooperative means. Likewise, to promise that all human beings can live as brothers is to deny the individuating experience of death (Heidegger 1959, 37).[57]

Beyond disillusionment with both major modern forms of egalitarian politics, however, the postwar American novelist and the postwar German philosopher came to strikingly different conclusions from a common insight. To come to terms with the ever-present possibility and inescapable necessity of one's own death, Heidegger argued, is to perceive the essentially temporal character of human existence. Human beings do not live in a series of isolated moments called "the present." They live instead by projecting their past experiences into the future. And they understand that past (and hence themselves) "traditionally," in terms of concepts that they have acquired—largely imbedded in the language itself—from the people among whom they were born (Heidegger 1967 [1927], div. 2, chs. 4 and 5).[58] Fundamentally, therefore, temporal existence is historical existence. But the fact that human beings live historically does not mean that their lives are entirely determined or unfree. On the contrary, the individual who sees that death is an ever-present possibility thereby also sees that he or she has actually always lived, if only implicitly, by choice. Human beings can make their lives—not only individual, but also communal—more authentic, by making that choice explicit. The choice is not an abstract determination among indefinite possibilities. Rather, it is a choice between continuing to live as one has lived in the past, in the particular circumstances in which one finds oneself, or ceasing to do so. To live historically is to live as part of a particular people, not as an isolated individual or as a member of the human race per se (See Blitz 1982; Gillespie 1984; Poeggler 1963; Schwan 1965).[59] Heidegger thus embraced the fascist reaction against both liberal individualism and communist universalism, because he thought that it was truer to the historical nature of human existence (See also Heidegger 1959, 31–32; Farias 1988).[60]

For Hemingway the fascist reaction against both liberalism and communism simply constituted yet another example of a political movement—originating in natural desires, but then serving primarily to justify official violence when those natural desires had dissipated. As the politics of "the people" (*Volk*) defined basically through ethnic ties, fascism could claim to have the same natural foundations as the family. Hemingway suggested that the desire to mate and procreate is as strong as, if not stronger, than the fear of violent death and the desire for human fellowship. But he also indicated that politics based on family ties have no more lasting or genuine natural foundations than those based on the fear of violent death or the pleasures of male camaraderie. Family relations do not guarantee future affection any more than childhood friendship. On the contrary, Hemingway reminded his readers through the historical vignettes, extended family relations in the form of ethnic ties merely provide an excuse, in America as well as in Europe, for the violent oppression of others.

Hemingway's insistence on the simple goodness of pure, natural sensation thus saved him not only from complete nihilism, but also from the fascist reaction to that nihilism (Heidegger 1982).[61] But it created a gap between nature and history that he found impossible to bridge.

Because they feel that life is good, Hemingway saw, human beings try to preserve it. Failing that, they engage in violent killing—they hunt and they war—in rebellion against their inescapable fate. Like the satisfaction of simple sensation or the more intense thrill of sexual pleasure, however, the exultation in conquest is short lived. In the death of another living creature, every human being cannot help but see prefigured his or her own demise.

Like Heidegger, Hemingway thought that the confrontation with death as one's own-most possibility revealed not only that the continuation of human life fundamentally constitutes a choice, but also that human existence is essentially historical. Therein lay the difficulty with which the novelist incessantly struggled without coming to a satisfactory solution: Why should a human being self-consciously choose to persist in the face of ultimate defeat? On what grounds can a son hope to live more satisfactorily than his father? To recognize the historical character of human existence is to recognize its essentially transitory character. If all human institutions developed basically to preserve human life, then—in time and with experience—the impossibility of achieving that goal will necessarily become clear. Having perceived the essential emptiness of family, church, and polity, the people in our time must confront the question of the value of life itself in an unprecedented way.

On the other hand, Hemingway recognized, confrontation with the possibility of one's own death would be neither so fearful nor so revealing if human beings did not fundamentally feel that life itself is good. Heidegger had reduced the present to the venue through which human beings project the past into the future. Hemingway contrasted the satisfaction that one can find in simple sensations at the present moment with both the anxiety produced by an uncertain future and the disillusionment necessarily associated with the past.⁶²

For Hemingway, there were two insoluble problems. First, he was unable to affirm what he himself saw as the distinctively human characteristic: the foresight into one's own death that makes human existence essentially historical. Because human beings are not the only sensitive animals, Hemingway identified what is good about life itself with nature as a whole. In thus opposing nature and history, he lost a sense or conception of *human* nature. Consequently, he was also unable to find any way human beings could relieve their alienation and suffering by joining together. Although he saw both that human beings are naturally attracted to one another and that they do not live happily in isolation, he did not think that they could form an enduring union that would not become an empty, inauthentic, and hence ultimately oppressive sham.

NOTES

1. See Catherine H. Zuckert, *Natural Right and the American Imagination* (Lanham: Rowman and Littlefield, 1990).
2. Philip Young, *Hemingway: A Reconsideration* (University Park: Pennsylvania State University Press, 1966), has pointed out some ways in which Hemingway's Nick Adams stories constitute a kind of retelling of the Huck Finn Saga. Like Huck, Nick grows up on the outskirts of civil society; further like Huck, Nick eventually runs away from home. But, again like Huck, Nick finally returns. But in some respects, Nick does not represent a latter-day version of Huck so much as he constitutes a twentieth-century reinterpretation of Natty Bumppo. The strongest echo of Natty in Nick Adams may be found in the fragment of an unfinished novel, "The Last Good Country," where Hemingway shows Nick take a rifle and flee from the law after catching trout out of season. Ernest Hemingway, *The Nick Adams Stories* (New York: Charles Scribner's Sons, 1972), 70–82. Cooper's novels had explicitly been dedicated to teaching his countrymen that there were natural principles of right that could form the basis of a just polity—the very claim Hemingway questions. Like Natty and unlike Huck, Nick acquires much of his formative education from the Indians. That education does not concern the skills of self-preservation or stoical endurance, however, so much as the complex interrelation of love, birth, and death. In a later story, Hemingway shows that Nick first learned both the pleasures of sex and the pangs of infidelity from an Indian. "Ten Indians," in Ernest Hemingway, *Men without Women* (New York: Charles Scribner's Sons, 1927), 97–102.
3. Hemingway grew up in Oak Park, Illinois, a suburb of Chicago, where his father was a physician; he and his family regularly spent summers on the upper peninsula of Michigan. Like Nick, Hemingway also left home to serve in World War I, became disillusioned as a result, and spent time in Europe trying to find himself and some form of satisfying companionship. See Carlos Baker, *Ernest Hemingway: A Life Story* (New York: Charles Scribner's Sons, 1969). The name Hemingway gave his protagonist, Nick Adams, is clearly associated, first, with the devil, who led the first "man" Adam into the temptation that resulted in his mortality (as well as his knowledge of good and

evil) and second, with the founder whose son also became president, but who both, unlike their predecessors, served only one term.

4. Nick's withdrawals are thus always rather explicitly temporary. For example, coming down from the mountains into the town in "An Alpine Idyll," he reflects: "I was a little tired of skiing. We had stayed too long. I was glad there were other things beside skiing, and I was glad to be down, away from the unnatural high mountain spring into this May morning in the valley." Hemingway, *Men Without Women*, 110.

5. Philip Young also observed, Hemingway: *Reconsideration*, 40, that Nick's relation to civilization is different from Huck's, just as Nick's relation to his father is much different from Huck's relation to Pap—in large part because Nick's father is utterly unlike Pap.

6. Hence the amalgam of Being and Time with In Our Time in the title of this essay.

7. I have concentrated on Hemingway's first collection of Nick Adams stories because I think this collection reveals most clearly both the promise and the problems that Hemingway saw in the return to nature. Examined carefully, this early collection contains all the themes and thoughts that animate his entire corpus. Hemingway himself suggested that the whole could be seen in the part, if that part were viewed carefully enough. See *Death in the Afternoon* (New York: Charles Scribner's Sons, 1932), 278: "Let those who want to save the world if you can get to see it clear and as a whole. Then any part you make will represent the whole if it's made truly."

8. By separating each story from its sequel and so destroying a facile sense of narrative continuity, the vignettes were intended to give the collection of stories something of the actual character of human experience, in which certain incidents stand out and are remembered as significant turning points even though the meaning or the reasons why they stick in the memory continues to elude the particular individual. Wesley A. Kort, "Human Time in Hemingway's Fiction," *Modern Fiction Studies* (1980): 582, has also pointed out that, whereas the action in the vignettes tends to be public and external, the stories themselves are more private and give an internal view.

9. See Robert M. Slabey, "The Structure of *In Our Time*," Clinton S. Burhams, Jr., "The Complex Unity of *In Our Time*," and Jackson J. Benson, "Patterns of Connection and Their Development on Hemingway's *In Our Time*," in Michael S. Reynolds, *Critical Essays on Ernest Hemingway's "In Our Time"* (Boston: G. K. Hall, 1983), 76–119, for somewhat different accounts of the structure and order. David Seed, " 'The Picture of the Whole': In Our Time," in A. Robert Lee, ed., *Ernest Hemingway: New Critical Essays* (London: Vision, 1983), has pointed out many of the thematic links among vignettes and stories. See also Charles G. Hoffman and A. C. Hoffmann, " 'The Truest Sentence': Words as Equivalents of Time and Place in In Our Time," in Donald R. Noble, *Hemingway: A Reevaluation* (Troy, NY: Whitston Publishing, 1983), 99–114.

10. E. R. Hagemann, " 'Only let the story end as soon as possible': Time and History in Ernest Hemingway's *In Our Time*," *Modern Fiction Studies* 26 (Summer 1980): 255–61, has shown that the vignettes cover the period from 1914 to 1923.

11. "Now the essence of the greatest emotional appeal of bullfighting is the feeling of immortality that the bullfighter feels in the middle of a great faena and that he gives to the spectators. He is performing a work of art and he is playing with death, bringing it closer, closer, closer to himself, a death that you know is in the horns because you have the canvas-covered bodies of the horses on the sand to prove it." Hemingway, *Death*, p. 213.

12. Stephen Cooper, *The Politics of Ernest Hemingway* (Ann Arbor: University of Michigan Research Press, 1987), 23, concludes that Hemingway omitted all political commentary in *In Our Time*, because Cooper ignores the interrelations between stories and vignettes.
13. "Where you see gratuitous cruelty most often is in police brutality," Hemingway observed in *Death in the Afternoon*, 187–188, "in the police of all countries I have ever been in, including, especially, my own.... After one comes, through contact with its administrators, no longer to cherish greatly the law as a remedy in abuses, then the bottle becomes a sovereign means of direct action. If you cannot throw it at least you can always drink out of it."
14. Hemingway originally planned to stress the transient, disordered character of both life and "the news" in our time not only through his title and his flat journalistic style, but also graphically by framing each page with a collage of newspaper articles. Baker, *Ernest Hemingway,* 115–116.
15. Hemingway read Nietzsche's *Thus Spoke Zarathustra*. See Michael S. Reynolds, *Hemingway's Reading 1910–1940* (Princeton, NJ: Princeton University Press, 1981), 163.
16. Hemingway was a personal friend of Picasso and a lifelong admirer of Braques, so it is not altogether surprising that he produced a rather "cubist" work—almost, but not quite, a novel—in which ordinary relations of sequence, time, and narration are fractured and reorganized on an apparently flat surface created by his studiedly simple, "objective," reportorial prose style. Kenneth G. Johnston, "Hemingway and Cezanne: Doing the Country," *American Literature* 56 (March 1984): 28–34, has traced the influence of postimpressionist painters on the novelist. Hemingway explicitly mentioned Cezanne's influence in "On Writing"—the conclusion that he drafted, but then excised, from *In Our Time*.
17. There is, in fact, a definite connection between each introductory scene and subsequent story. In a letter to Edmund Wilson, Hemingway explained that the introductory scenes "give the picture of the whole before examining it in detail. Like looking with your eyes at something, say a passing coastline, and then looking at it with 15X binoculars. Or rather, maybe looking and then going and living in it and then coming out and looking at it again." Edmund Wilson, *The Shores of Light* (New York: Farrar, Straus, and Young, 1952), 123.
18. Citations are to Ernest Hemingway, *In Our Time* (New York: Charles Scribner's Sons, 1925).
19. Hemingway made the same point about the inability of modern medicine to account for the ineradicable connection between birth and death in "The Quai at Smyrna," which he later added as an introduction to the entire collection. On a quai full of refugees—a British officer reports—women continued to have babies. The problem was that "you couldn't get the women to give up their dead babies. Had to take them away finally. Then there was an old lady, most extraordinary case. I told it to a doctor and he said I was lying." Brought before him on a litter, the woman drew up into a birthing position as she died. "I told a medical chap about it and he told me it was impossible" (10).
20. John Locke, *The Second Treatise of Government* (New York: Liberal Arts, 1952), ch. 5.
21. The story is introduced by a vignette describing the surprise on a German soldier's face when the Americans "pot" him as he reaches the top of a wall and is preparing to jump down into an unidentified garden. In the story itself, Marge is also surprised when she goes to meet her lover by the lake—in the apparent peace of a natural garden. There is no security or "Garden of Eden" free from the threat of death and the resulting inconstancy—however

apparently pacific and even idyllic the circumstances. Likewise, Hemingway suggests, there is no real innocence or loss thereof.
22. Hemingway indicates how thoughtless and cruel such camaraderie can become in the introductory vignette. Having set up a wrought-iron house gate as a road barrier, the narrator then celebrates the ease with which his team shoots down the German officers who try to climb over—forgetting the purpose of the war as well as any sense of humanity. The narrator reports, "We were frightfully put out when we heard the flank had gone, and we had to fall back."
23. By describing in the introductory vignette the execution of six Greek ministers shot against the wall of a hospital, Hemingway reminds his readers that institutions specifically established to preserve human life do not and cannot counteract the destructive effects of competition and conflict. Politics is an arena—even a cause—of such conflict, more than it is a solution.
24. Bugs is rather ambiguous, in fact, about Ad's relation to his wife. After insisting that "they wasn't brother and sister no more than a rabbit," Bugs twice reiterates that she "looked enough like him to be twins" (77–78). Hemingway suggests that there is a natural tendency toward incestual relations between brother and sister in the story "Soldier's Home" (see below in the text) as well as "The Last Good Country." In the latter, he shows Nick running off to the woods with his sister "Littleness."
25. Despite both his love for Maria and his sympathy for the Spanish republicans, Roberto in Hemingway's *For Whom the Bell Tolls* (New York: Charles Scribner's Sons, 1940), 463, comes to exactly the same conclusion. Unable to ride away from an attack with his girl and the gypsies because he is wounded, Roberto insists that she go on without him: "What I do now I do alone. I could not do it well with thee. . . . That people cannot do together. Each one must do it alone." As Hemingway demonstrates in the stories that follow Nick's wounding, love cannot overcome the fact of death.
26. All the protagonists of the next five stories have something in common with Nick, even though not one of them is identical with him. Wirt Williams fails to see the point of the difference between Nick and the other protagonists—they represent alternative possible outcomes—when he finds it hard "to accept Krebs as Nick in 'Soldier's Home,' and George as Nick in 'Cat in the Rain,' [although] the logic of the chronicle insists upon it." *The Tragic Art of Ernest Hemingway* (Baton Rouge: Louisiana State University Press, 1981), 36.
27. Since the unnamed soldier in the story following Nick's wounding has an affair with a nurse named Luz in the hospital—as Frederick Henry does with Catherine Barclay in Hemingway's subsequent novel, *A Farewell to Arms* (New York: Charles Scribner's Sons, 1929)—it is tempting to identify the soldier with Nick, and both with Henry. (Henry also has a friend named Rinaldi.) Like Catherine, Luz stays on night duty; and like Henry, the soldier on crutches does many of her rounds. Again like Catherine and Henry, "they wanted to get married, but there was not enough time for the bands, and neither of them had birth certificates. They felt as though they were married, but they wanted everyone to know about it, and to make it so they could not lose it" (84). They do lose it after the armistice, however, when the soldier goes home to find a job and Luz takes up with a major. The major never marries Luz as he promised, and "[a] short time after, [the soldier] contracted gonorrhea from a sales girl in a Loop department store" (85). Love does not enable human beings to conquer death, because—like all things human—love, too, is transitory. (Catherine does not leave Henry for another man, but she dies in childbirth.)

28. Just as in Chapter 5 of *In Our Time*, the six ministers are shot against the wall of a hospital, so the wounded soldier is pulled next to the wall of a church. Neither institution provides any real protection from death, Hemingway suggests. Readers learn that Nick was wounded at Fossalta only in a later story, "A Way You'll Never Be," in Ernest Hemingway, *Winner Take Nothing* (New York: Charles Scribner's Sons, 1927), 63–85. The fact that Richard Cantwell also returns to Fossalta as the place where he was wounded at the beginning of Hemingway's *Across the River and Into the Trees* (New York: Charles Scribner's Sons, 1950), 17–18, indicates the extent to which Hemingway has his protagonists share the same fundamental, formative, shattering experience.
29. In the next story, when Harold Krebs's mother urges him to settle down and get a job because "God has some work for everyone to do . . . There can be no idle hands in His kingdom," the ex-soldier thus responds, "I'm not in His kingdom" (98).
30. Having been at Belleau Wood, Soissons, then Champagne, St. Michel, and in the Argonne, Krebs does not want to talk about the war when he first arrives home. Later when he feels the need to talk, no one wants to hear about it. His town has heard too many atrocious stories to be thrilled by actualities. Krebs finds that to be listened to at all he must lie; and after doing this twice, he too has a reaction against the war and is against talking about it.
31. "All of the times that had been able to make him feel cool and clear inside himself when he thought of them; the times so long back when he had done the thing, the only thing for a man to do, easily and naturally, when he might have done something else, now lost their cool, valuable quality and then were lost themselves" (90).
32. Nausea at the emptiness of modern life is a theme of Nietzsche's work, as it became also a theme in the work of Jean-Paul Sartre. Unlike Hemingway, neither Nietzsche nor Sartre associated that nausea particularly with untruth, however. Hemingway made the association, because he thought that meaning is to be found in pure, unmediated, and hence true feeling. That truth is what Krebs lost.
33. In the sequel to the story Hemingway reminds his readers that there were women somewhat ready at hand. "He was still a hero to his two young sisters." Harold's favorite sister even tells all her friends that he is her beau.

    "Couldn't your brother really be your beau just because he's your brother?"
    "I don't know."
    "Sure you know. Couldn't you be my beau, Hare, if I was old enough and if you wanted to?"
    "Sure. You're my girl now." (97)

    As in the story of Ad, Hemingway again hints that incest may be the most natural—certainly it is the least conventional—form of association. Brother need not be introduced to sister; they are already tied by affection and common experience.
34. Whereas Plato *Republic* 414b–415c, suggested that a just government would have to be founded on a "noble lie," Hemingway concludes that all governments are based on lies and that none can therefore be just.
35. Hemingway had originally published the vignettes separately in a volume entitled *in our time*. But using no capitalization in the title was the publisher's idea, not Hemingway's. The absence of capitals in the title of the original collection provides a convenient way of distinguishing the earlier collection of vignettes from the later collection of vignettes and stories.) By leaving "L'Envoi" as an unnumbered postscript and making two of the original 18 vignettes from in

our time into "stories," Hemingway created a book of 15 chapters in which one of the original vignettes, "The Revolutionist," became central.

36. As a journalist, Hemingway reported both the revolutionary conditions in Italy following the disastrous Allied defeat at Caporetto and the likelihood of nationalistic fascist response. Although Northern Italian workers supported revolution—he observed—they were not willing to undertake the harsh measures necessary actually to bring it about. He also predicted the probability of a fascist reaction. See Robert O. Stephens, *Hemingway's Nonfiction* (Chapel Hill: University of North Carolina Press, 1968), 180–192.

37. Hemingway's first novel, *The Sun Also Rises* (New York: Charles Scribner's Sons, 1926), was also intended to be a response to, rather than an affirmation of, Gertrude Stein's comment, "You are all a lost generation." Although Hemingway took the title of the novel from the section of Ecclesiastes that he quotes after quoting Stein on the frontispiece, most critics seem to have ignored the significance of the recurring natural cycle: "One generation passeth away, *and another cometh; but the earth abideth forever.* The sun also rises, and the sun goeth down . . . ; unto the place from whence the rivers come, thither they return again" (emphasis added). Unlike the Biblical author, Hemingway regards the source to which all return as natural, rather than divine. In both *In Our Time* and his subsequent novel, he presents life or the generative cycle as a kind of response to European nihilism.

38. In the third of the émigrés stories, Hemingway shows that the young gentleman and his wife have been arguing, probably over the prospect of an abortion. (See the more explicit argument in "Hills Like Elephants," in Hemingway, *Without Women*, 39–44.) Their guide does not understand what is bothering them. Excited by the prospect of beginning a new life as a guide, he attributes all the misunderstanding to differences in language: "Part of the time he talked in d'Ampezzo dialect and sometimes in Tyroler German dialect. He could not make out which the young gentleman and his wife understood best so he was being bilingual. But as the young gentleman said, Ja, Peduzzi decided to talk altogether in Tyroler. The young gentleman and the wife understood nothing" (130). Misunderstanding is not merely the result of a failure to communicate, Hemingway indicates. It is rooted in a more fundamental form of alienation. The much older guide had hoped to become part of a new little free and egalitarian society. Having called the young man "*caro*" several times with no objection, Peduzzi is looking forward to repeating the expedition the next day. But the young gentleman warns him, "I may not be going . . . very probably not" (135). Hemingway later reveals that he omitted "the real end of it which was that the old man hanged himself. This was omitted on my new theory that you could omit anything if you knew that you omitted and the omitted part would strengthen the story and make people feel something more than they understood" (*The Moveable Feast* [New York: Charles Scribner's Sons, 1964], 75.) The statement refers to what has often been dubbed Hemingway's "iceberg" theory of writing after his earlier statement in *Death*, 192: "If a writer of prose knows enough of what he is writing about he may omit things that he knows and the reader, if the writer is writing truly enough, will have a feeling of those things as strongly as though the writer had stated them. The dignity of movement of an iceberg is due to only one-eighth of it being above water. [On the other hand, a] writer who omits things because he does not know them only makes hollow places in his writing." Hemingway may have taken this notion from the postimpressionist painter of whom he was so fond. Cézanne also intentionally left out a great deal. Richard W. Murphy, *The World of Cézanne 1839–1900* (New York: Time-Life, 1968), 77. The order of the stories in *In Our Time* points to the suppressed meaning, however. Like Peduzzi,

all the émigré couples are disappointed in their own desire to find a new life, because they fail to face the source of their dissatisfaction with the old.
39. The first such emigres depicted by Hemingway are "Mr. and Mrs. Elliot [who] tried very hard to have a baby," but—at 40—she proves too old. Fifteen years her junior, Hubert Elliot had not really intended to marry Cornelia. "He had been in love with various girls before he kissed Mrs. Elliot and always told them sooner or later that he had led a clean life. . . . He wanted to keep himself pure so that he could bring to his wife the same purity of mind and body that he expected of her. . . . Nearly all the girls lost interest in him" (110). Cornelia first praised his purity (she was Southern by birth), and then his lovemaking. They were married, and he took her to Europe—just as he later takes some friends who admire his poetry to the château in Touraine that he has rented for the summer. Touraine turns out to be hot, so Elliot's friends follow another rich (unmarried) poet to the seashore. The Elhots get tired of trying so hard to have a baby in the big hot bedroom. Ceding his bed finally to the older female companion whom his wife convinced him to bring to Europe, Elliot writes poetry late into the night in his own room. He has already sent the check to the publisher to bring out his volume. Hemingway leads the reader to doubt that Elliot's poems will have any more passion or perception than his married life. Neither art nor education constitutes a substitute for experience, and Hubert has very little. He remains a man of pure ideas.
40. In the following story, Hemingway shows another young American couple—living in Italy—in which the wife wants to settle down and have a child. Looking out the window of their hotel, she spots a kitty trying to avoid the rain by hiding under a table, and insists on going out to get it. Finding the cat gone, she returns to the room and expresses her sense of dissatisfaction to her husband George: "Don't you think it would be a good idea if I let my hair grow out? . . . I get so tired of looking like a boy" (120–121). When he responds that he thinks she looks "pretty darn nice," she continues: "I want to pull my hair back tight and smooth and make a big knot at the back that I can feet . . . I want to have a kitty to sit on my lap and purr when I stroke her. . . . And I want to eat at a table with my own silver and I want candles." Impatient with such domestic desires, George tells her to "shut up and get something to read." Like Nick as a boy at the cabin in the Michigan woods, George uses books as a means of escape.
41. Like the boy Nick who used to put down his book to go squirrel hunting, Joe in "My Old Man" loves his father. He does not know that his father helped fix races—trying to amass enough money to return home to the States with his son. Joe does remember his "old man" telling him about when "he was a boy in Kentucky and going coon hunting, and the old days in the States before everything went on the bum there. And he'd say 'Joe, when we've got a decent stake, you're going back to the States and go to school.' What've I got to go back there to go to school for when everything's on the bum there?' I'd ask him. 'That's different,' he'd say." (168) When his father is killed in an accident, Joe is thus shocked to hear a bystander comment as they take the body away: "The crook . . . had it coming to him." Although the old friend comforting the boy urges him not to "listen to what those bums said. . . . Your old man was a swell guy," Joe concludes, "I don't know. Seems like when they get started they don't leave a guy nothing" (173).
42. I therefore disagree fundamentally with Kenji Nakajima's presentation of *"Big Two-hearted River" as the Extreme of Hemingway's Nihilism* (Tokyo: Eichosha, 1979). Nakajima provides a useful summary of many different critical interpretations of the story.

43. Hemingway, *Moveable Feast*, 75. Sheridan Baker, *Ernest Hemingway: An Introduction and Interpretation* (New York: Rinehart, 1976), 31–38, has interpreted the whole story—especially the short tense sentences and Nick's stated desire not to think—as a reaction to his wounding in the war.
44. The fact that Nick does not return to his family's cabin—but goes, rather, to fish on another river in the same general neighborhood—is but one indication that he has not entirely settled the problem represented by his past, and particularly by his father.
45. Nick's satisfaction with finding a "good place" and making it his home should be contrasted with the waiter's meditations on the plight of the old man in "A Clean Well-lighted Place" in Hemingway, *Winner*. Having tried to commit suicide the week before, the old man stays in the "clean, well-lighted cafe" until forced to go home. "What did he fear?" The waiter muses. "It was not fear or dread. It was a nothing that he knew too well. It was all a nothing and man was nothing too. . . . Some lived in it and never felt it but he knew it all was nada y pues nada y nada y pues nada. Our nada who art in nada . . . Now, without thinking further, he would go home to his room. He would lie in the bed and finally . . . go to sleep. After all, he said to himself, it is probably only insomnia" (23–24). After he was wounded, Nick also suffered insomnia, but he conquered it—as he does his nihilistic disillusionment following the war—by going "back to trout-fishing, because I found that I could remember all the streams and there was always something new about them, while the girls, after I had thought about them a few times, blurred." "Now I Lay Me," in Hemingway, *Without Women*, 137. Nick finds himself at home and at peace only when he is alone in nature.
46. When Lieutenant Cantwell revisits Fossalta in Hemingway, *Across the River*, he stoops to relieve himself at the very place where he (and also Nick) was wounded. As part of the natural cycle, human beings first make dung, and then themselves finally decay.
47. Because Nick has been wounded, he is aware of his own vulnerability. As a result, he has an even keener sense of how good it is simply to feel alive. In *Death*, Hemingway argued that a matador has not really been tested until he goes back into the ring and faces death *after* being wounded.
48. Hemingway, *Nick Adams Stories*, 240–241.
49. "I found the greatest difficulty, aside from knowing truly what you really felt, rather than what you were supposed to feel, and had been taught to feel, was to put down what really happened in action; what the actual things were which produced the emotion that you experienced." Hemingway, *Death*, 2.
50. Ibid.
51. Hemingway, *Death*, 232–233: "One of [the] greatest pleasures [of killing] is the feeling of rebellion against death which comes from its administering."
52. Charles Fenton, *The Apprenticeship of Ernest Hemingway* (New York: Farrar, Straus, 1954), quoted by Slabey, "Structure of *In Our Time*." Jeffrey Meyers, "Hemingway's Second War: The Greco-Turkish Conflict, 1920–1922," *Modern Fiction Studies* 30 (Spring 1984): 25–36, gives the actual historical background for both this scene and the execution of the six ministers.
53. *Being and Time* was originally published in 1927, two years after *In Our Time*. Martin Heidegger, *Being and Time* (New York: Harper and Row, 1962).
54. Ibid., div. 1, ch. 5, sect. 30.
55. Ibid., div. 2, ch. I, sects. 46–53. "Own-most" represents a translation of *eigentlich*—often less precisely rendered as "authentic."

56. See ibid., div. 1, ch. 5, sect. 38.
57. See Martin Heidegger, *Introduction to Metaphysics* (New Haven, CT: Yale University Press, 1959), 37: "From a metaphysical point of view, Russia and America are the same; the same dreary technological frenzy, the same unrestricted organization of the average man"
58. Heidegger, *Being*, div. 2, chs. 4 and 5.
59. Most English- and French-speaking commentators have missed the historical definition of "possibility" and the connection between the individual's fate and his or her nation's destiny. Mark Blitz, *Heidegger's "Being and Time" and the Possibility of Political Philosophy* (Ithaca, NY: Cornell University Press, 1982), and Michael Allen Gillespie, *Hegel, Heidegger, and the Ground of History* (Chicago: University of Chicago Press, 1984), represent exceptions. See also Otto Poeggler, *Der Denkweg Martin Heideggers* (Pfullingen, FRG: Neske, 1963), and Alexander Schwan, *Politische Philosophie im Denken Heideggers* (Cologne and Opladen, FRG: Westdeutscher Verlag, 1965).
60. Heidegger's statement about the absence of any difference between America (the United States) and Russia (the Soviet Union) in his *Introduction to Metaphysics* continues thus:
    At a time when the farthermost corner of the globe has been conquered by technology and opened to economic exploitation; when any incident whatever, regardless of where or when it occurs, can be communicated to the rest of the world ... simultaneously; ... time as history has vanished from the lives of all peoples.... We are caught in a pincers. Situated in the center, our nation incurs the severest pressure ..., but our people will only be able to wrest a destiny from it if *within itself* it ... takes a creative view of its tradition. All this implies that this nation, as a historical nation, must move itself and thereby the history of the West beyond the center. (pp. 31–32, emphasis added)
    Although Heidegger was an active official of the Nazi party for only a short time—and the famous "turn" in his thought resulted in a much more passive stance toward the world—he never apologized for or disavowed his Nazi allegiance even though the Nazis finally sent him to the Eastern Front. On the contrary, when his *Introduction to Metaphysics* was translated and reissued in the 1960s, Heidegger kept a statement about the "essential truth of National Socialism" in the text. He very explicitly continued to maintain that both liberal and Marxist-Leninist political systems need to be superseded. Because his philosophy influenced writers on the left like Jean-Paul Sartre even more, perhaps, than it did thinkers on the right, the relation between Heidegger's philosophy and his politics continues to be a hotly debated topic. See Victor Farias, *Heidegger et le Nazisme* (Paris: Editions Verdier, 1988).
61. See Martin Heidegger, *Nietzsche: Nihilism* (New York: Harper and Row, 1982), for Heidegger's argument, first, that Nietzsche represents not the overcoming but the completion of nihilism, and, second, that people have to live through the nihilism necessarily associated with technology in order to see the light on the other side.
62. From Heidegger's point of view, Hemingway's attachment to a conception of nature in general and to pure sensation in particular kept the novelist within the traditional metaphysical understanding of "being" (originally equated with "nature" by the Greeks) understood as "presence." Heidegger would not, therefore, have been surprised that the American novelist proved unable to integrate his attachment to nature with his insight into the necessarily historical character of human existence—an insight that results from an authentic confrontation with the possibility of one's own death.

WORKS CITED

Baker, Carlos. *Ernest Hemingway: A Life Story*. New York: Scribner's, 1969.
Baker, Sheridan. *Ernest Hemingway: An Introduction and Interpretation*. New York: Rinehart, 1976.
Benson, Jackson, Jr. "Patterns of Connection and Their Development on Hemingway's *In Our Time*." In *Critical Essays on Ernest Hemingway's "In Our Time,"* edited Michael S. Reynolds, 88–102. Boston: G. K. Hall, 1983.
Blitz, Mark. *Heidegger's "Being and Time" and the Possibility of Political Philosophy*. Ithaca, NY: Cornell University Press, 1982.
Burhams, Clinton. "The Complex Unity of *In Our Time*." In *Critical Essays on Ernest Hemingway's "In Our Time,"* edited by Michael S. Reynold, 76–119. Boston: G. K. Hall, 1983.
Cooper, Stephen. *The Politics of Ernest Hemingway*. Ann Arbor: University of Michigan Research Press, 1987.
Farias, Victor. *Heidegger et le Nazisme*. Paris: Editions Verdier, 1988.
Fenton, Charles. *The Apprenticeship of Ernest Hemingway*. New York: Farrar, Straus, 1954.
Gillespie, Michael Allen. *Hegel, Heidegger, and the Ground of History*. Chicago: University of Chicago Press, 1984.
Hagemann, E. R. "'Only Let the Story End as Soon as Possible': Time and History in Ernest Hemingway's *In Our Time*." *Modern Fiction Studies* (1980): 255–261.
Heidegger, Martin. *Introduction to Metaphysics*. New Haven, CT: Yale University Press, 1959.
———. *Being and Time*. New York: Harper and Row, 1962.
———. *Nietzsche: Nihilism*. New York: Harper and Row, 1982.
Hemingway, Ernest. *In Our Time*. New York: Charles Scribner's Sons, 1925.
———. *The Sun Also Rises*. New York: Charles Scribner's Sons, 1926.
———. *Men Without Women*. New York: Charles Scribner's Sons, 1927a.
———. *Winner Take Nothing*. New York: Charles Scribner's Sons, 1927b.
———. *A Farewell to Arms*. New York: Charles Scribner's Sons, 1929.
———. *Death in the Afternoon*. New York: Charles Scribner's Sons, 1932.
———. *For Whom the Bell Tolls*. New York: Charles Scribner's Sons, 1940.
———. *Across the River and Into the Trees*. New York: Charles Scribner's Sons, 1950.
———. *The Moveable Feast*. New York: Charles Scribner's Sons, 1964.
———. *The Nick Adams Stories*. New York: Charles Scribner's Sons, 1972.
Hoffman, Charles and A. C. Hoffman. "'The Truest Sentence': Words as Equivalents of Time and Place." In *In Our Time*. In *Hemingway: A Reevaluation*," edited by Donald R. Noble, 99–114. Troy, NY: Whitston Publishing, 1983.
Johnston, Kenneth. "Hemingway and Cezanne: Doing the Country." *American Literature* 56 (1984): 28–34.
Kort, Wesley, A. "Human Time in Hemingway's Fiction." *Modern Fiction Studies* (1980), 579–596.
Lee, Robert. ed. *Ernest Hemingway: New Critical Essays*. London: Vision, 1983.
Locke, John. *The Second Treatise of Government*. New York: Liberal Arts, 1952.
Meyers, Jeffrey. "Hemingway'sSecond War: The Greco-Turkish Conflict, 1920–1922." *Modern Fiction Studies* (1987): 25–36.
Murphy, Richard. *The World of Cezanne 1839–1900*. New York: Time-Life, 1968.
Nakajima, Kenji. *"Big Two-Hearted River" as the Extreme of Hemingway's Nihilism*. Tokyo: Eichosha, 1979.

Poeggler, Otto. *Der Denkweg Martin Heideggers*. Cologne and Opladen, FRG: Westdeutscher Verlat, 1963.
Reynolds, Michael. *Hemingway's Reading 1910–1940*. Princeton: Princeton University Press, 1981.
———, ed. *Critical Essays on Ernest Hemingway's In Our Time*. Boston: G. K. Hall, 1983.
Schwan, Alexander. *Politische Philosophie im Denken Heideggers*. Cologne and Opladen, FRG: Westdeutscher Verlag, 1965.
Seed, David. "The Picture of the Whole: *In Our Time*." In *Ernest Hemingway: New Critical Essays*, edited by A. Robert Lee, 13. London: Vision, 1983.
Slabey, Robert M. "The Structure of *In Our Time*." In *Critical Essays on Ernest Hemingway's "In Our Time,"* edited by Michael S. Reynolds, 76–87. Boston: G. K. Hall, 1983.
Stephens, Robert. *Hemingway's Nonfiction*. Chapel Hill: University of North Carolina Press, 1968.
Williams, Wirt. *The Tragic Art of Ernest Hemingway*. Baton Rouge: Louisiana State University Press, 1981.
Wilson, Edmund. *The Shores of Light*. New York: Farrar, Straus, and Young, 1952.
Young, Philip. *Hemingway: A Reconsideration*. University Park: Pennsylvania State University Press, 1966.
Zuckert, Catherine H. *Natural Right and the American Imagination: Political Philosophy in Novel Form*, 161–195. Lanham: Rowman and Littlefield, 1990.

3 Hemingway, Hopelessness, and Liberalism

William Curtis

What does the literature of Hemingway mean for liberal politics? There are critics who would challenge the legitimacy of this question because they deny that art and literature are, or ever should be, relevant to political life.[1] Nevertheless, there is a venerable tradition in Western political philosophy, stretching from Plato to Richard Rorty, which insists that art and literature are intrinsically political and vital to politics. Art and literature are influential vehicles of cultural meaning. As such, they reflect, represent, interpret, teach, challenge, and transform society's values, values that lie at the foundations of moral and political life. Thus, on the Platonic-Rortian view, art and literature inform and influence the ethical and political ideas, identities, and behaviors of citizens, sometimes directly and obviously, and other times much more subtly, perhaps even subconsciously.

In Plato's *Republic*, Socrates famously argues that poetry and drama are integral to the moral and civic education of the Guardians because these art forms provide them with inspiring ethical and political exemplars. Stories glorifying bad examples, on the other hand, must be purged from the utopian polis lest they corrupt the Guardians' moral development. Rorty perceives a similarly important educational role for stories to play in the modern liberal polity. In contrast to the authoritarian *Republic*, however, Rorty cannot simply dictate the censorship of works that are politically illiberal. Liberals, after all, believe in tolerance and freedom of expression. Instead, Rorty suggests that liberals think of works of art (and philosophy, which for Rorty is a genre of literature) as falling into two categories: (1) works that are useful to the liberal political project of establishing the freedom and equality of all citizens; and (2) works that are valuable to individuals' idiosyncratic projects of private self-creation and the private pursuit of aesthetic entertainment and bliss (Rorty 1989, 65–69, 141–198).[2]

Literature in the first category guides liberal democratic citizens to better understand what our ideals of equality and freedom mean. A liberal community should pay particular attention to works of art that bolster, fruitfully challenge, and extend our conception of justice, thereby fomenting, in Hume's phrase, "a progress of the sentiments". According to Rorty, one way of understanding the liberal quest for justice is to see it as a process

> of coming to see other human beings as "one of us" rather than as "them" [which] is a matter of detailed description of what unfamiliar people are like and of redescription of what we ourselves are like. This is not a task for theory but for genres such as ethnography, the journalist's report, the comic book, the docudrama, and, especially, the novel. Fiction like that of Dickens, Olive Schreiner, or Richard Wright gives us details about the kinds of suffering being endured by people to whom we had not previously attended (Rorty 1989, xvi).

Political philosophy in Category 1 might contain analytical arguments which, for example, contend that liberal justice requires affirmative action policies for historically oppressed minorities. A novel from this category might tell a story that makes us newly identify with and better appreciate the struggles of those oppressed minorities and convince us in this way that affirmative action is perhaps warranted. Rorty's first category thus includes literature like Upton Sinclair's *The Jungle,* John Dewey's *Democracy and Education,* and Walt Whitman's poetry celebrating the egalitarian spirit of American democracy. These works inform our liberal ideals and inspire hope in liberal political progress.

The second category includes literature that glorifies illiberal fantasies or attacks liberal ideals, and also works that are cynical about or merely uninterested in the pursuit of liberal justice. Literature in this category might include Dostoevsky's *Grand Inquisitor,* the novels of Proust, and Foucault's *Discipline and Punish.* Although, arguably, none of these works bolsters the liberal political project, liberal society does not censor them. Rather, we enjoy and struggle with them in our private lives, apart from our mandate to be good and just liberal democratic citizens.

This article applies Rorty's framework to Hemingway's opus and places it in the second category: They are not works that are very relevant to the public task of constructing a more liberally just society. This is not simply because Hemingway powerfully illustrates the failures of liberal politics; to the contrary, such critique is essential to the liberal project. Rather, Hemingway's stories are politically unhelpful because they are so deeply cynical and pessimistic about politics and the possibility of liberal progress. Indeed, there is a robust streak of anti-intellectualism in Hemingway's work suggesting that speech and thought are themselves useless instruments at best, and obstacles at worst, for solving modern ethical and political problems. This political skepticism strikes at the heart of the liberal project, which ideally maintains that citizens can achieve a just political compromise between their competing views of the good life through deliberative institutions based on their shared freedom and equality. Faith that liberal society can remedy injustices through liberal political institutions is a *sine qua non* of the commitment to liberal justice. Hemingway's work, however, disparages any such faith as hopelessly naïve by suggesting that politics and political power are inevitably corrupt and invariably bring oppression and even war. Indeed, his fiction shares important themes with the writings of one of liberalism's most trenchant critics: Jean-Jacques Rousseau.

Section I presents a brief overview of the disparate interpretations of Hemingway's politics and argues that the primary political commitment embraced by his protagonists is an anti-establishment romanticism. Section II discusses the ethical and political commitments of liberalism that are largely absent from Hemingway's fiction. Section III shows how Hemingway's work importantly shares themes with Rousseau's philosophical critique of liberal politics and society. It concludes, however, that while Rousseau ostensibly suggests positive political solutions to the problems of modern politics, Hemingway does not. Section IV argues that Hemingway's anti-intellectualism and skepticism about self-reflective thought and rational dialogue is fundamentally at odds with the liberal project, which crucially requires both.

Although Hemingway's political hopelessness is problematic for liberal politics, I conclude with the suggestion that there may be a way to redescribe Hemingway's work as politically relevant to liberalism after all. Liberals can read Hemingway as pointing out the dangers of hopelessness, and learn from his broken characters that hopelessness is something that must be recognized and politically attended to. Such redescription, if plausible, is encouraged by Rorty's pragmatic understanding of liberalism, and Rorty would no doubt appreciate the irony if Hemingway deplored the use of his art to bolster liberal politics.

I. HEMINGWAY AND POLITICS

Although there are a variety of political ideologies represented in Hemingway's work, his own political views were enigmatic, and have been the subject of considerable debate among scholars. Keith Kinnamon, for example, asserts that Hemingway was reliably leftist, which is corroborated by his support of the Communists in Cuba and the Republicans in the Spanish Civil War, and by his journalistic contributions to leftist magazines (1996, 157–159). However, while Hemingway sometimes supported Communist *revolutionary activity*, he rejected Communist *politics*. He wrote in a letter, "I can't be a Communist because I hate tyranny and, I suppose, government. . . ." (1981, 360). He also wrote to Russian critic, Ivan Kashkeen, in 1935 that he couldn't be a Communist "because I believe in only one thing: liberty. . . . All the state has ever meant to me is unjust taxation. . . . I believe in the absolute minimum of government"(1981, 419). This anti-government sentiment is even aimed at the New Deal by one of his characters in *Green Hills of Africa*, who calls it "Some sort of Y.M.C.A. show. Starry eyed bastards spending money that somebody will have to pay. Everybody in our town quit work to go on relief" (1935, 191). It is difficult to reconcile these statements with an allegiance to leftist politics.

In contrast to Kinnamon, Scott Donaldson claims that Hemingway had a life-long allegiance to "the ideas of conservative Republicanism" (1977, 123). Stephen Cooper agrees with Donaldson's assessment of the author's radical individualism and distrust of government, but concludes that Hemingway is more accurately described as a libertarian (1987, 134). This label, however, is also problematic. While libertarianism is admittedly a big ideological tent, libertarians tend to be well-disposed toward the commercial world and free market competition. In Hemingway's writings, however, there is as much criticism of capitalism and commerce as there is of Communism.

The difficulty with placing Hemingway on the left-right spectrum is that his deepest political commitment consists of being romantically anti-establishment, regardless of whether the establishment is politically right *or* left. This at least partly explains Hemingway's apparently conflicting political views and his rejection of any systematic political theory. Whatever the political context, if Hemingway could identify disenfranchised, downtrodden rebels courageously struggling against well-entrenched fat cats, he immediately sympathized with the former. This is how he saw the struggle of the Republicans against the Fascists in Spain, the Cuban Communists against the Batista regime, as well as his own battle against the literary critics. Moreover, in Hemingway's fiction, it is unclear that the ultimate consequences of the battle even matter. What is important is the fight itself, against a tough opponent, which pushes his protagonists to achieve an existentialist authenticity through the performance of daring, heroic feats. Winning and establishing a more "just" system is not the point; Hemingway's political skepticism does not allow him to embrace the utopian ideals promised by the theories of rebel intellectuals.

Indeed, Hemingway holds such intellectuals in contempt because of their typical refusal to get their hands dirty in the fight; they are all talk and no action or sacrifice. This sentiment is memorably displayed in *To Have and Have Not*, when the fashionably leftist novelist, Richard Gordon (based on Dos Passos), asks the tall, scarred Nelson Jacks, a WWI vet and Communist organizer, what Jacks thought of his novels:

> "Didn't you like them?"
> "No," said the tall man.
> "Why?"
> "I don't like to say."
> "Go ahead."
> "I thought they were [shit]," the tall man said and turned away (1937, 210).

The sentiment is further illustrated in a scene in *For Whom the Bell Tolls*, when Robert Jordan, in the midst of an urban firefight, meets a famous left-wing British economist who has casually wandered onto the scene. When the economist begins to ask Jordan academic questions about the fighting, Jordan tells him, in censored prose, to "Go muck yourself" (2003, 241).

If Hemingway despises intellectuals, he is also wary of ideologically-driven men of action, who are prone to excesses of cruelty and violence. We see this in *To Have and Have Not*, when the murderous Cuban revolutionary, Roberto, pointlessly kills the poor fisherman, Albert, and Harry Morgan thinks to himself: "F—- his revolution. To help the working man he robs a bank and kills a fellow who works with him and then kills that poor damned Albert that never did any harm. That's a working man he kills. He never thinks of that" (168). Likewise, in *For Whom the Bell Tolls*, the brazen massacre of the Fascists in Pablo's village at the start of "the movement" (99–130) and the "devotion to stern justice" exhibited by the Italian battle police, who summarily execute the officers of the retreating army in *A Farewell to Arms*, serve to illustrate Hemingway's skepticism about ideology and the fanaticism and self-righteous violence it brings (200–203).

Hemingway's work rejects political theory because modern politics is a corrupting, lost cause. The Hemingway protagonist typically recognizes this corruption, perhaps losing the political faith he once had, and consequently attempts to find meaning and redemption in the private realm, whether it be predominantly through his personal relationships (e.g., *A Farewell to Arms*, *The Sun Also Rises*, *For Whom the Bell Tolls*), or perhaps through an engagement with nature, which can be—like Hemingway's portrayals of human relationships—antagonistic, harmonious, or both at the same time (e.g., *In Our Time*, *The Sun Also Rises*, *The Old Man and the Sea*, and his tales of hunting and bull-fighting). Furthermore, it is evident that even these nonpolitical, private efforts made by his protagonists, often set amidst social turmoil that is the product of politics gone wrong, have ambiguous results.

For example, in perhaps Hemingway's most hopeful story, *The Old Man and the Sea*, Santiago indeed triumphs over the monstrous marlin and regains his dignity, but sharks demolish the fish before he can bring it home, and Santiago remains, at the end, a starving old man with naught but his wistful dreams of lions. Does Nick Adams really find a satisfactory solution to the modern human predicament by living in solitude in the Michigan woods? Is Robert Jordan's death in *For Whom the Bell Tolls* glorious or pointless, given the corruption, cruelty, and incompetence of the Republican leaders under whom he fights? It is fair to conclude that not only does Hemingway's work have no hope for politics and justice, but that it is even ambivalent about private attempts to find something to be hopeful about in the context of a nihilistic modern world.

To better understand the challenge that Hemingway's political skepticism presents to liberal politics, however, we must first identify the commitments of liberal politics.

II. LIBERALISM AND HOPE

Jeremy Waldron tells us that, generally, "In politics, the term 'liberalism' denotes a family of positions centered around constitutional democracy, the rule of law, political and intellectual freedom, toleration in religion, morals and lifestyle, opposition to racial and sexual discrimination, and respect for the rights of the individual" (1998, 598). This concise definition is helpful, but it cannot capture the dynamism inherent in the deliberative practice of liberal politics and its goal of implementing a liberal conception of justice in the political community.

Liberal conceptions of justice require that the rights of all citizens be respected, which renders them free and equal. But the meaning and substance of these civil and political rights is not static. Liberal politics is an ongoing process—which theorists sometimes call *public justification*—through which citizens deliberatively determine what "free and equal" amounts to in practice, especially in light of the fact that they hold pluralistic, and sometimes conflicting, ethical visions of the good life. Liberalism requires citizens, some of whom may be government officials, to engage in political dialogue to justify to one another why particular government policies are warranted in light of the freedom and equality that they share. Rorty refers to this process when he writes that, "Liberal society is one whose ideals can be fulfilled by persuasion rather than force, by reform rather than revolution, by the free and open encounters of present linguistic and other practices with suggestions for new practices" (Rorty 1989, 60).

Public justification takes place, of course, in formal political and legal institutions, like the legislature and courts. It also takes place more generally in what Jurgen Habermas and Charles Taylor call the "public sphere": those spaces of civil society where people can openly and critically discuss politics, which include town meetings, radio and television shows, op-ed pages, the blogosphere, and even the ever-trite congregation around the water cooler (Habermas 1991; Taylor 1995, 257–287). Although these latter engagements are less proximate to the deployment of state power, they nevertheless serve to hold government accountable through democratic mechanisms and public pressure.

It is through these inclusive and deliberative engagements that liberal democratic political communities carry on politics in order to compromise upon the authoritative, but always evolving, conception of justice that is enforced by the state through its laws and policies. Public justification, Stephen Macedo tells us, requires that "the application of power should be accompanied by reasons that all reasonable people should be able to accept" (1990, 41). Ideally, citizens consent to the publicly justified use of government power because they accept the reasons that have been given for it. This is how the liberal political order achieves legitimacy and stability, and why liberal democracies claim to be the most successful societies in terms of peace, prosperity, freedom, and humaneness.

There will always be citizens, however, who challenge the political order and accuse it of falling short of justice; indeed, we would worry about a dangerous political complacency if critical voices disappeared. Because establishing liberal justice is an ongoing and arduous task, faith in the process of liberal politics is an essential virtue that citizens must possess: They must believe that progress is possible and not give up on public justification. While there are certainly other virtues and qualities that are essential to good liberal citizenship—like tolerance and open-mindedness, moral imagination, an ability to engage in critical normative discussion, and a command of politically relevant historical knowledge—Rorty emphasizes that liberal hope is crucial because it motivates us to continue to politically engage with one another and improve our conception of liberal justice. Without this motivation, liberal politics cannot succeed.

Hemingway's fiction, however, is bereft of liberal hope and its commitment to deliberative public justification. To the contrary, Hemingway's work shares some prominent themes with the work of an important thinker who also has no hope in liberalism: Jean-Jacques Rousseau.

III. HEMINGWAY AND ROUSSEAU

Rousseau reacts against certain Eighteenth Century Enlightenment ideas about moral and social progress that are central to modern liberalism including: that society can be made better through more widespread liberal education; that men are endowed with reason that enables them to free themselves from "irrational" sources of authority, such as the throne and altar, and create a just and rational political system; that modern science and technology allows man to become, in Descartes's phrase, "lords and masters of nature", and thus make the world safer, healthier, and more productive; and that commerce makes men more humane and cooperative, and brings the material prosperity and security that they seek. Although the Enlightenment *philosophes* had diverse views about religion and politics, they agreed that men could and should create a society in which all individuals can be happy and free, and that men can achieve this if they properly develop their rational faculties and set them to the task of rationally organizing society.

Rousseau began his intellectual career among the *philosophes* and even contributed articles to Diderot's monument of Enlightenment learning, the *Encyclopedie*. Nevertheless, he was highly critical of the emerging modern commercial societies of Europe and of the Enlightenment conception of progress upon which they were founded. Indeed, in the *Discourse on the Sciences and Arts*, Rousseau attacks the modern arts and sciences for their corrupting influence on man. In contrast to Thomas Hobbes, who notoriously depicts man as naturally rapacious, Rousseau argues throughout his work that man is naturally free, happy, and good but becomes oppressed, corrupted, and vicious as he becomes "civilized" and "enlightened."

In the *Discourse on the Origins of Inequality*, Rousseau presents his conception of the "natural man," stripped of all qualities that are produced by society. Rousseau's philosophical anthropology begins with a presocial "state of nature" in which man is a simple animal: He lives a self-sufficient, solitary, and indolent life, wandering about the wilderness. A bountiful Nature provides him with everything he needs, which is very little by civilized standards: "I see him satisfying his hunger under an oak, quenching his thirst at the first stream, finding his bed at the foot of the same tree that furnished his meal; and therewith his needs are satisfied" (1992, 20). Natural man has no language, reason, foresight, imagination, fear or conception of death, morality, politics, love, companions or family, property, or even a residence, and neither has he any need or desire for these things. He must, of course, beware of the various dangers of the wild, but because he has been born amidst them, he is much more physically vigorous than civilized man, who is subject to a multitude of illnesses that are the product of civilization (21–25, 43–44). Sex and reproduction occur with the same casualness with which natural men and women satisfy their other natural needs; children leave their mothers as soon as they can be independent, mother and child ceasing even to be able to recognize one another after a short while (30, 43).

In this state, above all else, man is free, and because of this he is spiritually whole and happy. Echoing Epicurus, Rousseau asserts that natural man's ability to always satisfy his (simple) desires amounts to happiness: "Whoever does what he wants is happy if he is self-sufficient; this is the case of the man living in the state of nature" (1979, 85). Furthermore, a by-product of natural man's happiness is a natural goodness because "man never becomes wicked except when he is unhappy" (44).

Rousseau writes that natural man has two fundamental emotional dispositions: (1) a healthy self-love (*amour de soi*); and (2) a natural sense of pity. Rousseau contrasts *amour de soi* with *amour-propre*, an unhealthy self-love that only emerges as man becomes a social and political creature. While *amour de soi* is a solitary and innocent species of self-concern, *amour-propre* involves the opinions of others, and is thereby rendered contingent and ultimately corrupting. Dennis Rasmussen elaborates, "*Amour de soi* seeks only absolute goods such as security, health, and pleasure—that do not involve comparing oneself to others—whereas *amour-propre* seeks comparative goods and so is the source of vanity, pride, resentment, anger, envy, jealousy and in fact all of the hostile passions" (Rasmussen 2008, 21–22).

The natural pity that Rousseau attributes to natural man means that he immediately and unreflectively sympathizes when he sees another animal in pain. He lives by the "maxim of natural goodness": "Do what is good for you with the least possible harm to others" (*Discourse on the Origins of Inequality,* 37–38). Thus, natural man is innocently self-concerned, and is bereft of any inclination to harm or dominate others. Yet underlying both of these qualities is the genuine source of happiness: natural man's sentiment of his existence (43). "This sentiment of existence, stripped of any other emotion, is in itself a precious sentiment of contentment and peace which alone would suffice to make this existence dear and sweet to anyone able to spurn all the sensual and earthly impressions which incessantly come to distract us from it and to trouble its sweetness here-below" (*The Reveries of the Solitary Walker* 1992, 46). Indeed, it is this primary, sublime sentiment of existence that gives rise to *amour de soi,* and motivates natural man to live his independent, harmless, and happy life.

In the *Discourse on the Origins of Inequality,* Rousseau describes natural man's fall from this idyllic state, as he ultimately becomes the sociable and, consequently, dependent, self-alienated, wicked, unhappy man of modern society. Bountiful Nature in Rousseau's story abruptly becomes more harsh, and natural men through the centuries begin to cooperate and compete for survival. Their increasing social interaction causes *amour-propre* to stir in their breasts as they begin to compare themselves to one another (*Discourse on the Origins of Inequality,* 44–45). But there is a pertinent middle period in this tale of descent that is particularly relevant to a pervasive theme in Hemingway's fiction. Rousseau describes this period as one in which bands of savage families live together in primitive "Hut societies": "although men had come to have less endurance and although natural pity had already undergone some alteration, this period of the development of human faculties, maintaining a golden mean between the indolence of the primitive state and the petulant activity of our [modern] *amour-propre,* must have been the happiest and most durable epoch (48)." Rousseau is thus not merely enamored of the animal-like existence of natural man; he shows certain appreciation for the development of what we normally think of as humanity's most noble capacities: morality and virtue, dignity, friendship, and love. The problem is that inextricably linked to these capacities is the sort of social competition for power and esteem that ultimately makes us all unfree and miserable. The noble savages of this middle epoch, however, are in a balanced state where they have developed these positive capacities that go hand-in-hand with *amour-propre,* but their *amour-propre* has not yet become disastrously problematic for their freedom and happiness.

Inevitably, however, this golden epoch deteriorates, especially as a division of labor emerges and social and economic inequalities dramatically increase. According to Rousseau, economic development enables the rise of all the other sophisticated arts and sciences of civilization, which are fruits of and further facilitate our corruption (*Discourse on the Origin of Inequality,* 49–51). The end result of this fall is modern, liberal, commercial society, in which no one is free, equal, or happy, not even the rich since they are dependent upon the poor and jealous of each other. Contrary to the *philosophes*, modern commerce, which, to paraphrase Oscar Wilde, puts a price on everything but knows the value of nothing, does not make us humane, cooperative, secure, and happy. Rather, it stokes the flames of our unnatural desires and turns us into grasping, materialistic frauds. As Rousseau puts it, "Suspicions, offenses, fears, coldness, reserve, hate, betrayal will hide constantly under that uniform and false veil of politeness, under that much vaunted urbanity which we owe to the enlightenment of our century (*Discourse on the Sciences and Arts* 1992, 6)." Indeed, as Arthur Melzer observes, Rousseau believes that "the modern commercial republic . . . necessarily creates a society of smiling enemies, where each individual pretends to care about others precisely because he cares only about himself" (Melzer 1997, 282).

In different works, Rousseau suggests three solutions to the dependence and misery of modern society: (1) citizenship in a virtuous republic, the solution depicted especially in *The Social Contract*; (2) a highly contrived course of education and socialization that enables one to retain one's naturalness amidst society, which is the solution found in *Emile*; and (3) the path of the philosopher or artist, found in Rousseau's autobiographical writings, by which one achieves natural goodness through genius, self-knowledge, solitude, and strength of spirit.

Hemingway's work provocatively shares Rousseau's negative assessment of modern commerce and politics. A central theme in his work is the fallenness and corruption of modern society, which tries to hide its crass commercialism and blimpish nationalism under a thin veneer of pollyannish liberal propaganda. For Hemingway, modern politics, in all of its forms, has resulted in hypocrisy, oppression, and war. Moreover, as in Rousseau's writings, Hemingway's work contrasts modern civilization with the essential goodness of apolitical Nature. It is telling that Hemingway claimed that all genuine American literature can be traced back to *Huck Finn*, and Philip Young (1966) has suggested that *In Our Time* is a retelling of the Huck Finn saga (Young 1966). Twain himself exhibits Rousseauian themes in his novel: Huck Finn, who has affinities with Rousseau's savage, sets out to escape pretentious, oppressive civilization to find a more authentic existence in nature on the river. Catherine Zuckert notes that Hemingway reverses the action of *Huck Finn* in *In Our Time*: "Whereas Huck traveled from civil society to the state of nature and back, Nick [Adams] grows up in the Michigan woods, runs away from home to join the war in Europe, and then returns home to find peace and satisfaction living all by himself in the state of nature. For Hemingway, that which is good in human life is to be found in nature" (Zuckert 2010, 19–49). Indeed, many of Hemingway's protagonists aspire to be the self-sufficient, unsociable, unreflective Rousseauian natural man, an aspiration that emerges in the wake of a great pain that has been suffered as the result of being involved with "civilization."

But like Rousseau, Hemingway also indicates that the aspiration is ultimately futile: Once one has been civilized, one cannot recapture the happy, innocent state of natural man.

These Rousseauian themes are poignantly developed in *The Sun Also Rises*. The initial setting of Paris provides the perfect Rousseauian scene of the moral corruption and misery of modern society. Jake arrives at the *bal musette* with a prostitute (with whom we know he cannot have the traditional transaction) and presents her to his friends as his "fiancée," and the petty dissembling ensues (18). Lady Brett enters with two effete homosexual men, at whom Jake feels an inexplicable rage, perhaps because they can physically perform with a woman (like Brett) but, of course, do not. The torment that Jake and Brett feel in each other's presence because they cannot be together is palpable. Robert Cohn is instantly bewitched by Brett and is poised to leave his wife, the hapless Frances, which results in Brett shortly thereafter using him as a temporary sexual distraction with a tryst in San Sebastian. This tryst, of course, sets the stage for Cohn's climactic jealous rage in Pamplona toward the end of the novel. The whole Parisian scene—the dialogue, mannerisms, and motives—is awash with blasé affectation and a disdain for any kind of moral seriousness or sense of responsibility; these quaint notions apparently no longer exist for this jaded postwar generation (14–28). In direct contrast to Rousseau's natural man, all of the characters have feverish desires that far outstrip their abilities to satisfy them.

When Jake and Bill go fishing in the Spanish countryside, however, we get a blissful respite from the insidious social competition that subsequently resumes and intensifies when they meet up with Brett, Mike, and Robert in Pamplona for the fiesta. The moment the two friends get on the bus and start their journey to Nature, they get away from the insecure and lovesick Cohn, who is an exemplary Rousseauian specimen of civilization: While he is very "nice," he is also utterly torn apart by conflicting passions and indulgent illusions—the very opposite of the unified soul of Rousseau's natural man—which ultimately lead him to commit violence against his "friends." On the bus to the countryside, Jake and Bill have a fiesta with the simple, unpretentious Basque folk who pass around the wineskin and joke with the two Americans (103–108). The penurious Basques insist on buying them drinks when they stop at a posada. When Jake buys a round and tries to leave a tip, the naïve waitress gives it back to him, thinking that he has misunderstood and overpaid (106). Avarice is clearly not something that afflicts these country folk. The Basques and the village waitress resemble the savages of Rousseau's primitive "Golden Age": obviously communal, but also relatively unspoiled, free, and happy.

Indeed, Hemingway's admiration for the natural virtue of the simple peasant is a prominent theme in his work. The peasant *partizans* in *For Whom the Bell Tolls*, particularly faithful old Anselmo, and the intrepid trio, Sordo, Agustín, and Andrés, fit the mold. The relatively worldly Pilar and the fallen Pablo are more complex, but still demonstrate noble peasant virtues. Pilar is perhaps the most admirable character in the book, and Pablo, although he is utterly (and predictably) corrupted by becoming a village leader of the Loyalist political movement, ultimately retains a chance of redemption at the close of the novel. But perhaps the most famous example of the naturally virtuous peasant in Hemingway's corpus is the impoverished, courageous fisherman, Santiago, in the *The Old Man and the Sea*.

In *The Sun Also Rises*, when Jake and Bill reach the rural town of Burguete, they curiously find that commercial *amour-propre* has preceded them: The country innkeeper guiltily charges them what they paid at the big hotel in Pamplona because it is the "big season" (109–110). They get their revenge by "utilizing" large quantities of wine, which is included in the fixed price. Nevertheless, when they hike out to the Irati River the next day and fish, Jake finally finds his soul at rest and is happy. He and Bill banter about fishing and current events, including politics, though in a detached, light-hearted way. They engage in friendly—not hostile or destructive—competition to see who has caught the biggest trout (Hemingway 1926: 120–121). As Bill returns for lunch from fishing downstream, Jake observes that "His face was sweaty and happy," and the reader knows that this is true of Jake as well (120). There is an easy-going absence of politics between them.

When Jake is absorbed in fishing, he seems to truly experience the sentiment of existence, just as Rousseau does on his solitary nature walks and when he rows on the lake in the *Reveries* (119–120; Rousseau, *Reveries of the Solitary Walker,* 41–48). It is only when Bill maladroitly though innocently broaches the subject of Brett that Jake's soul begins to stir unhappily again, but they agree not to talk about it and have four more happy days of fishing (123–125). This bliss, however, cannot last for civilized man, just as Rousseau's moments of happiness do not last in the *Reveries*. A telegram arrives from Brett, pulling them back to the social morass of Pamplona. Jake briefly finds respite once more toward the end of the novel after he has left his friends and is swimming in solitude at the beach in San Sebastian (237–238). But again he is yanked out of this state by Brett, who calls on him to come collect her in Madrid after she has done what she believes to be an act of virtue, making the young bullfighter she has seduced, Pedro Romero, leave her.

Romero presents an interesting Rousseauian figure as well. He resembles Rousseau's character, Emile: a young man who has been brought up to retain his natural purity amidst a corrupt civilization. All the bull-fighting aficionados agree that Romero is a prodigy and, although we do not get Romero's first person perspective, we can speculate that when Romero is absorbed in his perfect, pure art "for himself," he experiences his sentiment of existence (167–168). Montoya, who Scott Donaldson calls "bullfighting's conscience" (2002, 93), worries that Romero will be corrupted if he gets involved with the decadent, sophisticated crowd over at the Grand Hotel: "Look," said Montoya, "People take a boy like that. They don't know what he's worth. They don't know what he means. Any foreigner can flatter him.

They start this Grand Hotel business, and in one year they're through. . . . He's such a fine boy. . . . He ought to stay with his own people. He shouldn't mix in that stuff (*The Sun Also Rises*, 172)." Montoya is relieved when Jake agrees that Montoya should not deliver the Grand Hotel invitation that has arrived for Romero, and Jake ironically comments that there is an American woman at the Grand Hotel who "collects bull-fighters." Like Emile's Tutor, Montoya acts to control what Romero is exposed to, usurping the boy's autonomy to ensure that he stays uncorrupted.

The climactic moment of Rousseau's *Emile* occurs when the Tutor arranges for Emile to fall in love with the supremely innocent Sophie (414–417). Indeed, it is only because Emile wishes more than anything to be worthy of Sophie's love that he commits himself to being a virtuous member of society. Before he falls in love, Emile is self-sufficient (or believes himself to be) and merely practices the asocial "maxim of natural goodness": He does not harm anyone else. It is through his love for Sophie that he becomes denatured and fit to be a socially moral being, though, if the Tutor's machinations succeed, a social being who naturally resists the degenerative excesses of *amour-propre*.

In *The Sun Also Rises*, there are intriguing, if twisted, parallels to *Emile*: The worldly, rapacious Lady Brett is substituted for Sophie, and Jake for the Tutor, who delivers Romero up to her with predictable results. Montoya, knowing Jake has done this, won't even come near his one-time friend after this betrayal (177, 228). Not only does Romero fall for Brett, but he consequently gets physically brutalized by the jealous Cohn (201–202). Despite his injuries, Romero is still able to perform successfully in the ring the next day, but the pain is visible on his face (219–220). Afterwards, he and Brett abscond to Madrid, where he naively proposes marriage and to make her into his own Sophie by having her grow her hair out and become a proper Spanish wife. Romero's aspiration is, of course, laughable: Far from being a Sophie, Brett's corruption rivals that of Laclos's notorious *femme fatale*, the Marquise de Merteuil in *Les Liaisons Dangereuses* (Laclos was influenced by Rousseau's writings). Though Brett is infatuated with the beautiful, nineteen-year-old matador, she has a crisis of conscience in the face of his purity and sends him away because she is "not going to be one of these bitches that ruins children (243)." She consoles herself by telling Jake, "I don't think I hurt him any." Rousseau and Montoya, however, would share a very different assessment of her actions.

Hemingway also clearly joins Rousseau in his criticism of modern commerce. Again, this can be seen in *The Sun Also Rises*, which displays obsession with money and cost. Indeed, Scott Donaldson sees the central moral theme of the book, the "morality of compensation," emerging from the metaphor that one must pay for what one gets. This ethic flies in the face of the basic preoccupation of most members of modern commercial society, which is always to pay less or not at all. Donaldson suggests that Hemingway depicts Jake, Bill, and Romero as moral exemplars by showing them to be models of financial responsibility. They are contrasted with the "morally aberrant" trio of Brett, Mike, and Robert (Donaldson 2002, 86). Mike is a bankrupt, Brett equally profligate, and Robert is idle and financially callous because of his unearned allowance. Jake, Bill, and Romero, on the other hand, are always picking up the tabs and making sure all debts are paid. Donaldson concludes that "Hemingway's insistence on the need to earn, and to pay for, what you get is in no way a statement in support of materialism, for it is accompanied by disgust with the crooked and corrupting values of the commercial world" (93). He goes on to discuss Hemingway's clear condemnation of the modern commercialization of the Pamplona festival, noting that, for Hemingway, commercialism is a "cancer" that even threatens the purity of bull-fighting.

To Have and Have Not furnishes an even more bluntly negative portrayal of the modern commercial world, as Harry Morgan, trying to make it as an honest fishing guide, is ripped off by an allegedly wealthy tourist and starts his downward spiral to smuggling and murder, ultimately meeting his ignominious fate at the hands of bank robbing revolutionaries whom he is ferrying to Cuba. Crime and commerce go hand-in-hand in this novel. When Mr. Sing, the Chinese "business man," contracts with the financially desperate Harry to smuggle twelve Chinese aliens to U.S. soil from Cuba, he pleads with Harry: "Captain, have you no trust in me? Don't you see that our interests are identical" (34)? Identical, indeed: Harry, in order to avoid the risk of being caught by the authorities, strangles Mr. Sing after taking his money, and dumps the twelve Chinese refugees back on the Cuban beach. This scene aptly illustrates Rousseau's view that in commerce, interests are never aligned; at best, commerce is a system of barely suppressed aggression fueled by inflamed *amour-propre.*

As in Rousseau's thought, it is not only the poor who are made unfree and unhappy by the system. Hemingway skewers the "Haves," ensconced on their yachts, in several keen sketches toward the end of the book. Not only is the existence of the crooked and alcoholic "sixty-year-old grain broker" shown to be precarious and morally empty, but even the "happy family," who made their money the "right way" by selling some nameless product at a several thousand percent mark-up, is an object of disgust and derision (233–240). On the *New Exuma II* lounge two unhappy, Harvard-educated aesthetes: the rich and spoiled Wallace Johnston and his ashamed, 36-year-old catamite, Henry. The adulterous pair on the *Irydia IV*—the insecure addict, Dorothy, and Eddie, the drunken, phlilandering "professional son-in-law"—help to round out this delicious scene of Rousseauian corruption and misery among the millionaires (227–233; 214–246).

Hemingway clearly describes a Rousseauian view of commercial life, and he joins Rousseau's criticism of the misguided idealism and hypocrisy of modern politics as well. In *For Whom the Bell Tolls*, there is a clear sense in which Robert Jordan's heroic fight has become only *against* the Fascists, but not *for* the Communists, because of the cynicism, hypocrisy, and excess violence that he witnesses on the part of the latter. The Rousseauian, and patently bourgeois scene at Gaylord's in Madrid, where Communists and their Russian sponsors mingle, symbolizes the fallen state of political ideology: "Gaylord's itself seemed indecently luxurious and corrupt" (231). It was there that Jordan learns the lesson that, "If a thing was right fundamentally the lying was not supposed to matter. There was a lot of lying though. He did not care for the lying at first. Then later he had come to like it. It was part of being an insider but it was very corrupting business" (229). Jordan remembers how he had once been an idealist but came to realize that idealism was exactly what made you a "bore" at Gaylord's (235–237). He resolves not to take his love, Maria, there because she retains a certain natural innocence, thanks to Pilar's ministrations, despite having been previously gang-raped by the Fascist Falangists (228).

One of the most striking descriptions of the corrupting force of political ideology comes in Pilar's story about the beginning of the Loyalist movement when Pablo led the revolt in his village and cruelly executed the Fascist sympathizers by making them run the gauntlet and off a cliff (98–130). Pilar describes the degeneration of the decent peasants, who are initially akin to Rousseauian savages and are therefore mostly uncomfortable with participating in the brutal executions. Ultimately, however, they turn into a drunken mob that slaughters the aristocrats like animals, "Because the people of this town are as kind as they can be cruel and they have a natural sense of justice and a desire to do that which is right. But cruelty had entered into the lines and also drunkenness.... (116)".

Pilar does not get a chance to tell about the revenge of the Fascists when they retook the town. However, in the wake of her narrative, Jordan admits to himself the problematic nature of his politically-driven, *partizan*-guerilla operations: "The *partizans* did their damage and pulled out. The peasants stayed and took the punishment. I've always known about the other, he thought. What we did to them at the start. I've always known it and hated it and I have heard it mentioned shamelessly and shamefully, bragged of, and boasted of, defended, explained, and denied" (135). Nevertheless, he remains committed to the fight as a matter of his own ethical, existential identity even if he has lost his political faith.

In Hemingway's work, modern politics at best leads to injustice and oppression and at worst leads to war. He agrees with Rousseau that there is redemptive power to be found in Nature, though Hemingway is also more prone to describe and celebrate the challenges that Nature presents, whether it be inclement weather, wild predators, enormous marlins, or magnificent bulls in the Plaza de Toros. Nature, while not always kind, is at least honest and respectable, unlike human beings and most human social interaction. Nature forces one to be honest with oneself.

But Hemingway does not follow Rousseau in proposing suggestions for how one might remedy the problems of modern society that they both acknowledge. Hemingway does not imagine a political solution to the degradation of modern politics as Rousseau does in *The Social Contract*; indeed, one can scarcely imagine him doing so, given his pervasive political skepticism. Hemingway also shows such hostility to intellectuals, theorists, and writers that he appears to dispute the possibility that mere contemplation, even in the natural surroundings depicted in the *Reveries*, could bring redemption by itself. Lastly, Hemingway offers no educational solution, like the one we find in *Emile*, unless the education is that of war.

Indeed, there is a sense in Hemingway that only veterans of some kind of intense struggle—*physical*, not just intellectual—can truly come to appreciate their sentiments of existence, even if this experience inevitably proves fleeting. It is the experience of the immediacy of risk and death that makes love, as well as solitude in nature, take on meaningful existence for the veteran. It is clear that Jake, Count Mippopolous, Robert Jordan, Frederic Henry, and Santiago can achieve these moments of meaningfulness, while Robert Cohn and Richard Gordon cannot. But having experienced war or other risky physical struggle, the Hemingway protagonist walks a fine line between experiencing ephemeral moments of peace and happiness, and letting the experience of the struggle, with the wounds that it inflicted, drive the hero over the edge into madness and self-destruction.

Rousseau, too, believes that those moments in which the intellectual experiences the sentiment of existence are ephemeral (though they are experienced as timeless), but the intellectual's struggle is primarily just that: intellectual and/or artistic. Hemingway is too anti-intellectual, too infatuated with the strength and purity of the man of action, to agree with the Swiss thinker here. One could say that while both Rousseau and Hemingway are attracted to the Rousseauian natural man, Rousseau also recognizes that the natural man is ultimately a simplistic amoral brute. Hence, even Emile must be socialized and made moral. Hemingway's protagonists, on the other hand, seem nevertheless to strive to regain the existence of Rousseau's natural man: They want to stop thinking, stop talking, and rid themselves of their past. Hemingway is too pessimistic and skeptical to explicitly offer any theoretical remedies for the moral diffidence that plagues modern man, who is, like Frederic Henry, "embarrassed by the words sacred, glorious, and sacrifice," and finds "Abstract words such as glory, honor, courage, or hallow [are] obscene.... (169)". Yet such concepts are essential to Rousseau's political solution to modern fallenness presented in *The Social Contract*.

While Rousseau harshly criticizes the goals and fruits of Enlightenment philosophy and the emerging liberal commercial societies that are based upon it, he does not embrace anti-intellectualism and exalt action at the expense of thought. We must beware of reason and language corrupted by *amour-propre*, but reason and language might be cured by Rousseau's three solutions. Hemingway, however, indicates that anti-intellectualism is the only honorable, sane reaction to the corrupt reason and language that surround his protagonists.

IV. HEMINGWAY'S ANTI-INTELLECTUALISM AND LIBERALISM

Hemingway's work exhibits a disdain for the proposition that human deliberative reason can find a solution to the nihilism and injustice that afflicts the modern world. As Robert Evans puts it, Hemingway's anti-intellectualism is "an act of calculated retrenchment, involving a deliberate refusal to admit the free play of the higher intellectual faculties—reason, speculative thought, and imaginative vision—as legitimate guides for conduct and as potential means for clarifying, ordering, and enriching human experience" (Evans 1966, 164). Hemingway's protagonists typically seem exempt from, or even desperately try to avoid, meaningful reflection. For example, near the end of *In Our Time*, Nick Adams feels happy upon setting out into the wilderness alone because he has "left everything behind, the need for thinking, the need to write, other needs" (134). After Nick sets up camp and begins to reminisce about his comrade, Hopkins and his method of making coffee, Nick becomes aware that "His mind was starting to work." Fortunately, "He knew he could choke it because he was tired enough" (142). Evans observes that "Hemingway opposes the thrust of thought with the counter-thrust of action: Carrying a heavy pack for miles uphill on a hot day, pitching camp, stowing your gear away—sheer, draining physical activity—this is the great thought-preventive, the central weapon in the unremitting warfare against the mind" (Evans 1966, 167). Other "weapons," Evans notes, soon show up in Hemingway's work, including drinking, sex, hunting, and war, but these are essentially variations on the primary theme of action as a distraction from thought (170).

Frederic Henry, in *A Farewell To Arms*, is also anti-thought, which includes being anti-meaningful conversation. When he and the priest are discussing the war and he concludes that the war is not coming to an end, he confesses, "That's why I never think about these things. I never think and yet when I begin to talk I say the things I have found out in my mind without thinking" (165). As he says later in the novel, "I was not made to think. I was made to eat. My God, yes. Eat and drink and sleep with Catherine (210)", and still later to Catherine, "Let's not think about anything" (228). Henry here aspires to be Rousseau's unthinking, sensuous, and happy natural man.

Hemingway also negatively juxtaposes the three cautious, reflective doctors who first come to see Henry's badly wounded knee, to the flamboyant Dr. Valentini. The three doctors closely examine the wound, discuss their opinions with one another, and ultimately determine that it would be safest to put Henry's surgery off for six months. In contrast, Valentini sweeps in, takes a quick peek at the knee, announces that he will operate immediately, and then proceeds to have a drink with Henry and discuss women and food (91–95). The surgery is, of course, successful. Valentini is Hemingway's kind of doctor: a man of action who trusts his instincts. The three deliberative doctors are painted as timid incompetents.

In *The Sun Also Rises*, an important aspect of Hemingway's literary style is the fact that we must often glean what the apparently stoic first-person narrator, Jake Barnes, is really feeling by paying close attention to his interlocutors' reactions to him. Self-reflection is scarce in Jake's narrative. While occasionally, and only at night, Jake's thoughts burst through his attempts not to think them ("To hell with you, Brett Ashley"), for the most part Jake, the good journalist, emotionlessly reports the scene, even when he loses his friend Montoya, and even when he delivers his love, Brett, to Romero for their affair. Robert Jordan, likewise, frequently admonishes himself and those around him not to think or talk about things that might distract them from the actions that they must take (*For Whom the Bell Tolls*, 8–9, 17, 21, 34, 43, 168, 171, 340, 469).

Evans argues that "thinking" only means two things in Hemingway: worry and memory. This "makes thought only a subspecies of unpleasant emotion, for both worry and that sort of memory which the Hemingway hero tries to repress are characterized by ineffectual preoccupation with circumstances which cannot be altered and by an accompanying inner distress and pain. Small wonder that the protagonist flees from such 'thought' to the bright fields of danger, where he can at least encounter the immediacies of sensation and deed!" (Evans 1966, 168) The problem with the Hemingway protagonist in Evans's view is that he "lacks the intellectual resources to achieve a distance from his suffering, to contemplate it, and to learn from it something fundamental about himself." Hemingway's protagonists typically suffer from the lingering pain of a "wound," and Evans recognizes that the "relentless denial of thought" is supposed to be justified as a reaction to that pain. Nevertheless, this denial renders Hemingway's world "remarkably boring and narrow" because of the "vast reaches of moral, intellectual, aesthetic, and even social experience that are forever hopelessly beyond anyone penned in these novels by the author's private geography of despair" (174).

The "denial of thought," which includes the denial or evasion of memory, means that the Hemingway protagonist tries to escape his history. History has wounded the protagonist, undermined his values and ideals, and left him with no hopeful vision for the future. As a result, Evans notes, Hemingway is prone to render "A world devoid of a sense of history and time, of past actions and future consequences, of speculative thought and imaginative vision [that] is not a human world at all. It is an animal world, a world of weathers and immediate sensations. It is not surprising, then, in such a world, that language and the values funded in language become suspect and embarrassing"(176). Evans concludes that Hemingway's is an emotionally immature response to the world, that the Hemingway heroes are in fact moral cripples, and that, "For all its blood and thunder, Hemingway's world is not quite man-sized" (176).

More recently, critic James Wood adds to this verdict, judging Hemingway's "nullification of thought" to be little more than a "ratification for permissible male reticence": "It has the effect, throughout [*True At First Light*] and elsewhere in Hemingway's writing, of making the hero not an active mind but merely a voyeur of his own obscurities" (Wood 1999, 15). The "Hemingway revolution," Wood writes, was "to take first-person narration and make it into the original style of a third person author," which, Wood admits, can produce undeniable force and beauty. Nevertheless, Wood warns that this style of writing is problematic because it "moves like the mind but has no mind in it," and "stifles feeling and then stylizes the very stifling." Hemingway's famous stylistic reticence is ultimately just the author giving up on language—thought and speech—a curious surrender for a *writer* to make. Moreover, it leaves Hemingway's macho literary preoccupations—bull-fighting, sex, drinking, hunting, etc.—unexplained. Indeed, Wood suggests that these preoccupations amount to a tiresome metaphysical provincialism in Hemingway's work, because it "has no interest in explaining itself and there little interest in admitting the reader."

In Hemingway's defense, Lionel Trilling argues that Hemingway's reticence and emphasis on the authenticity of action over speech and thought was perhaps justified in the tragic wake of WWI. It is not cynicism or despair behind Hemingway's ubiquitous understatement, but rather that "Men had made so many utterances in such fine language that it had become time to shut up.... [i]t is not so much *reason* as it is *rationalization* he resists" (Trilling 1961, 65). While Trilling's point is well-taken, it is nevertheless difficult to find Hemingway making a distinction between reason and rationalization. Liberals can join Hemingway's condemnation of the eloquent political speech that led to the unspeakable horrors of WWI, but still finally agree with Wood that if, "for a brief historical moment, it was important for literature that Hemingway insist on what was not describable—that he make a hard clearing through the more untruthful descriptions of other writers—that moment soon passed, even in Hemingway's lifetime, and then was left without proper enemies, and with merely the defense of his own forlorn lack" (Wood 1999, 15).

It is understandable that Hemingway would want to turn away from the corruption, hypocrisy, and stupidity of the politics that resulted in WWI. The attempts by his protagonists to reject this politics and forge meaning for themselves through risky, existentialist rebellion are without doubt aesthetically inspiring. Nevertheless, Hemingway's denigration of thought and the possibility of productive, rational, political dialogue cannot be reconciled with a commitment to liberalism as a form of politics based upon deliberative rationality. Clearly, liberals believe that action must be taken too, but only actions that one can rationalize and articulate as consistent with a publicly justified conception of liberal justice. Good liberal citizens cannot simply act unthinkingly and instinctually as Hemingway's characters do. Nor can they repress history and avoid understanding their political identities in relation to their history. It is, after all, a political community's history that provides the substance of politics and the context in which injustice can be identified and ameliorated.

Liberal citizens do not have to be superhumanly reflective, of course, but they must be appropriately open to reasoned argument that some of their practices may be unjust and be prepared to abandon them if they cannot be publicly justified. The evolving liberal compromise is created through the exchange of reasons with fellow citizens. Hemingway's assertion that, "So far, about morals, I know only what is moral is what you feel good after and what is immoral is what you feel bad after," will not cut it in the court of public justification (*Death in the Afternoon* 1960, 4). Tellingly, Hemingway's grounding of morality on sincere, authentic feeling is once again akin to an important thread in Rousseau's philosophy (*Emile*, 289–291).

Thus, while one does not have to agree with Evans that Hemingway's protagonists are merely moral cripples, liberals must acknowledge that they are failures as liberal citizens. They do not believe in liberal politics and its ongoing project to deliberatively articulate the substance of liberal justice. Instead, they attempt to turn off their rational faculties and live by mere physical feeling. As Wood notes, Hemingway and his protagonists are anti-explanation and anti-justification. Do we ever discover why Frederic Henry joins the Italian cause? Why Nick leaves home? Are they even capable of formulating answers to these questions? Hemingway's characters shun self-reflection as well as the reflective dialogue that is at the core of the liberal project and instead engage in, as several critics suggest, "baby talk" (Lewis 1934, 28; MacDonald 1952, 267; Wood, 1999, 15). But baby talk will not do for a pluralistic citizenry trying to accomplish the complex task of identifying and compromising on a conception of justice that treats all as free and equal. Indeed, as liberal societies progress, their political dialogue becomes more refined. *Contra* Rousseau, this does not mean evermore corrupt. Rather, it means, we hope, that liberal society can establish an even more nuanced and improved conception of justice as it takes into account facts and injustices to which it was previously blind. But for Hemingway, as for Rousseau, there is no progress to be found in liberal politics. For him, if one is honest and acknowledges the truth of reality, one ends up just where Jake Barnes does at the end of *The Sun Also Rises*: ultimately hopeless.

V. CONCLUSION

While Hemingway's exaltation of the tragic modern rebel's existentialist struggle on the backdrop of a corrupt modern world may be romantically attractive, it provides little substance for a positive, realistic politics. Critic Dwight MacDonald is perhaps harsh when he remarks that, in Hemingway's work, "A feeling that loyalty and bravery are the cardinal virtues and that physical action is the basis of the good life—even when reinforced with the kind of nihilism most of us get over by the age of twenty—these don't add up to a philosophy" (1952, 171). This judgment might nevertheless be echoed by liberals engaged in the political struggle to create a just society: Hemingway's agonistic, existentialist romanticism doesn't add up to much of a political philosophy.

Although we do not want Hemingway's hopelessness infecting our political life, the liberal solution for what to do with ostensibly non-liberal works of art is to relegate them to the private realm where they can remain important for the private ethical and aesthetic projects of individuals. Liberal citizens like all human beings, experience moments, even periods, of hopelessness. Hemingway has a unique and artful way of portraying this very human experience that has clearly resonated with many people. Moreover, as illustrations of what can happen to modern people who experience the ravages of war and the inevitable cruelties of political and commercial competition, Hemingway's stories might remind us to be more aware of these harms and of the dangerous hopelessness they produce, despite the fact that his characters cannot serve as political exemplars since they cannot overcome their hopelessness.

In fact, this observation might suggest that there is a liberal public use for Hemingway after all. While Rorty's framework plausibly places Hemingway's work in the private realm because of its political hopelessness, Rorty also reminds us of the power of redescription, that "anything can be made to look good or bad by being redescribed" (1989, 73). Can we redescribe Hemingway's literature in such a way that it can helpfully inform the liberal political project? Perhaps there is at least one way that liberals *qua* liberals can fruitfully learn from Hemingway's work: by treating it as an historical artifact that bears witness to a time when liberal hope was desperately under siege. After all, it is crucial for liberals to be historically reflective, as Hemingway's characters are not. Yet Hemingway's tragic, unforgettable characters can serve as poignant reminders to liberals of what can happen when people are wounded, become hopeless, and give up on politics, communication, and even thought itself. His stories can serve as cautionary tales that elicit empathy among liberals for the hopeless, and motivate liberals to politically attend to them. We must admit, however, that given his own political predilections, Hemingway might deplore the use of his art for this purpose. Providing liberal aid to his protagonists would rob them of their risky, rebellious meaning. But liberals need not concern themselves with his likely disapproval: This is the risk all artists run.

NOTES

1. The Nineteenth Century Aesthetic Movement, for example, famously claimed that art should be for art's sake alone. On this view, to see art through a political lens inevitably misses or even bowdlerizes its aesthetic value.

2. Richard Rorty, *Contingency, Irony, and Solidarity*, Cambridge: Cambridge University Press, 1989), xvi, 65–69, 141–198. Rorty suggests that the novel is a much more effective vehicle for evolving our liberal sensibilities than are works of political philosophy. I would argue, however, that this depends on things like the issue and the audience. It seems plausible, for example, that a systematically constructed analytical argument is going to be more persuasive to logophile types than a melodramatic narrative, which might be very convincing to another sort of mind. As a pragmatist, Rorty should be for what works when it comes to persuading people to be liberally just.

WORKS CITED

Baker, Carlos. *Ernest Hemingway: A Life Story*. New York: Charles Scribner's Sons, 1969.

Cooper, Stephen. *The Politics of Ernest Hemingway*. Ann Arbor, MI: UMI Research Press, 1987.

Donaldson, Scott. "Hemingway's Morality of Compensation." In Ernest Hemingway's *The Sun Also Rises: A Casebook,* edited by Linda Wagner-Martin, 81–98. Oxford: Oxford University Press, 2002.

———. *By Force of Will: The Life and Art of Ernest Hemingway*. New York: Viking, 1977.

Evans, Robert. "Hemingway and the Pale Cast of Thought." *American Literature*, 38 (2) (1966): 161–176.

Habermas, Jurgen. *The Structural Transformation of the Public Sphere*. Cambridge, MA: The MIT Press, 1991.

Hemingway, Ernest. *In Our Time*. New York: Charles Scribner's Sons, 1925.

———. *The Sun Also Rises*. New York: Charles Scribner's Sons, 1926.

———. *Green Hills of Africa*. New York: Charles Scribner's Sons, 1935.

———. *To Have and Have Not*. New York: P. F. Colliers and Son, 1937.

———. *Death in the Afternoon*. New York: Charles Scribner's Sons, 1960.

———. *A Farewell to Arms*. New York: Scribner, 1929 (1979).

———. *For Whom the Bell Tolls*. New York: Scribner, 1940 (2003).

———. *Ernest Hemingway: Selected Letters, 1917–1961*. Edited by Carlos Baker. New York: Charles Scribner's Sons, 1981.

Kinnamon, Keith. "Hemingway and Politics," In *The Cambridge Companion to Hemingway*, edited by Scott Donaldson, 149–169. Cambridge: Cambridge University Press, 1996.

Lewis, Wyndham. *Men Without Art*. New York: Russell and Russell, Inc., 1934

Macedo, Stephen. *Liberal Virtues: Citizenship, Virtue, and Community in Liberal Constitutionalism*. Oxford: Clarendon Press, 1990.

MacDonald, Dwight. *Against the American Grain*. New York: Random House, 1952.

Melzer, Arthur M. "Rousseau and the Modern Cult of Sincerity." In *The Legacy of Rousseau*, edited by Clifford Orwin and Nathan Tarcov, 274–295. Chicago: University of Chicago Press, 1997.

Rasmussen, Dennis Carl. *The Problem and Promise of Commerical Society: Adam Smith's Response to Rousseau*. University Park, PA: Pennsylvania State University Press, 2008.

Rorty, Richard. *Contingency, Irony, and Solidarity*. Cambridge: Cambridge University Press, 1989.

Rousseau, Jean-Jacques. *The Collected Writings of Rousseau*, edited by Christopher Kelly, 128–224. Vol. 4, Hanover, NH: University of New England Press, 1994.

———. *Emile or On Education*. Translated by Allen Bloom, A., New York: Basic Books, 1979 [1762].

———. "Discourse on the Sciences and Arts." In *The Collected Writings of Rousseau*, edited by Rogers Masters and Christopher Kelly, 3–22 Vol. 2, Hanover, NH: University of New England Press, 1992 [1750].

———. "Discourse on the Origins of Inequality." In *The Collected Writings of Rousseau*, edited by Rogers Masters and Christopher Kelly, 1–95. Vol. 3, Hanover, NH: University of New England Press, 1755 (1992b).

———. "*The Reveries of the Solitary Walker.*" In *The Collected Writings of Rousseau*, edited by Christopher Kelly, 3–90. Vol. 8, Hanover, NH: University of New England Press, 1992c.

Taylor, Charles. *Philosophical Arguments*. Cambridge, MA: Harvard University Press, 1995.

Trilling, Lionel. "Hemingway and His Critics." In *Hemingway and His Critics*, edited by Carlos Baker, 61–70. New York: Hill and Wang, 1961 (1939).

Waldron, Jeremy. "Liberalism." In *Routledge Encyclopedia of Philosophy*, edited by Edward Craig. London: Routledge, 1998.

Wood, James. "The Lion King," *New York Times*, 11 July, 1999.

Young, Philip. *Hemingway: A Reconsideration*, University Park, PA: Pennsylvania State University Press, 1966.

Part III
The Politics of Morality, Manliness, and God

4 Ethics Without Theodicy in Ernest Hemingway's *A Farewell to Arms*

Sayres Rudy[1]

> For even though no one cares to admit it openly, consolations would be needed, the great inexhaustible consolations, the possibilities of which I often felt at the bottom of my heart, almost frightened to be containing them, the boundless, in so limited a vessel. It is certain that the divinest consolation is contained in humanity itself—we would not be able to do much with the consolation of a god; only that our eye would have to be a trace more seeing, our ear more receptive, the taste of a fruit would have to penetrate more completely, we would have to endure more odor, and in touching and being touched be more aware and less forgetful–: in order promptly to absorb out of our immediate experiences consolations that would be more convincing, more preponderant, more true than all the suffering that can ever shake us to our very depths.
>
> Rainer Maria Rilke 1972 [1915]: 138–139

> I believe that the Evil—and acute fear of Evil—which [literature] expresses has a sovereign value for us. But this concept does not exclude morality: on the contrary, it demands a 'hypermorality.'
>
> Georges Bataille 1985 [1957]: ix

I. A NOVEL POLITICS

In Ernest Hemingway's *A Farewell to Arms* (Hemingway 2003[1929])[2], a novel in five acts, ambulance driver Frederic Henry falls for nurse Catherine Barkley and gets wounded at the Italian front; impregnates Catherine in a hospital bed; abandons the Caporetto retreat to avoid execution for disloyalty; flees from Italy to Switzerland with Catherine; and watches her die giving birth to a stillborn boy. The novel, a feverishly tragic and haunted and bruising love story, suffuses with cruelty and despair. What *jouissance* the narrative evinces or attracts with its relentless suffering has long been interpreted as necessary for Hemingway's doctrine of stoic heroism. The final scene encapsulates, in this view, the lesson of *A Farewell to Arms*: In this brutal, pointless world Frederic can only trudge off in the rain with war and death behind but no peace or life ahead. This putative "code" heroism would render Hemingway a nihilist, staging morbid death-in-life scenarios to enforce a life-as-death ethos of mere survival. But *A Farewell to Arms*—brimming with play, love, energy, and decency—embodies an ethics of desire, fidelity, and multiplicity that rejects precisely this euthanasiac either/or moralism of nihilism/theodicy.

In *A Farewell to Arms* Hemingway refuses a brutal, indifferent world that affords us only providential saintliness *or* dignified resignation. Instead, as Murdoch described in her metaphysics of morality, we realize that "Everyday moral decisions normally involve consideration of details; political and social reflections tend to avoid these (*de minimis non curat lex)* but are sometimes felicitously forced to notice them. As we move from generalities toward the accidental and particular we introduce muddle but also variety and space" (Murdoch 1992, 349). Murdoch captures the sense of Hemingway's novel. Morality is more interesting, more complicated, and more contingent than any theodicy or ideology.

A Farewell to Arms portrays neither spiritual seekers in a purposeful universe nor fatalist survivors in a lifeless cosmos. The book casts impassioned people into a beautiful, vibrant world poisoned by arrogance, violence, bad luck, and moral abstraction. In *A Farewell to Arms* human subjectivity thrives on curiosity, mystery, dreams, fantasy, memory, hope, affection, and pain that make life, *living*, intrinsically valuable—not merely endurable. His magical humanity inhabits horrendous violence as majestic nature does torrential rain. Human and natural landscapes combine throughout *A Farewell to Arms* in their irrepressible vitality, irreducible to sheer miserable devastation. *A Farewell to Arm's* burdened subjects and heavy weather signal not ontological gloom but willful struggle against singular, extimate injury. If the universe, humanity, and nature are not essentially hostile, meaningless, or lifeless, then we may find value *in them* rather than *in overriding them*. Therefore, morality, as described by Wittgenstein in *Tractatus* "is fundamentally an attitude of acceptance of the world of facts which is viewed as a whole" (in Murdoch 1992, 27). Hemingway's story gets its emotive force precisely by denying, by breaking, the ontology of suffering over passionate willing. This takes us from the descriptive to prescriptive registers, as it were, of Hemingway's anti-nihilistic anti-theodicy.

Frederic and Catherine fantasize their union by conjoining their war-wounds (her dead fiancé, his physical-spiritual damage) without clear understanding or speech.[3] Their love grows not by communicating or resolving each other's pain but living anew with it—not despite their suffering, which shapes who they are, but through it. They are not autonomous sovereign subjects joined by an articulately shared identity that precludes or removes conflicting interests. Rather, they are fragmented, dislocated, or "depressed" people attached by an affinity of injury and desire that solves nothing and abhors happy endings *yet makes love*.

Thus Hemingway dismantles the sinister derivation of ontological misery from solitude, loss, or disaffection. Just as loneliness, alienation, suffering,

Ethics Without Theodicy in Ernest Hemingway's A Farewell to Arms

and death do not constitute existence, neither do they preclude love, hope, healing, or life. More radically, Hemingway suggests, it is our unspeakable wounds and unconscious (psychic or erotic) drives that generate our resolute life-force and ground our passionate love. Like Wittgenstein's study of the limits of communication: "The solution of the problem of life is seen in the vanishing of the problem . . . .There are, indeed, things which cannot be put into words. They *make themselves manifest*. They are what is mystical" (in Murdoch 1992, 30). Between the heaven of theodicy and the hell of nihilism, Hemingway traces the love-becoming of people despite, within, particularly *through* their "pieces of tragic utterance"" (Murdoch 1992, 95).

Outside the ordered testimony of being, Frederic and Catherine come together without dissolving into some new romantic sameness; outside the confines of a shared identity their love attracts beyond speech, beyond perspicuous exchange-values. Hemingway describes love as the love of love itself, life as the life of life itself, in this sense, as that which cannot be captured, mastered, or commanded. Thus in *A Farewell to Arms* unions of language and feeling, intention and action, meaning and experience, utterance and reception, one and another always fail or deceive. Yet those indelible gaps create the situation of love, only corrupted when subordinated to some "higher" meaning. *A Farewell to Arms* posits an experiential ethics without domination, where "it is a matter of experience, rather than of faith or definition, that the [mystical] man is a good man" (Murdoch 1992, 355). Frederic and Catherine construct a space for living and loving in which people touch rather than teach, are overcome rather than overcome, by *becoming more fully themselves* through a coruscating physics of sub- and supra-conscious desire and attachment. Hemingway's work embraces life rather than some therapeutic theory of the world or its inhabitants that decides what life is about.

Amid infinite forces moving the affective reactions of vulnerable souls, Hemingway finds love in his characters' *fidelity to difference/immanence* and *disavowal of reconciliation/transcendence*. I extrapolate from this "ethics" of intimacy/extimacy a "politics" of co-existence, pragmatism, and affection without domination. There is a clear separateness between the inner and the outer, the public and the private and "The separateness is to do with the difference between political morality and private morals, and the rough-and-ready unavoidably clumsy and pragmatic nature of former" (Murdoch 1992, 381). It is often supposed that all the suffering and death in love and war exhaust Hemingway's "nihilistic" vision, his advocacy of tough and resigned detachment in a painfully meaningless universe. This perspective reduces Hemingway's aesthetics and ideals to his bleak battles and laconic loners, and his artistic depths to his atmospheric and behavioral surfaces. Hence, the standard ethical view foisted on Hemingway is that to deny life's *transcendent purpose* is to deny life's worth altogether. In either its religious or secular guise, theodicy associates the value of human life with a supra-human *meaning*; bereft of providential Reason, Spirit, or "Good" humans become merely neurotically conscious animals. Humanity must be valued, paradoxically, *outside itself*, in an *explanatory* or *compensatory* account of our suffering as redeemed by or serving a hidden blessing (Geuss 1999). Otherwise, for theodicy, *ontological suffering* entails an *ethics of mere survival*, such as achieving dignity in a senseless world. In a universe of monistic naturalization, the *fact of disenchantment* entails *the value of nihilism*. This elaborate construct that perceives nihilism in any non-transcendent valuation of human becoming is itself wholly nihilistic, as it abstracts value from the "merely" human. By this metric Hemingway's anti-theodicy implies a nihilism that baselessly laments the human-beast that only persists.

The ruse of theodicy is to exclude by fiat sources of human value *outside dualistic metaphysics* and *ethics*. The trick of theodicy-speak is to claim, perversely, that Hemingway's aversion to ontological suffering amounts to a groundless ideology or aesthetic, not a cogent ethics. This fusion of a *meaningless world* with *ethical nihilism* asserts what it claims to abhor: a terrible existence that precludes inherent human worth by definition (Nietzsche 1998 [1887]).[4] The idea that life offers only death or survival, so often attributed to Hemingway, *A Farewell to Arms* rejects vigorously. This ideology of nihilistic theodicy generally conceives desire, play, or will as *anti-ethical*: We recuperate ethics, or supra-beastly human worth, from a disenchanted world by imposing some system on these human motivations from without, above, or beyond. Any theory of an ethics founded *in humanity* (instincts, passions, affectivities, desire, fantasies, or aesthetics) rather than in *overcoming or negating humanity*—any ethics of *humanity-as-human*—theodicy defines as incoherent, echoing justificatory schemes of sovereignty.[5] Hemingway deplores any such ontology or ethics in *A Farewell to Arms*. To Hemingway, any dualistic mystification that subordinates the value of human life to greater "transcendent" or "beneficent" orders like Reason, Divinity, Providence, State, or Law constitutes the true, and truly dangerous, nihilism. It is just this moralistic closure—the humanity-hatred of nihilistic theodicy—that Hemingway denounces in *A Farewell to Arms*.

Hemingway detests, then, the *ontology and normativity of theodicy* and so *A Farewell to Arms* burns with resistance to any justification of suffering on metaphysical conceits of "higher" forces, causes, purposes, or meanings. In *A Farewell to Arms* humanity bursts from savage war in the proliferating textures, sensations, uncertainties, sexualities, sacrifices, flirtations, friendships, dreams, discoveries, desires, flights, madness, games, wills, and "wildness" of Frederic, Catherine, Rinaldi, the Priest, and others. In parallel, nature smothers political hubris as the rivers, trees, mountains, horses, birds, fields, leaves, and dark of night, and light of day overflow the landscape. *Human and natural lives* inhabit, resist, and defeat the wretched occasions of death in war or childbirth. Such suffering confronts but does not obviate human and natural vitality. The passion and fantasy, imagination and fear, loyalty and love that drive characters in *A Farewell to Arms* cannot be subsumed, legislated, regulated, or otherwise expended. They supplement the living of integral, if enduringly and singularly wounded, individuals. Despair, injury, and death are not "the human condition" but the harsh climes where Hemingway reclaims devotion, resolve, and beauty. Cherishing human abandon over divine abandonment Hemingway inverts theodicies of religious church or secular state. Imbuing humans with value to be fulfilled by self-exploration and immersion in their vibrant becoming *A Farewell to Arms* rejects the nihilism that evacuates humanity. From Hemingway's rejection of ontological suffering and ethical survivalism of nihilistic theodicy we may, with caveats, infer the "politics" of *A Farewell to Arms*.

Hemingway's conception of subjectivity affronts the overlain-sovereignties of the (1) self-contained, self-articulated liberal democratic figure disciplined and aggregated by (2) representative institutions. Frederic and Catherine do not choose their pain or desire but are chosen by them; their fidelity is to events that motivate them *as subjects without language, autonomy, or self-determination*. *A Farewell to Arms* abounds in reciprocal excesses: violence and eroticism that exceed comprehension; speech and action that exceed violence and eroticism. In *A Farewell to Arms*, subjects who speak fully and accurately their condition are inconceivable, as desire lies precisely *in this excess*, in the unspeakably abundant drives to war and love. In theories of sovereignty communicative citizens and reflective state apparatuses meet in the mutual transparency of political subjects who present (and bend) their identities toward public agreement. But Hemingway inscribes subjectivity *against* these sovereign fixtures: urges *beneath* the conscious selves and sensations *among* the energized bodies that escape the sanctioned emotions and official semiotics of governing institutions. Hemingway scorns military, matrimonial, and medical formalities of course; but more incisively, he assails the conventional articulation of state and citizen, war and soldier, lover and loved through the prolific means of social regimentation—all the bureaucratic and technological regularities that coerce human and natural life. *A Farewell to Arms* is a treatise on passionate devotion *in the absence of translation, clarification,* and *rationality*. Frederic and Catherine, principally, "enter into the composition of *one* loving subject who exceeds them both" (Badiou 2000 [1997], 43). True to distinct wounds and fantasies, they do not reconcile, overcome, or understand their differences but remain attached to each other *and* themselves. They construct a dream for their life, one forever interrupted by "the real" of their divided fates, but it is a life worth living—more, a dream worth dreaming. Their fantasies, like their repetitive and insipid vows of utter oneness, express the futility of speech-acts to secure love—but *not* the futility of love. In *resisting* standardizing apparatuses of capture (war, state, marriage, party) we remain true to the particular and defining situations that form us as desiring subjects while loving across the abyss of alterity.

A Farewell to Arms embodies two theories of subjectivity, concerning human multiplicity and singularity. *Multiplicity* means that since all animate life is infinitely differential it has no reliable, nameable "identity" outside of "essentializing social constructions." Reality is always in flux; there is no "being," only "becoming." *Singularity* refers to an event that ruptures a given way-of-being such that subsequent experience or understanding must refer back to it, or is arranged according to it. We become subjects under such events: love, war, the Resurrection,[6] "to which we must respond." Without subjectivizing events, we would be like rocks or wildebeests: "multiple" but physical, instinctual, and non-conscious. Thus singular events arrange our subjectivity in cohesive desires, symbols, and meanings. *Singularity* "structures" subjects in ways *multiplicity* denies; the subject *becomes* by being jolted out of a naturalized state to engage in conscious actualization. Simply, *subjectivity is a structure* that links an event with conscious activities and unconscious desires; it is a *moving* structure, of course, but the Real always returns to constitute the subject of fantasy. If singularity conditions subjectivity in this way, then it rejects multiplicity.[7] Hemingway reworks this opposition. In *A Farewell to Arms* wounds and romance are defining events to which Frederic and Catherine must respond impulsively, fantastically, passionately;[8] tirelessly declaring feelings, naming themselves, making promises, and stating demands, they neither seek nor reach "understanding." Bound by the event of their love, they are also subjects of previous events, that is, bound to previous ways-of-being. Their attachment grows, their love intensifies, and they *unite* without betraying their fidelity to their distinct paths—and without the consensual assimilation or tolerance of alterity that disparate liberals suppose might eliminate conflict. Frederic and Catherine—remaining true to their singular events, wounds, and desires—fall "madly" and "truthfully" in love. Yet Hemingway suggests that it is in loving *from our own subjective positions*—foreswearing harmonious or homogeneous social "identities" and working through our own robust subjectivities toward others—that we achieve multiplicity.

A Farewell to Arms rebuffs the facile identity politics of universalism (humanity-based) or multiculturalism (group-based). Constituted by traumatic events, we must shatter our stable orientation and insular identities to belong among others. But we do not replace our personal-psychic identity with new social-political ones, or simply pile them up and get *many* (clear and distinct) identities. We break our ways of being in the world, our profoundly patterned survival strategies, to reach others who are doing the same. This rupture itself—perilous, boundless—expresses and constitutes love. To leap into this permanently disruptive liminality and decentered subjectivity, is, for Hemingway, to live courageously. In singular subjects' desiring and risking themselves without Gods, guarantees, or happy endings, Hemingway's *A Farewell to Arms* locates the flight from repressive human insularity *and* punitive administration to reckless multiplicity—that

Ethics Without Theodicy in Ernest Hemingway's A Farewell to Arms 81

is, the sacrifice of sovereignty for love, closure for openness, and certainty for discovery.

II. A FAREWELL TO ARMS

The voluminous literature on *A Farewell to Arms* has two tendencies. There is a scholastic strain focused on biographical or symbolic structure of the text and a philosophical strain concerned with psychoanalytic, political, or philosophical extrapolations from specific passages.[9] In this section I explore the text's rhythm, trajectory shifts, and repetitions to unpack the philosophical and psychological theme of ethics in terms of human multiplicity and singularity. Analysis of the novel highlights the meaning of morality in terms of nature, war, identity, communication, and the complexity and contingency of interpersonal connection.

1. Nature and Morality

A Farewell to Arms erupts rather than starts. The opening's poetic, mysterious imbrication of war and nature is legendary:

> In the *late summer of that year we lived* in a house in a village that looked across the river and the plain to the mountains. In the bed of the river there were pebbles and boulders, dry and white in the sun, and the water was clear and swiftly moving and blue in the channels. Troops went by the house and down the road and the *dust they raised powdered the leaves of the trees. The trunks of the trees too were dusty and the leaves fell early that year* and we saw the troops marching along the road and *the dust rising and leaves, stirred by the breeze, falling* and the soldiers marching and afterward the road bare and white except for the leaves . . . There was fighting in the mountains and at night we could see the *flashes from the artillery*. In the dark it was *like summer lightning*, but the nights were cool and *there was not the feeling of a storm coming*. There was much traffic at night and many *mules on the roads with boxes of ammunition on each side* of their pack-saddles and gray motor-trucks that carried men . . . There were big guns too that passed in the day drawn by tractors, the long barrels of the guns covered with *green branches* and *green leafy branches* and vines laid over the tractors . . . There were mists over the river and clouds on the mountain and the trucks splashed mud on the road and the troops were muddy and wet and in their capes; their rifles were wet and under their capes the two *leather cartridge-boxes* on the front of the belts, gray *leather* boxes heavy with the packs of clips of thin, long 6.5 mm. cartridges, bulged forward under the capes so that the *men*, passing on the road, *marched as though they were six months gone with child* . . . At the start of the winter came the permanent rain

and *with the rain came the cholera. But it was checked* and in the end *only seven thousand died of it in the army* (3–4, my italics).

Urgently Hemingway presents his tropes—leaves, mules, trees, rivers, dust, lightning, branches, and mountains mix with soldiers, capes, cartridges, clips, ammunition, and motor-trucks. "Late summer of that year we lived," he writes, without clarifying. He mystifies time (what year?) and identity (what "we"?) to subordinate them to something else perhaps. It is unclear whether natural, nurturing life becomes or defies machine-like, martial death.

2. Nature and War

What would give "the feeling of a storm coming," and does he mean war or weather? He distinguishes "green branches" from "green *leafy* branches"; modifies "leather cartridge boxes" with "gray *leather* boxes"; repeats "the dust they raised" and "the dust rising"; and recites the leaves, the leaves, like a mantra. Is he lulling us to sleep with such hypnotic reiterations or is he jarring us awake with its affront to stylistic convention? Or is he just belaboring his symbols? Will we learn *why* he stresses not just green branches, but green *leafy* branches; why he describes leather boxes as made of . . . leather? Is he challenging us to decide between poetry and bad writing?[10] Rain and cholera kill off "only seven thousand . . . in the army." Is this a pathetic[11] revenge scenario in which noble nature strikes back at a *number* (not "men") of "the army" and "the fighting"?[12] Does his "only" express contempt or cynicism toward, war, humanity, modernity, or machinery?

And soldiers carrying little killing machines recall women carrying little living beings. This inaugurates the long arc of death that, surviving the absence of war, will kill Catherine and child. If Hemingway really associates burdened soldiers with pregnant women then it is one of the more bizarre and alarming comparisons in literature. Why would he go so far afield just to impeach gender norms? It seems on multiple planes that Hemingway is de- or re-constructing the ethical subject.

3. Identity

A sensible response to such uncertainties is to find in Hemingway a radical renunciation of conventional thinking about war/nature, fate/drive, and man/woman. We hardly needed the posthumous *Garden of Eden* to discover Hemingway's heterodox sexual or gender codes, for instance; *A Farewell to Arms* announces them constantly. But most critics convert Hemingway's rebellious gestures into counter-orthodoxies; his gender-bending signals his *homo*sexuality, his absent signifiers indicate his *post*-modernity, his wartime bitterness registers his *anti*-war stance, and so on. These inane negations are the domain of identity theorists combing through Papa's corpus to re-identify, re-essentialize, and re-simplify him as *no-longer* X, but *now not-X*. But this is the polarity that *A Farewell to Arms* renounces throughout toward an ethics of living with ambiguity and loving through *dis*-identification. The cascading beauty of his first pages expresses just this unmasterable profusion of meanings and images, without registering, indexing, or signaling hidden answers to their mystery. So it is throughout the first of the five books, which start and end with an uncertainty that refuses appropriations of identity-fetishism.

4. Beyond Language

When Catherine meets Frederic (18) we already know he is depressive, passive, observant, sensitive, and quiet, though we do not know what lack motivates him. When we first encounter Frederic he says, "I saw a cloud coming over the mountain . . . I watched the snow falling" (6). He neither acts nor reflects, but action and reflection surround him, embodied by the ribald Rinaldi and pacific Priest. Frederic's first action is this: "I smiled at the priest and he smiled back across the candle-light" (8). Preceding speech, Frederic and the priest express their affection, however filial, queer, fraternal, or spiritual; again, Hemingway suspends this decision, retaining an expansive space of indefinite intimacy. A rush of Italian chatter follows about "beautiful young girls" and places Frederic ought to go in Italy, but *he* says nothing. When he returns "to the front" Frederic is still impenetrable but now responds in single words: "Magnificent . . . Yes . . . Wonderful . . . " (11–12). Asked where he had traveled Frederic lists several cities and Rinaldi says, "You talk like a time-table" (11). The meaningful smile with the priest and meaningless speech with Rinaldi privilege the implicit but also denigrate language, making Frederic the oddly charismatic model of silence. But Frederic regrets not visiting the priest's beloved Abruzzi: "I myself felt as badly as he did and could not understand why I had not gone. It was what I had wanted to do and I tried to explain how one thing had led to another . . . I explained, winefully, how we did not do the things we wanted to do; we never did such things" (13). Suddenly Frederic starts rambling about sex "and the strange excitement of waking and not knowing who it was with you, and the world all unreal in the dark and so exciting that you must resume again unknowing and not caring in the night, sure that this was all and all and all and not caring" (13). This is his confession to the priest about sexual escapades but also much more. In guilt Frederic babbles about understanding, explanation, and agency; in the drink he slurs along about the excitement of not knowing his lovers; and in ecstasy he recalls those mornings-after "still pleasant and fond and warm and breakfast and lunch" (13). Frederic the apologetic sybarite is also a frustrated intellectual,[13] a man who has felt and thought his way into a false or performative negation of feeling and thought.

In his reverie Frederic announces,

84   *Sayres Rudy*

> I tried to tell about the night and the difference between the night and the day and how the night was better unless the day was very clean and cold and I could not tell it; as I cannot tell it now. But if you have had it you know. He [the priest] had not had it but he understood that I had really wanted to go to the Abruzzi but had not gone and we were still friends, with many tastes alike, but with the difference between us. He had always known what I did not know and what, when I learned it, I was always able to forget. But I did not know it then, although I learned it later (14).

Passions continue to stir where language fails and communication is not necessary to confirm the veracity of experience.

5. Complexity and Contingency

Even if taken literally as the iconic conditions of Frederic's fantasies and *Angst* (Baker 1994 [1951], 103),[14] day and night also signify his ambivalence over "the world all unreal in the dark [and] better unless the day was very clean and cold . . . " He is torn among excitement, mystery, eroticism, clarity, and "niceness"—in his staggering inebriation he overflows in oppositions. He is not vacuous but inhabited by warring impulses that produce profusion or paralysis. As if these rapid and perplexing shifts were not enough Hemingway then abruptly doubles Frederic, displacing the narration into its own future tense (Phelan 1990, 56; Davidson 1973, 127). The split temporality of the alienated narrator pronounces desire, his romantic nostalgia or erotic longing, the author-editor of his memory. Frederic's passion tells his story as much as he tells the story of his passion (See also Wexler 1981, 112–113).[15] Instead of truth that sense grasps, sensation "tells the truth."

From the start, then, Hemingway experiments with "the games of truth and error through which being is historically constituted as experience; that is, as something that can and must be thought" (Foucault 1990 [1984]: 6–7). To communicate and emulate "the way amoral fact is experienced" he adopts this nearly technical style of blurred lines, shadowed lights, and blended colors (Berman 2005: 27; See also Watts 1980 [1971], 307).[16] He writes his sober anti-drama to study by instantiating the uncontainable force of "creative-destructive bonding" (Gajdusek 2002, 304ff.; See also Deleuze 2006 [1981], 185–6).[17] *A Farewell to Arms* builds a nuclear reactor to concentrate and capture, even at a glance, human fission and fusion. Hemingway wants to portray (and protect) experience and expression as intrinsic verities. "[I]f the conclusion becomes in the process a little less conclusive, it may, for that very reason, approach nearer to the truth" (Woolf 1980 [1927]: 10; 1927: 85ff; Stewart 2001, 98ff, 99).[18]

Frederic, post-oneiric reverie, abruptly hits a wall of puerile self-pity. The war is a "nuisance" and "the battery, . . . protected by the little hill,

Ethics Without Theodicy in Ernest Hemingway's A Farewell to Arms   85

... fired twice ... and made the front of my pajamas flap" (15). Greeting mechanics, he bemoans "a false feeling of soldiering": "It evidently made no difference whether I was there to look after things or not ... Evidently it did not matter whether I was there or not ... The whole thing seemed to run better while I was away" (16–17). So when our hero meets Catherine Barkley (18) we meet him already as a polar, morosely ponderous, womanizing, false-soldiering, fantasist man-boy in pajamas. From the first, then, we are compelled to compare Catherine's Frederic in some sense, to our own. Here they meet (18–19):

> "How do you do, Miss Barkley said. "You're not Italian, are you?"
> "Oh, no."
> "What an odd thing—to be in the Italian army."
> "It's not really the army. It's only the ambulance."
> "It's very odd though. Why did you do it?"
> "I don't know. There isn't always an explanation for everything."
> "Oh, isn't there? I was brought up to think there was."
> "That's awfully nice."
> "*Do* we have to go on and talk this way?"
> "No."
> "That's a relief, isn't it?"
> "What is the stick?" I asked. Miss Barkley was quite tall. She wore what seemed to me to be a nurse's uniform, was blonde and had tawny skin and gray eyes. I thought she was very beautiful ...
> "It belonged to a boy who was killed last year."
> "I'm awfully sorry."
> "He was a very nice boy. He was going to marry me and he was killed in the Somme."
> "It was a ghastly show."
> "Were you there?"
> "No."
> "I've heard about it ... "
> "Had you been engaged long?"
> "Eight years. We grew up together."
> "And why didn't you marry?"
> "I don't know," she said. "I was a fool not to. I could have given him that anyway. But I thought it would be bad for him."
> "I see."
> "Have you ever loved anyone?"
> "No."
> "I wanted to do something for him. You see I didn't care about the other thing and he could have had it all. He could have anything he wanted if I would have known. I would have married him or anything. I know all about it now. But then he wanted to go to war and I didn't know."
> I did not say anything.

"I didn't know about anything then. I thought it would be worse for him. I thought perhaps he couldn't stand it and then of course he was killed and that was the end of it."

"I don't know."

"Oh, yes," she said. "That's the end of it."

Calling the Italian front "silly" but "beautiful," she remarks that when she and her fiancé signed on to the war she had imagined him ending up in her hospital "with a saber cut, I suppose, and a bandage around his head . . . If they [realized what France is like] it couldn't go on. He didn't have a saber cut. They blew him all to bits." Again Frederic "didn't say anything."[19]

From this cyclonic exchange we stumble back toward Babel. Rinaldi, (Helen) Ferguson, Frederic, and Catherine chatter: "'No understand.' 'Abbastanza bene,' I translated. He shook his head. 'That is not good. You love England?' 'Not too well. I'm Scotch, you see.' Rinaldi looked at me blankly. 'She's Scotch, so she loves Scotland better than England,' I said in Italian. 'But Scotland is England.' I translated this for Miss Ferguson. 'Pas encore,' said Miss Ferguson. 'Not really?' 'Never. We do not like the English.' 'Not like the English? Not like Miss Barkley?' 'Oh, that's different. You mustn't take everything so literally" (20–21). In eight pages (13–21), then, we circuit through our hero's key experiences and Hemingway's key tropes: escapist fantasy (promiscuity), depressive reality (futility), seductive intimacy (vitality), and fragmentary language (incongruity). Frederic is loutish, fraternal, funny, filial, sullen, ruminative, childlike, flirtatious, aggressive, diplomatic, dishonest, and, all along, opaque—a cipher for Hemingway's unsettled philosophies of self, other, war, love. All action and no motivation, Frederic could be seen as unmoored sociopath or repressed bureaucrat, a vacuous vessel suitable (literally) for either of two polar American male prototypes: drifter cowboy or caged salesman. But Frederic is not more cowboy or salesman than Catherine is a saint or a whore; rather they are singular creatures irreducible to such seamless caricatures.

III. CONCLUSION

It is perilous to call literature "political" or "ethical." A valuable work of art rarely "argues for" the moral ideas it takes up. Hemingway's portrayal of Frederic and Catherine may not, moreover, *endorse* that portrayal. One writes of a novel as having "an ethics" at great risk also of appropriating the story or, perhaps worse, intellectualizing its emotional impact. Hemingway wrote *A Farewell to Arms* to evoke, and provoke, an experience, not to defend an ethical position. But it does not necessarily offend his intention to infer from the experience an ethical sensibility. The narrative provides radically disconcerting conceptions of subjective becoming: An absorbing love affair that breaks traditional norms of communication,

Ethics Without Theodicy in Ernest Hemingway's A Farewell to Arms 87

growth, family, sexuality, and marriage, ending in the death of mother and child; a desultory, decorated anti-hero who "deserts" an army he is not really part of after pointlessly executing a retreating soldier and nearly being shot for treason; a manic-depressive, Post Traumatic Stress Disorder-impaired nurse who, alternatively, dominates and submits to others but has a febrile willfulness. This immensely traumatized and perverse social landscape is the site of passionate contact, ferocious loyalty, and eruptive hope among the Priest, Rinaldi, Frederic, Catherine, and others around them.

If Hemingway, or we, value this will to hope and dream and love without theodicy, without a "theory," then those things matter in themselves, intrinsically. Similarly, "the point of making a distinction between the political and the private 'moral scene' is itself a political point" (Murdoch 1992, 390). To advocate for the inherent value of experience is, by extension, specifically to seek release from the exclusive, dualistic value-endowment of the Law, Right, or Good—that is, to favor and find praiseworthy a life *against* morality. The novel's political relevance focuses most clearly on "an awareness of the particular non-totality of political situations" (Murdoch 1992, 378). *A Farewell to Arms* is, in this sense, "ethically" against ethics and "politically" against politics. Hemingway shows people inventing deeply humane commitments without ethical or political belief.

A careful reading of Hemingway's *A Farewell to Arms* situates his "political rebellion" not in any straightforward opinion about war or democracy or gender but in his conception of subjectivity that strives within its animating force to risk love and loss. It is this view of humanity—not his trivially idiosyncratic political convictions—that profoundly contest the grounds of (individual and collective) sovereignty and necessarily the repressive apparatuses of psychic-juridical-moral closure. Hemingway exiles his silent, solitary, desperate, and aimless boy to an automated killing field, an anti-cowboy at the dawn of American hegemony snorting at patriotism and honor and finally taking flight with the lover he cannot save. After telling Catherine, "Now if you aren't with me I haven't a thing in the world" (257), Frederic feels her die—"it did not take her very long" (331)—and says, "There's nothing to say" (332). But how does such devastation embrace life, love, flight? A good response comes from Kant "who tells us that tragedy joins the sublime and the beautiful together" (Murdoch 1992, 99–100). Hemingway's audacious method is to afford his reader that embrace, to make our reaction to that scene define its meaning, *to force us to measure our strength to endure without theodicy by experiencing their fate as life-affirming rather than nihilistically tragic*. Every Hemingway critic "engages his or her own desire" (Moddelmog 1999, 191), of course, as he himself said: "Read anything I write for the pleasure of reading it. Whatever else you find will be the measure of what you brought to the reading" (Plimpton 1961 [1958]: quoted in Baker, 29). But this means *not* that readers decide the meaning of the text, superficially enough, but that the text decides the meaning of readers. In

A *Farewell to Arms*, Hemingway's ethical confrontation divides us by our own reactions to it, into those who need a theodicy to keep going and those strong enough to love without further reward.

NOTES

1. I thank Vishnupad, Adam Sitze, Elliott Prasse-Freeman, and David Stout for support and insight. I am most grateful to Lauretta Frederking for her grace and grit in creating this volume. My essay is dedicated to Hector Risemberg, siempre mi compinche.
2. I will always refer to Ernest Hemingway, *A Farewell to Arms* (Scribner 2003 [1929]) *by citing page numbers only in parentheses.*
3. In Lacanian terms they speak their *demands* and *desires* throughout until gradually their demands and desires reveal their drives as they fall in love. I am grateful to Vishnupad for extensive discussion of this interpretation of the novel.
4. As Nietzsche claimed in the *Genealogy of Morality*, those who attack life and sacralize "after"-life must see life-affirmers as nihilistic.
5. Contractual or dialectical conceptions of political sovereignty "overcome" human tendencies to irrationality, conflict, or desire.
6. Hemingway emphasizes just these features of event-singularities central to Badiou's philosophy of truth (Badiou 2001 [1998], 28ff.).
7. Surely *singularities* are *multiple*; each of us is animated distinctly. The debate concerns the extent of difference, i.e., whether each of the multiple singularities is internally differential or structurally fixated (Badiou 2000 [1997]: 24–25; Deleuze 1990 [1969], pp. 52ff).
8. *A Farewell to Arms* is, more radically, saturated with sadomasochistic, transsexual, and homosexual fetishism (Fantina 2005, Eby 1999).
9. Scholastic *and* philosophical readers disagree over the deliberateness of Hemingway's stylistic and thematic innovations.
10. It is bewildering that Hemingway's writing is considered "bland," "plain," "flat," "simple," or "monotonous." Indeed *A Farewell to Arm's* style is inconsistent, innovative, and experimental. Space constraints allow me only one example; note that within Book I Hemingway changes his quotation form three times. After conventional quoting (5–58), he does this: "The medical captain, 'What hit you?' Me, with eyes shut, 'A trench mortar shell'" (59). Then, dropping quotation marks: "Why don't I get wounded? Maybe you will, I said. We must go, said the major. We drink and make noise and disturb Federico. Don't go. We we must go. Good-by. Good luck. Many things. Ciaou. Ciaou. Ciaou . . . I found I was quite drunk but went to sleep" (77). Hemingway uses style to portray the sodden inosculation of drunken consciousness and speech, but also to signal vagaries of subjective coherence. In several conversations he makes it hard to discern who is saying what to whom, as if to emphasize the porosity of subject positions (e.g., 139–140, 262).
11. Surely Hemingway was taunting his critics with his schematic pathetic fallacy (rain = tragedy, mountain:plain::happy:sad, etc.).
12. "Now the fighting was in the next mountains" (5) gives a parallel anthropomorphism, pairing the pathetic and martial fallacies.
13. To wit, a social scientific specialist in methods. Frederic is either intellectual or anti-intellectual in his fascinated preoccupation with causality, interpretation, and meaning. Frederic returns over and over to such irresoluble dilemmas when speaking about war and love.

14. Literal schematics of the "symbolic structure" of *A Farewell to Arms* convert the "image of life and home (the mountain) and the image of war and death (the plain)," or light and rain, etc., into "Hemingway's first study in doom," its allegedly "dominant mood" (Baker 1994 [1951]: 103).
15. His passion decides the memory; the memory does not depict the passion. This split narrator opens up the space of his difference. Telling of his *past shame*, he *now lacks that shame* (or he would hide it now as before). This same space creates ambiguity about Frederic and Catherine, allowing that he may be narrating their time together *thematically*: That is, building into the "factual" story his desire to, for instance, have grown to match her maturity (Wexler 1981: 112–113).
16. Hemingway's admiration for Cézanne's aesthetic was philosophical. For both "the landscape, although realistically described, still represents something more, some metaphysical or emotional or symbolic expression of the artist" (Watts 1980 [1971]: 307).
17. Francis Bacon "distinguishes between the violence of spectacle, which does not interest him, and the violence of sensation as an object of painting . . . [M]oving from horror to the cry . . . [brings an] increase in sobriety and the ease of figuration falls away" (Deleuze 2006 [1981]: 185–186). Hemingway's sober experiments disfigure similarly, to seize ecstasy in the ordinary.
18. Stewart (2001: 98ff.) argues that *A Farewell to Arms* (1929) summates *In Our Time* (1925), rendering *The Sun Also Rises* (1926) a relatively sunny response to it. However the towering *SAR* and *A Farewell to Arms* interrelate, we must not presume Hemingway's "final vignettes . . . undercut . . . his provisional hopefulness" (p. 99). This confusion of linear periodization across and within his works oversimplifies his sense of truth.
19. This dialogue shows why *A Farewell to Arms*-the-film *must* undermine *A Farewell to Arms*-the-novel, and why Hemingway hated both major releases of *A Farewell to Arms*. The 1932 version [Frank Borzage, dir., Ben Glazer, scr., with Helen Hayes and Gary Cooper] is criminally bad while the 1957 version [Charles Vidor, dir., Ben Hecht, scr., with Rock Hudson and Jennifer Jones] is piously good; but either way, the films erase the silences that pull readers into the character's uncertainty. *Viewers are told* whether Frederic's line, "That's awfully nice," is resigned or petulant. But *readers experience the uncertainty that Catherine must have felt*, hearing that sentence. When we read "I did not say anything" we *experience* Frederic's blankness as *positing or willing silence*. Cooper and Hudson do not posit an absent reaction; they just stand there.

WORKS CITED

Badiou, Alain. *Deleuze: The Clamor of Being*. Translated by Louise Burchill. Minneapolis: University of Minnesota Press, 2000 [1997].

———. *Ethics: An Essay on the Understanding of Evil*. Translated by Peter Hallward. London: Verso, 2001 [1998].

———. *Saint Paul: The Foundation of Universalism*. Translated by Roy Brassier. Stanford: Stanford University Press, 2003 [1997].

Baker, Carlos. "The Mountain and the Plain." *Critical Essays on Ernest Hemingway's A Farewell to Arms*. Edited by George Monteiro. Boston: GK Hall & Co., 1994 [1951].

Bataille, Georges. *Literature and Evil*. Translated by Alastair Hamilton. London: Marion Boyars, 1985 [1957].

Berman, Ronald. *Modernity and Progress: Fitzgerald, Hemingway, Orwell.* Alabama University Press, 2005.

Davidson, Arnold. "The Dantean Perspective in Hemingway's *A Farewell to Arms.*" *Journal of Narrative Technique* 3:2 (1973): 121–130.

Deleuze, Gilles. *The Logic of Sense.* Translated by M. Lester. New York: Columbia University Press, 1990 [1969].

———. "Painting Sets Writing Ablaze." *Two Regimes of Madness: Texts and Interviews, 1975–1995.* Edited by David Lapoujade. Translated by Ames Hodges and Mike Taormina. New York: semiotext(e), 2006 [1981].

Eby, Carl. *Hemingway's Fetishism: Psychoanalysis and the Mirror of Manhood.* Albany: State University of New York, 1999.

Fantina, Richard. *Ernest Hemingway: Machismo and Masochism.* New York: Palgrave MacMillan, 2005.

Foucault, Michel. *The Use of Pleasure: Volume 2 of The History of Sexuality.* Translated by Robert Hurley. New York: Vintage, 1990 [1984].

Gajdusek, Robert. *Hemingway in His Own Country.* South Bend: University of Notre Dame, 2002.

Geuss, Raymond. "Art and Theodicy." *Morality, Culture, and History.* Cambridge: Cambridge University Press, 1999.

Hemingway, Ernest. *A Farewell to Arms.* New York: Charles Scribner's Sons, 2003 [1929].

Moddelmog, Debra. *Reading Desire: In Pursuit of Ernest Hemingway.* Ithaca: Cornell University Press, 1999.

Murdoch, Iris. *Metaphysics as a Guide to Morals.* London: Penguin Books, 1992

Nietzsche, Friedrich. *On The Genealogy of Morality.* Translated by Maudemarie Clark and Alan Swensen. Indianapolis: Hackett Publishing Co., 1998 [1887].

Phelan, James. "Distance, Voice, and Temporal Perspective in Frederic Henry's Narration: Success, Problems, and Paradox." *New Essays on A Farewell to Arms.* Edited by Scott Donaldson. Cambridge: Cambridge University Press, 1990.

Plimpton, George. "An Interview with Ernest Hemingway." *Hemingway and His Critics: An International Anthology.* Edited by Carlos Baker. New York: Hill and Wang, 1961 [1958].

Rilke, Rainer Maria. "Letter to Princess Marie von Thurn und Taxis-Hehenlohe." *Letters of Rainer Maria Rilke, 1910–1926.* Edited by Jane Greene and M. D. Herter Norton. New York: W. W. Norton & Co., 1972 [1915?].

Stewart, Matthew. *Modernism and Tradition in Ernest Hemingway's In Our Time.* New York: Camden House, 2001.

Watts, Emily. "Landscapes." *Hemingway.* Edited by H. Weber. Wege der Forschung, Bd. 546. Wissenschaftliche Buchgesellschaft, 1980 [1971].

Wexler, Joyce. "E.R.A. for Hemingway: A Feminist Defense of *A Farewell to Arms.*" *Georgia Review*, 35 (1981).

Woolf, Virginia. "An Essay in Criticism." *New York Herald Tribune* (9 Oct). In *Hemingway.* Edited by H. Weber. Wege der Forschung, Bd. 546. Wissenschaftliche Buchgesellschaft. 1980 [1927].

5 Manly Assertion

Harvey Mansfield[1]

Let us now leave the gray, flat, featureless domain of science to look for something new. Our science rather clumsily confirms the stereotype about manliness, the stereotype that stands stubbornly in the way of the gender-neutral society. But we already knew before science told us that men are more aggressive than women: Is there also something to be learned in this fact? In this chapter I will elevate manliness from aggression to assertion and thereby discover its connection to politics.

Aggression is a vague word because it applies to any action that increases your power. *Power* is a vaguer word because it doesn't tell you for what purpose power will be used. Any action, even a smile, can look like aggression if you don't see the point of it; and if you deliberately refrain from looking at its purpose, like the scientists we have studied, you leave it to be inferred that its only, all-purpose purpose is to increase power. But let's suppose, against that view, that power has a point. Let's suppose that it is used to assert something, which means to assert the worth of something, to make a claim on behalf of someone or something. Pay attention, says the manly man, which means pay attention to *me*. Manliness is not mere generalized pushiness but rather a claim on your attention. That is why the male animal displays and the manly man struts and boasts (Moynihan 1965, ch. 3).[2] He has a point to make and the point is important! His aggression takes the specific form of an assertion of importance applying both to himself and to the matter he raises. If you want to be manly, you have to be assertive (so a fashion among women for "assertiveness training" arose in the 1970s). Modern science overlooks assertiveness because it feels uncomfortable with the notion of human importance. It wants to explain human events by means of universal laws that give no respect to our sense of self-importance and offer no solace for our delusions of grandeur. Manliness, too, is about the universe, but it claims a place in it for human importance.

To see assertive manliness, we will look at literature rather than science. We will go to Ernest Hemingway, the writer in our time (or just before) most celebrated for manliness, and to Homer, whose hero Achilles is the paragon and paradigm of manliness. Literature has the same aim as science, to find and tell the truth. But literature, unlike science, also seeks to entertain—and it could not entertain if it did not know some truth not well known by science about the human resistance to hearing the truth. Literature uses fictions that are images of truth while science tries to speak truth directly and succeeds only in speaking abstractly. Literature requires interpretation, and interpreters will disagree, a situation that science cannot abide and literature welcomes. Literature is open to different degrees of understanding from a child's to a philosopher's, while science speaks in a monotone and wants its audience of other scientists to be on the same level so that its results will be replicable. Science relies on non-scientist publicists to address the multitude of nonscientists. Science has fruits that benefit the body; literature nourishes the soul. Literatures takes on the big questions that scientists set aside and ignore, and so literature has more to say about manliness. The evidence literature offers for its insights comes from the intelligent observation of those who produce it. Great writers are both witnesses to truth and judges of what they see. We readers can replicate their insights according to our capacities, and we have to do so without the guarantee supposedly provided by scientific method that the truth conveyed is the same as the truth received. In studying human affairs, the trouble with the scientific guarantee of replicable evidence is that it's also a guarantee of clumsiness and mediocrity.

Manliness is not too modest to assert itself, to tell us the value of the manly man. Here is a small collection of manly assertions: "It is what a man must do." "But I will show him what a man can do and what a man endures." "And pain does not matter to a man." The most famous one: "But man is not made for defeat. . . . A man can be destroyed but not defeated."

These quotations come from Ernest Hemingway's masterpiece, *The Old Man and the Sea*, a novel published in 1952 (22, 66, 84, 103). They would probably not be written today, but Hemingway is almost today and his book, though out of fashion, is still read. It offers our most convenient access to manliness as something we do not quite recognize but is not yet over the horizon. Hemingway was a macho fellow and a seeker of adventure when coupled with fun; he was ridiculed in his own lifetime—by Noel Coward, for example, in a special rendition of Cold Porter's "Let's Do It"—when manly foibles were received more with amusement than indignation.[3] But this book is a serious work and we should consider it.

It is clear from its title that the book is about man and nature. Man is the old man and nature is the sea. The old man fishes for marlin, a big fish that is a challenge to catch and that can also be sold for food. The old man is named Santiago and is called so not by the narrator but only by the boy he mentors, who is called Manolin by the old man. No mature man is a character in the book although two or three persons are mentioned and there are several references to the "Great DiMaggio," the Yankee baseball player whom the old man admires. The old man stands for man because of his intelligence and his experience, working together. A mature man would be closer to his physical peak, but the old man has just enough strength and more knowhow, "tricks" of the trade. One particular thing he knows is to be patient. If you want to catch a big fish, you must wait for your luck to come. To be sure, when after a succession of failures the old man finally goes out by himself—the boy having been discouraged by his family from going along with one so unlucky—he quickly hooks his fish. The manliness of catching a big fish can be taught but has to be done alone.

The old man goes out on the sea, which represents nature because the land is divided into countries with various regimes that do not permit direct contact with nature. To be manly on land you would have to deal with a particular social context, as Hemingway did in his earlier book on bull-fighting, *Death in the Afternoon*, which is about Spain (1932).[4] In this book, Hemingway's manliness is unpolitical. The old man fights with a fish and as a fisherman he stands for man more easily than if he were Cuban or American. He contends with a marlin and several sharks, and he dreams of lions on the beaches of Africa. It is not that he is not Cuban, but he is described in a way that makes his manliness accessible to all regardless of political difference or diverse "values." The old man's love of baseball is shared by both Cubans and Americans (Sylvester 1999, 165–84).

Is man the dominant animal, as Darwin says? No, the old man thinks (for sometimes he thinks and sometimes he talks to himself) of the marlin whom he kills as his brother. The battle could have gone the other way, but the old man won through trickery. The marlin is more noble than man, whose integrity is compromised by his intelligence. Human intelligence works with nature as well as against it, for the stars that show the old man where he is are his friends, as is the bird that helps him catch his bait. After he has caught, fought, killed, and taken possession of the marlin, the old man has to bring him back to shore. He runs the gauntlet of sharks, who are not his brothers; he fights them off, but there are too many and they succeed in stripping the marlin of flesh, leaving the old man with its skeleton. He comes back with the evidence of his exploit but without profit from it. It is a trophy he deserves because he won the battle with the fish and because he did not conquer all nature to do so. What he won, he won fair and square.

Through the sharks nature gets even with him. "And what beat you, he thought. Nothing, he said aloud. I went out too far." He went out too far because the marlin pulled him out to sea, but the old man takes responsibility as if this had been his error. Then he can say aloud—*assert*—that nothing beat him, only himself. "I went out too far," says this very reflective manly man of himself. Manliness is the willingness to challenge nature combined with the confidence, inspired by the knowledge that one can succeed. It is also defined by the knowledge that one can fail, depending on the chance of catching a great fish and handling it successfully. Chance prevents nature from dominating us, and us from dominating nature. You win some, you lose some. If we could conquer nature and eliminate risk, we would not need manliness.

Manliness is an assertion of man's worth because his worth does not go without saying. So too, because worth needs to be asserted it needs to be proved; in asserting, one must make good the assertion. Did the old man go out too far, as he admitted? He did; he could not bring back his prize. Yet of course most of Hemingway's readers—those who do not think him sentimental—will not agree that the old man went out too far, and the marlin's skeleton proves that his deed was not a dream or a fisherman's lie about the one that got away. The old man thinks a lot; he seems to be a kind of self-taught philosopher. He has thought out the difference between being defeated and being destroyed, and he has decided that despite what you might think, being defeated is worse. The boy "keeps him alive," being a sort of student, and the old man found it pleasant to talk to him after his battle with the great fish. His manliness includes the analysis and the teaching of manliness. It does not have much religion. "I am not religious," the old man says before reciting his prayers "mechanically." He thinks (and does not say aloud) that he has no understanding of sin, but "there are people who are paid" to think about sin. He does not oppose those people or the Church, and in describing his story Hemingway actually supplies obvious parallels to Christ's agonies on the hill of Calvary (Hemingway 1995, 65, 105, 107, 121; Bloom 1999). He shows, however, that the old man suffers for his manliness and not to redeem himself from sin. It seems the old man does not like the idea of being dependent on divine help but does not object to others' belief. His manliness is full of contrivance in the clever ways he knows to subdue the fish, but it does not rely on advanced technology. It happened today; it could have happened in any age. Manliness does not depend on newly acquired power over nature; it is if anything, endangered by such power. Manliness contends with nature but respects nature because it is prompted by nature. We, Hemingway's readers, can see the manliness of Hemingway's hero because we, too, are prompted by nature to appreciate it. The old man is aware that he serves as an example to others who will be inspired by the news of his deed. It inspires us too, Hemingway's readers, but it also makes us envious. We see the definition of man summed up—displayed in deeds and asserted in accompanying speech—in the best one of us (Sylvester 1999, 183).[5] Hemingway is enough of a Christian to want to displace Christ (Bloom 1999, 5).[6]

Hemingway's old man gives us access to the heights of manliness that cannot even be glimpsed by modern science. The old man is not necessarily of our time but he is not repugnant to our time. His humanity, unlike Christ's, is somewhat withdrawn from what most people feel and know. At the end of the story, a woman tourist and her male companion look ignorantly at the long backbone of the great fish and mistake it for a shark. Not having read Hemingway's book, they do not appreciate the old man's feat.

The old man's manliness is not political; it cannot claim the recognition of a community as opposed to that of a young student.[7]

Next we go to Achilles, the manly hero par excellence without whom a book on manliness can hardly be composed, the archetype of the he-man and the asserter of his worth and the worth of his kind (Benardete 1985; 1997; 2000).[8] Achilles, let's admit, is a bit difficult for us. In contrast to the old man, Achilles is a warrior in the prime of life; he has a name and especially a lineage; he consorts with gods; he distinguishes himself undemocratically from the hoi polloi, the *anthropoi* or the human beings; and he finds himself not alone but in combat and competition with other heroes and in a relationship with nonheroic human beings, thus for both reasons in a political situation.

Achilles is a he-man (*aner*) above and distinct from human beings. We are used to holding the broader designation to be higher: humanity, mankind, humankind are nobler and more generous than any group of humans, which as such will necessarily have parochial interest at odds with the whole. To be devoted to humanity is a life well spent. But in Homer's *Iliad* the he-man of the Greeks (Achaeans) and the Trojans are presented as nobler than mere human beings, who lack individuality because they are incapable of great deeds. *Humanity*, it appears, is a collective word that has no singular, for to be an individual you have to be a great one. He-men are few, and they are identified with heroes. All the he-men are males, but most males are mere human beings along with all women and children. You could taunt he-men by calling them women, much as we might say to an adult, "stop acting like a child." When Hector, hero of the Trojans, challenged the Greeks to a duel and none responded, Menelaus rebuked the Greeks as women, calling them Greeks in the feminine plural (*Iliad* 7:96).

Instead of submerging themselves in the category of humanity, he-men or heroes connect themselves to the gods. They are sons of gods or they can trace a lineage to a god. Achilles was the son of Peleus, who was the son of Aeacus, the son of Zeus. There you are: Zeus is his great-grandfather. Not surprisingly, Zeus takes an interest in Achilles and the other heroes. He and other gods intervene on behalf of heroes; for example, at the beginning of the *Iliad*, Athena directly prevents Achilles from killing Agamemnon, appearing to him while invisible to others and pulling him back by his hair. Zeus is a father to the he-man, the heroes, but a ruler of human beings, who do not get his individual attention. Human beings suffer neglect and would be excluded from the care of the gods if they did not constitute a kind of audience before which the he-men display their heroism. Thus patriarchy in the style of the *Iliad* is not the fatherhood of God over the brotherhood of men but a compound of fatherly care of heroes and fatherly indifference to human beings outside the family. The gods care for the best men, and the best men seek to resemble the gods; they are even called demigods (*Iliad* 12:23).

Among the Greek heroes, however, there is a quarrel between Achilles and Agamemnon over Bryseis, Achilles' slave woman, stolen by Agamemnon. Agamemnon is king by virtue of his lineage, and when first presented in the *Iliad*, he is not called by his name but his father's, "Atreides lord of men" (*Iliad* I:7, cf. I:24). Achilles, knowing himself to be the better man, disdains Agamemnon's claim to his respect and obedience, and the two exchange furious insults. We see enacted the "wrath of Achilles" with which the *Iliad* begins, a wrath said to be "divine" and prompted, or supported, by the wrath of Apollo, who is also involved in the incident. The quarrel is not so much over the woman as between the two parties, Agamemnon claiming the authority of his lineage and Achilles the power of his virtue. The eternal dispute between ancestral and natural right opens up among the he-men because lineage, even to the gods, does not guarantee virtue, or as we would say, birth is one thing and merit another. Agamemnon relies on his scepter, symbol of his authority and made by the god Hephaestus, but Achilles swears by a scepter of his own and relies on his spear (*Iliad* I:134–139, 243–244, 303; 2:100–108). Manliness appears first not as a claim of authority but as the assertion of virtue against authority, an assertion always required because authority is always in the way of virtue and virtue never gets a free welcome from authority. In the course of asserting itself against authority, virtue becomes a possible claim on the basis of which one can assert one's worthiness to rule, thus a claim to authority. Even then it is only one of several claims and must expect to face resistance from other claims.[9]

Or does virtue not need to be asserted when it can be recognized, as today, in a competitive examination taken by all? Our "meritocracy" may seem to have solved Homer's problem of combining virtue and authority without fuss from the virtuous and condescension by those in authority. But to do this, meritocracy must understand virtue in conventional ways so that it can be recognized and scored by those in authority. We are aware that true virtue is rarely the winner of a competitive examination; and if it is, it cannot take success for granted and still needs to assert itself. Meritocracy does not eliminate the necessity of advertising one's merits, and we should not look down upon Achilles' boastful vaunts.

To vindicate his wrath, to make good on his claim, Achilles faces great risk as it has been foretold to him by his mother, Thetis, that if he returns to war to avenge the death of his friend Patroclus, he will die soon after (*Iliad* I:416, 18:95). He has a choice between returning home to live in peace or staying at Troy and going to battle to be killed with great glory. Eventually he chooses glory, dies, and goes to Hades (Brann 1997, 317–322).[10] When Odysseus later sees his shade there and asks him how things are going, Achilles replies, "Better slave on earth than king of hell!" He was dissatisfied with the choice he had made. Manliness rejects the safety of self-preservation in favor of the glory of risking one's life to vindicate one's rights and deserts. Homer shows us Achilles ruing his decision, and he wrote in the *Odyssey* of Odysseus' finding his way home through many risks, having made the choice that Achilles declined. Homer does not endorse either the wrath or the repentance of Achilles, it seems. He sings of his wrath and its consequences to remind human beings of the need for heroes, and heroes of the need for humanity. Achilles' assertiveness causes him to sulk in his tent—which is the aloofness of the manly man, as we have remarked—and to vindicate his right by avenging the death of his friend, a return to battle and a kind of entry into politics. For Odysseus, the return home permits him to resume his family life and his rule in Ithaca, after asserting his right to both against the suitors of his faithful wife.

What most obviously distinguishes Homer from Hemingway is the presence of the gods as actors in the story. The gods are a reminder of the need for authority in human affairs, of a higher power to which human beings can point when claiming their rights. Gods are necessary to manly assertion because without them assertion is mere assertion, arbitrary and unsupported. But gods also get in the way of manliness, as Hemingway indicates, by forcing men, even he-men, to call on and thus depend upon them. Possibly Hemingway's readers are supposed to supply the prayers of thanks that the old man seems to forget after he returns from fishing; in this way prayers ratify what heroic men have already done on their own and do not imply dependence on the divine. Even so, Hemingway seems less humane than Homer, more adamant in his aristocratic disdain. His manliness, while not trampling on the weak, offers them no succor, no recognition. Those who cannot catch a big fish are to admire those who can, perhaps in the way we all—all of us fans—admire the grade of Joe DiMaggio. A baseball player doesn't threaten us but doesn't help us either. By hobbling the heroes, the Homeric gods keep them restrained within our category of the *anthropoi*, not the same, not equal, but comparable and subject to human weakness. Achilles thought himself human only because he was not immortal and not because he was weaker than a god. That's a delusion Homer makes us see—makes Achilles see.

In our time there are many who say that heroes lack humanity and few who will admit that humanity needs heroes. But at all times heroes have to assert themselves. The question is, what is in it for us?

We have seen two instances of manly assertion, one recent, the other ancient, one outside politics, the other political. They have in common the assertion of oneself and the desire to prove a point to others, even if the point is not directly political like the demonstration by Hemingway's old man of how to catch a big fish. To make the point, the manly man stubbornly insists on himself, and when he does that, he *stands for* stubborn insistence on himself. Not only is he manly, but he also represents the need for manly men. He does this against any rational arrangement—including that of our gender-neutral society—by which one might wish to dispose of the irritating self-centered stubbornness of manly men. Yet manly assertion is a mode of speech and speech has a certain rationality: It makes sense, though often in deplorable fashion. What we must understand now is the combination of stubbornness and rationality in manly assertion. Out of that combination comes the political.

Let's start from the example of *patriarchy*, a political term used today. *Patriarchy* referring to male domination, is the name by which the women's movement has dubbed all previous human societies, somewhat as the French revolutionaries gathered all preceding eras in one category, "the old regime," to designate the age-old castle of oppression. And the women's movement is right: Every previous society, including our democracy up to now, *has* been some kind of patriarchy, permeated by stubborn, self-insistent manliness. Even our reason is infected and effectually controlled by the manly types; contrary to reason, for example, men have dominated the professions that require learning, not excluding the academic profession that is supposed to be devoted to learning. In protest, some of the braver sisters turned against reason itself, calling it "phallic," accusing it of a bossy attitude toward women's feelings, and condemning it for trying to direct or foreclose their choices.

It may go too far to accuse reason itself of being patriarchal. As Socrates said, a reasoned argument has a "logic" of its own that the reasoner cannot control but has to follow. But the accusation is right to suggest that stubbornness is added to rationality in manly assertion. An assertion, one could say, is a statement or proposition that the asserter *tries* to control. So there's no doubt that "Father knows best" is the very spirit of patriarchy, in which Father's authority is mixed with Father's knowledge. The phrase is usually spoken by Mother, often ironically, though Father is not above saying it himself if the occasion seems to demand the assertion of authority. Think of Jackie Gleeson on the *Honeymooners* saying "I'm the King" to his ever skeptical wife Audrey Meadows. "Father knows best" is a family motto that is easily translated into politics when those in power claim to know what's good for those in their control. The claim to knowledge is not added on like an accidental extra, however. Manly assertion appears first as stubbornness, but it is more than that; it claims to be knowledge. Patriarchy would not have grown up and flourished everywhere if there were not more to it than the tyranny of fathers. We will easily underestimate the difficulty of getting rid of patriarchy if we are not more careful about the reasons why it has survived.

What are those reasons? *Reasons*—because the one reason of survival is not enough; it no longer holds in the leisurely ease of our civilization, and in any case, it never was enough. Human beings want quality time in their sojourn on the planet; they want more than self-sacrifice for the sake of keeping the species going. They are interested in *why* the species should be preserved—the point overlooked by Darwin. Why did primitive peoples, desperately poor by our standards, living on the margin of existence, and subject to daily risks we can hardly imagine, waste their time and substance on religion? They wanted to know that they matter, that's why; and they were willing to spend heavily for the answer to that question from time and resources they might have saved for their material well-being. Other animal species seek to survive; humans want to survive with honor. It is through manliness that humans insist that they are worthy of the attention of the gods or have an honored place in the scheme of things.

Manliness might not seem to be involved in the meaning human beings want for themselves. The stereotype tells us that manly men are not necessarily the smartest or cleverest of human beings; they are men of action like John Wayne, not thinkers. Indiana Jones is an anthropology professor but seems to spend most of his time in the field. Hemingway's old man is a thinker, an exception to the rule, but then the professorial critics of the work, who don't care for men of action, don't notice that this one thinks (and thinks more than they do). We will not ignore the fact, as do the scientists who study sex differences, that the best thinkers, the philosophers, have been almost exclusively male (Stove 1999, 113–136).[11] But let us put it aside for the time being. The philosophers, though male, do not seem to be manly men of action. And the men of action, in their irrational, very unphilosophic way, seem to represent stubborn resistance to any reasonable scheme such as a gender neutral society that sets aside sex. The more extreme feminists may be wrong to imply that philosophers can never rise above the self-interest of males, but they would be right to say that *manly reasons is assertive* ("phallic").

What, then, do manly men contribute to the meaning of life since they do not think deeply or objectively about it? Strangely, their very stubbornness is a contribution. Instead of thinking deeply, and acting often in a petty way, the manly man makes an issue of himself; he asserts himself in some way. That is what his "aggression" means; he is stubborn for the sake of something and yet also and always on his own behalf. He connects himself—his personal stubbornness—to something bigger than himself— the issue in which, he claims, he and his honor are involved. When the scientists of stereotypes say that men are more aggressive than women, they leave out the end for which men are aggressive and the reasoning by which they support it. It's what men do with their aggression that matters, for however childish and self-interested they may be, they advance a cause for their complaints. Manly stubbornness is often, even usually, negative and selfish, but it is never merely that. To make an issue of something is a positive act. Even with a sulker like Achilles you can work out the principles by which he lives. Manliness is both irrational and rational: irrational because the manly man insists on his own importance no matter what; rational because he has reasons for doing so.

Now, to make an issue is a political act. It is to bring to general attention some unnoticed injustice done to you. The injustice harms you, but in making an issue of it you claim that it affects others too. Achilles expands his complaint against Agamemnon from stealing his girlfriend to not honoring the best of the Greeks (*Iliad* I:240, 412).[12] The latter is a more serious matter as it implies a general proposition that rulers should honor the best, a proposition of course including Achilles, in his humble opinion, but not confined to him. This claim transforms a private wrong, which you might suffer patiently, into a public wrong for which you insist on a remedy. The injustice will sometimes be done by society or the government, the powers that be; so to make an issue of it suggests that you are willing to challenge authority to get justice done. How far would you take this challenge? If you are a responsible person, and not a mere complainer, you might decide that it's up to you to step in to straighten things out. Not only do you make your claim public, but to be consistent, and to carry your point further, you take up the reins of control yourself, perhaps even leading a revolution against the status quo in extension of your manly logic. This is manly aggression when it is carried out to its conclusion, good or bad. What manly men contribute to the meaning of human life is its actualization in society. Biased as they are, they may not see justice well; they may be guilty of disastrous mistakes, as was manly Ajax in the *Iliad*. But when confronted with a problem, manly men get busy.

We in our liberal society speak often of the distinction between private and public, believing as we do that our liberties are safe only when a line is drawn to keep the public from interfering too much with the private. We don't want people to pick up the habit of crossing this line, of raising issues too often on subjects for which we have an established law, custom, or policy. The right of private property builds fences that protect us from too much interference either from fellow citizens or from the government, reacting to their pressure. But we also have a right of free speech, a right to address our fellow citizens, to raise issues, and thus to create a public question out of a previously private matter. It takes a certain quality of soul to do this, and the quality is manliness, the manly responsibility we have defined. The feminists had a slogan, "the personal is the political." They meant that what had previously been considered private, male-female relationships, had to be redefined by political means. They meant, too, that the original relationship had been defined by an act of political oppression done by males. The redefining from private to public is a manly act, in this case done by angry women who had a grievance and wanted a new society that would make room for their remedy. There are many injustices—such as this one, done to women—that remain latent until someone has the gumption to speak up and "act up," as the gay activists say.

One cannot assume that the distinction in our society between private and public is where it is because it has to be there. Surely there are matters that are private in all societies—somehow sex comes first to mind—but still, they are treated differently in different societies. Coming of age in Samoa is not the same as in an American high school (Caton 1990).[13] The difference is enacted and enforced by the public either in legislation or by custom. But the American high school is not the same as it used to be. When it is changed, the source of change is either public, the public changing its mind, or private, when the previous public is persuaded to change its mind or is just plain overthrown. In the latter cases, what was private opinion becomes the public rule, for example, our new gender-neutral society. The gender-neutral society replaced patriarchy, which also got its start from a previous change. There are different kinds of patriarchy, and the one that allowed women to vote in 1919 took over from the one before that time that did not.[14]

We must not look at public and private statically as a distinction that never changes; we must remember that the public emerges from private, latent interests or opinions that find expression. The public, the political, needs to be asserted; what is public now was once asserted, what will be public in the future will be asserted against what is public now. Politics is assertive, and assertiveness is a kind of aggression—the kind that is unwilling to let things be as they are. It is aggression that has received a certain form in an organization or regime and that acts for a certain end or ends.

Yet because the public emerges from the private, it does not follow that the public is created by the private, as most modern political thinkers say. No, the public is always there; always a ruling status quo exists that establishes for any society what is public and what is private. Aristotle said that man is by nature a political animal. He connects this to the fact that man is by nature a rational animal, with opinions on good and bad, just and unjust, harmful and advantageous (Aristotle *Politics* 1253a1–18). When you have an opinion you have a reason, and the reason applies not only to yourself but also to others like yourself. If you, a male, assert "my wife shouldn't fight in the army," you need a reason why wives or women generally should not do this. That reason keeps your assertion from being a mere whim, and it transforms your assertion from a personal statement to a principle that ought to rule others besides yourself. Our rationality prevents us from living on the basis of idiosyncratic preferences. Of course our reasoning may be unsound or biased; it usually is. But the attempt to reason renders us political animals. We cannot live without giving reasons to justify how we live. So we cannot live without a notion of the public, of a political association that attempts to enact and enforce what we assert, using reasons. Without reasons, our assertiveness would be mere unfounded aggression, a pure power move; without assertiveness, our reasoning would be dormant and ineffectual.

Aristotle is more assertive about the rationality of man, more discreet about the assertiveness. He tells us directly that having reason or speech (*logos*) makes us naturally political animals. But he doesn't set forth the argument for assertiveness that I have made. He doesn't want to encourage assertiveness. In his time, he thought, men were already tougher than they needed to be. As we shall see, the philosophers generally take a dim view of manly assertiveness. When Aristotle says "man" is by nature political, he says "human being" (*anthropos*), including women, not he-man (*aner*). Using the same distinction as Homer in the *Iliad*, Aristotle disagrees with Achilles that only he-men have the virtue to be political. Women share in human rationality, and they also share in assertiveness. Aristotle admits this latter fact in a subdued manner, and we have seen it again in the manly assertiveness of the women's movement in our day (See Manfield 2006, ch. 7).¹⁵ It would seem that we have the basis for the gender-neutral society in the very call for that society by the women's movement. If women can take their personal grievance and make it political, isn't that enough to show that women are as assertive, and therefore as political, as men?

NOTES

1. This chapter is reprinted from Harvey Mansfield, "On Assertion" pp. 50–63 in *Manliness*. New Haven: Yale University Press, 2006.
2. "The very essence of the male animal, from the bantam rooster to the four-star general, is to strut." Daniel Patrick Moynihan, *The Negro Family* (U.S. Department of Labor, march 1965), ch. 3.
3. "Ernest Heminway can *just* do it!"
4. *Death in the Afternoon* (1932) shows too that manliness is about knowledge and courage together, but the knowledge mixes the ways of bulls with the conventions of bullfighting.
5. Sylvester remarks on the "human community's discomfort with those rare individuals upon whom the survival of the many depends".
6. The judgment of William Faulkner: "His best. Time may show it to be the best single piece of any of us, I mean his and my contemporaries. This time, he discovered God, a Creator." Bloom, ed. 5
7. In *Death in the Afternoon*, Hemingway argues with an uncomprehending old lady about bull-fighting.
8. For what follows on Achilles, I rely on the work of the late Seth Benardete, *Argument of the Action*, ch. 2; *Bow and the Lyre*, 2, 4, 44; "Achilles and Hector," 31–58, 85–114.
9. See the seven claims to rule given in Plato, *Laws* 690a–c.
10. *Iliad* 9:10–16. Did Achilles have a choice or was it fated that he would die young? See Brann, *Past-Present*, 317–322)
11. See Stove, "Intellectual Capacity of Women," 113–136. No experiments on this matter, he says, would weigh with him "if their results were inconsistent with the verdict of ordinary experience" (132). But Stove does not make a point of our lack of experience with women philosophers. (In speaking of philosophers, here and elsewhere, I am not referring to philosophy professors but rather to thinkers of the highest rank).
12. Whether a ruler can always honor the best is a question, as Achilles comes to see.
13. It is not, however, as different as Margaret Mead said.
14. In 1878 the Supreme Court ruled that polygamy is not protected by the Constitution in part because it "leads to the patriarchal principle"—obviously not thought to be in force at that time; *Reynolds v U.S.* 98 U.S. 145 (1878).
15. See the discussion of Aristotle's *Politics* in Mansfield, ch. 7 *Manliness*.

WORKS CITED

Bernardete, Seth. "Achilles and Hector: The Homeric Hero." *St. Johns Review* 36 (1985): 31–58, 85–114.

———. *The Argument of the Action*. Chicago: University of Chicago Press, 2000.
———. *The Bow and the Lyre: A Platonic Reading of the Odyssey*. Lanham, MD: Rowman and Littlefield, 1997.
Bloom, Harold, ed. *Ernest Hemingway's The Old Man and the Sea*. Philadelphia: Chelsea House, 1999.
Brann, Eva. *The Past-Present*. Annapolis: St. John's College, 1997.
Caton, Hiram, ed. *The Samoan Reader: Anthropologists Take Stock*. Cambridge: Harvard University Press, 1990.
Hemingway, Ernest. *The Old Man and the Sea*. New York: Scribner, 1995.
———. *Death in the Afternoon*. New York: Scribner, 1960.
Mansfield, Harvey. *Manliness*. New Haven: Yale University Press, 2006.
Moynihan, Daniel Patrick. *The Negro Family*. U.S. Department of Labor, 1965.
Stove, David. "The Intellectual Capacity of Women." In *Against the Idols of the Age*, edited by Roger Kimball, 113–36. New Brunswick, NJ: Transaction, 1999.
Sylvester, Bickford. "The Cuban Context of *The Old Man and the Sea*." In *Ernest Hemingway's The Old Man and the Sea*, edited by Harold Bloom, 165–85. Philadelphia: Chelsea House, 1999.

6 Hemingway, Religion, and Masculine Virtue

Joseph Prud'homme

A vast number of literary critics have deemed Ernest Hemingway a nihilist. As an individual, they contend, Hemingway spurned religious truth and espoused absurdist nihilism. Many of these same literary critics have also long maintained that Hemingway's fiction expresses equally the thoroughgoing nihilism and rejection of religious claims they see as defining the writer's own values: The art and the artist express the same worldview. Noted critic Alan Lebowitz, for example, asserts that Hemingway gives readers but "one single, simple truth ... that life is harsh and dull ... and that man, under sentence of annihilation, is while he lives only a human punching bag" (quoted in Donaldson 1977, 232)." Scott Donaldson in his classic biography maintains similarly that Hemingway, in his most philosophical of moments, recognizes "only a universe stripped of meaning" (Donaldson 1977, 233). In a later biography Kenneth Lynn reiterates the traditional assessment: In Hemingway's world, "human life is hopeless" (Lynn 1987, 114, 317). Echoing such a sentiment many biographers have maintained for decades that Hemingway's life and art spurn religious values. Biographer Jeffrey Meyers among many others holds without equivocation that both Hemingway's personal thought and his literary output "are consistently skeptical about religion" (quoted in Stoneback 1991, 111).

Seen in this light it is small wonder that Hemingway has long been associated with philosophical existentialism. Critic William Barrett, for example, sees Hemingway's thought as deeply consonant with the views of Continental existentialist philosophers (quoted in Hoffman 1990, 173). Indeed, Steven Hoffman notes that an affirmation of existentialism represents the "thematic as well as stylistic climax, to which Hemingway's writing tends and which yields it a deep unity of meaning" (Hoffman 1990, 173). The same point is made by John Killinger in his classic piece *Hemingway and the Dead Gods: A Study in Existentialism*. Killinger holds that the "arc of existentialism ... runs all the way through Hemingway's work" (1960, 15); the "nothingness of the existentialists, the strange, unknowable, impending threat of nihilation" is ubiquitous in his work (15). Hence, "the hero is very much alone in this world, because he has no God and no real brother (99)." "There is not even real lasting love for him (99)." Killinger notes coldly that

"It is a brutal code" (99).¹ But it is one Hemingway's critics simply cannot escape, since, "For Hemingway as for the existentialists . . . God is dead in our time and the traditional ethic invalid" (See also Aeschliman 1998, 85)² (Killinger 98; See also Lehan 1973, 46–56; Donaldson 1977 234).³

However, an alternative line of scholarship concerning Hemingway the individual, and the values his work can be seen to espouse, has amassed strong evidence questioning this traditional assessment. Perhaps the most prominent critic in this camp is H. R. Stoneback. Stoneback contends strongly that Hemingway, far from being a nihilist, was a sincere Catholic who wrote with a strong Catholic sentiment, and that Catholic values are endorsed everywhere in his writings, a point, Stoneback asserts, that should be clear to all who approach Hemingway with an open mind. He was "very Catholic," Stoneback holds (Stoneback 1991, 114). Most critics he contends fail to cite specifics for their charge that Hemingway is a nihilist. And "it's a good thing," he notes wryly, since upon closer examination, "it is simply not there" (Stoneback 1991, 114). Standard critical work on Hemingway, Stoneback asserts, fails to appreciate how Hemingway's personal life manifests a sincere commitment to the Catholic faith. Rendering his personal spiritual journey "bogus," scholars then fail to appreciate how Hemingway's famous indirection, understatement, and partial concealment of underling points can mask a deeply religious undercurrent. A writer who speaks proudly of his work as an iceberg, with vast material beneath the surface, and who states clearly that "my style is suggestive rather than direct," and so declares unambiguously that "the reader must often use his imagination or lose the most subtle part of my thought,"—such a writer, if his personal religious life not be condemned as an utter sham, must be viewed with an eye open to religious messages coursing through his texts (Tylor 2007, 156; See also Stoneback 2003, 53).⁴ Further, Stoneback argues that critics fail precisely to employ the proper imaginative framework for understanding Hemingway since a lack of interest in or knowledge about religion—and especially the Catholic religious tradition—allows layers of meaning to remain unearthed.

Stoneback's research establishes a compelling case that Hemingway cannot be read as a consistent nihilist. Stoneback's work establishes very good grounds for questioning the thesis that a few lines of a *Clean, Well-Lighted Place* summarize Hemingway's life and the *tendance* of his writing: "Hail nothing, full of nothing, nothing is with you." Such a view of Hemingway, in light of Stoneback's cogent reasoning, seems unsupportable. In light of Stoneback's exhaustive research it would appear then that if we are to credit the standard assessment of the nihilistic orientation of Hemingway and his work, it must be that we see Hemingway not as a thoroughgoing nihilist but, at most, as one whose life and work expresses deep ambivalence.

Approaching Hemingway as a writer with deep complexity and ambivalence can free the student of Hemingway from what has been a customary mode of literary criticism of his work: the drive to exegete his writings as a whole, to discern an underling path, a grand vision and a sweeping undercurrent. Hemingway as complex and ambivalent problematizes this attempt: If his writing contains multiple threads and competing expressions of value, there may be no sense in attempting to develop a theory of *the* "Hemingway hero," as has so often been done by literary critics (For example Gurko 1968).[5] There may be multiple coherent threads in Hemingway's writing and, thus, multiple expressions of heroism.

When Hemingway is approached in this way his work, I argue, becomes especially revealing for contemporary political and moral philosophy. If one looks at his work for coherent expressions of various competing values and perspectives on life, and not for overarching visions, it becomes quite possible indeed to see that there are elements in the Hemingway corpus that depict a very real kind of Catholicism, a sincere and genuinely positive orientation toward Catholic values. There are points at which quite plausibly we can say that a genuine form of Catholic piety and Catholic set of values are both expressed and endorsed—even if they are not endorsed consistently across Hemingway's entire body of writing.

Hemingway's threads of Catholicism, I argue, are highly important for contemporary disputes in political and moral philosophy, and especially for pressing questions concerning masculinity in moral, political, and religious thought. That Hemingway, the famed author of bold tales of adventure and whose writings have so long been associated with notions of an overarching hero form, might prove relevant to discussions surrounding manliness may seem unsurprising. What might be surprising, however, is that when we approach Hemingway's work as expressing multiple coherent threads, a specifically Catholic Hemingway male hero emerges. Further, such a Catholic Hemingway Hero represents a mode of life and an approach to value that I argue is highly relevant for contemporary efforts to theorize masculinity in contemporary moral, political, and religious discourse.

Since the development of feminist theory in the 1970s, questions about maleness have assumed great importance in political and moral thought. How can maleness be affirmed without endorsing untoward forms of gender differentiation, and without implying the superiority of whatever one deems to be the male attributes? The Hemingway Catholic Hero I argue can provide a form of masculinity applicable to the post-feminist world. I advance this view by arguing that the Catholic Hemingway Hero serves suitably well as a means to revive manliness, precisely by the way it transcends two views of manliness which have emerged in recent religiously grounded forms of masculine revivalism: The masculinity of a certain form of Catholic thought typified in the work of Mel Gibson, and the idea of masculinity expressed in the Promise Keepers movement.

Hemingway's Catholic masculinity is plausible in the post-feminist world and superior to these competing expressions of religiously sanctioned manliness. Moreover, as itself an expression of religiously informed maleness this understanding can supply a sense of masculinity that can not only be a response to these other forms but perhaps a view that can persuasively engage them as well, as it operates within the same economy of religious concepts. Hence, Hemingway's thought does indeed appear to have very real relevance and importance for contemporary political and moral philosophy.

To establish this argument I first document the points where Hemingway can be seen as articulating elements of a code for a Catholic male hero. I do so by providing assessments of important features of three Hemingway works. I then provide a brief summary account of this form of masculine being in the world. Subsequently I apply this view to questions of contemporary manliness, and argue it provides a superior view than rival religious understandings and supplies a plausible account of manly virtue in contemporary life.

I. THREE WORKS AND THE ARC OF THE CATHOLIC HERO

I shall look first at the work *For Whom the Bell Tolls* from the 1940's and then the earlier short story produced in the mid-1920's, "Today is Friday," followed lastly by an assessment of the epic masterpiece of the 1950's, *The Old Man and the Sea*. This might appear to be a peculiar way to assess the religious thought in Hemingway's fiction; perhaps a strictly chronological approach would appear more satisfactory. I do however have a reason for grouping the works in this way. Stoneback's research has advanced compelling arguments to the effect that Hemingway's religious life can be periodized in the following way: That from 1925 to 1937 Hemingway entered a phase of "rather intense Catholicity" that was intellectually and emotionally profound. In the period lasting from 1937 to 1947, Hemingway experienced some real measure of "confusion" and "spiritual dryness," a period marked by an increasing openness to questions about faith—though not a period, Stoneback asserts, where the writer ultimately rejected the Church in unambiguous terms (1991, 117). From 1947 to 1960, Hemingway is seen to have entered a period of "resurgent belief," where a "profoundly Catholic" sentiment pervades his work. Only in the dreadful years of 1960 and 1961 does Hemingway come to experience complete despair and to see the world as devoid of meaning. In the aftermath of failed medical interventions to ease this depression, a darkness enveloped Hemingway, and the world would come to lose one of its towering literary geniuses (1991, 117).

If this periodization is accurate, it would be especially important to look first at works from a high point in the period of his openness to a questioning of faith, the period from 1937 to 1947. If we can establish that even at this point his work expresses a commitment that renounces existentialism and nihilism, we will have made substantial progress in delineating the religiosity discernible in Hemingway's texts. Indeed, as we shall see, even at this stage there are expressions of resistance to nihilistic existentialism.

Following this recognition we can then proceed to explore works from the period from 1925 to 1937, and finally the *magnus opus* from 1952, *The Old Man and the Sea*. Again, the goal is to explore his works for a coherent thread of Catholic values, not to provide one conclusive construction of a univocal Hemingway Hero. With this in mind, the three works I will explore can divulge precisely such a viewpoint.

1. *For Whom the Bell Tolls* and the Negation of Nihilism

Written in Havana in the late 1930s, and published in 1940, *For Whom the Bell Tolls* is rightly regarded as a classic work of fiction. The story unfolds during a highpoint in the Spanish Civil War. A college professor from the United States, Robert Jordan, has entered Spain with the goal of assisting the Republic cause. He is assigned to the especially dangerous mission of destroying a Fascist-held bridge as one part of a larger Republican offensive. Robert Jordan is guided by Anselmo, a Republican of noble character whose personal views are inconsistent with full Republican orthodoxy, and his group has as its real leader a warrior named Pilar, a courageous Republican woman, who though physically unprepossessing many find captivating. Along the way Robert loses faith in the Republican ideology, and also meets a woman from the local area, Maria, with whom he falls in love. Crushed by a horse during the assault, Robert must part from Maria, at least physically. Robert, mortally wounded, awaits his death while he lies on the pine floor determined to perform at least some good deed by fulfilling his duty and weakening, as he can, the advancing Fascist forces.

For Whom the Bell Tolls can be read as endorsing an ultimate nihilism about the human condition. Yet, I argue, there are also real expressions in the work of a rejection of nihilism—and the work in fact may express a quite traditional endorsement of older moral and religious values. I shall focus on events in the concluding chapter, Chapter 43, and will explore the arguments for reading the work as endorsing a nihilistic orientation followed by the arguments for an alternative account.

First, the final chapter of the novel sees Robert Jordan apparently rejecting the truth of religion, and also accepting the ultimate nothingness of his own existence. At one point he asks, "Who do you suppose has it easier? Ones with religion or just taking it straight? It comforts them very much . . . but we," he says, "know better, "we [who] know there is nothing to fear" (1940, 468). He is here—it appears—rejecting religion, and he seems to be holding that death is simple annihilation in a void of ultimate meaninglessness. On this view, death, in the tradition of the Epicureans, might indeed hold no terror as it would usher in simply utter emptiness. He can further be read as claiming that there is nothing beyond death when he asks, "Whom are you talking to?" during his final moments alive. Is he actually speaking with his revered grandfather, he asks? To the question of whether there is anyone whom he is actually conversing with during his final hours he says, simply, "nobody" (469). Additionally, in describing what his impending death will be like he says, "It will be just nothing. That's all it will be. Just nothing" (470). Death will be nothing because, in the end, his life, we could hear him say, has itself been nothing. Given these assertions of nothingness, and the preeminence of Robert Jordan in the novel as a whole, the piece can be read as articulating an ultimate nihilism—a view that man has no lasting value and a journey to the meaningless void, his only true polestar.

This interpretation, however, is not the only one that can plausibly be found. For Hemingway seems to contradict such a reductionist view in his discussion of how Robert Jordan and Maria will in fact be together following his death—a claim with a genuine metaphysical reference, one that is inconsistent with a thoroughgoing nihilism. As Robert and the group come to acknowledge that Robert's wounds are fatal, and that he must be left to die lest the mission have no hope of success, Robert and Maria exchange heart-rending words of love and commitment. Robert says that he and Maria have become one person and so Maria will never lose Robert: He will always be with her. It seems that Robert means this in a powerfully real sense; he is not professing in doggerel poetry that he will live in Maria's memory: They ARE now one, and will remain so forever, he asserts. Such a bold view, it would seem, negates the claim of there being nothing in man transcending physical death. For Robert Jordan's claim is a metaphysical one about survival and transcendence that no nihilist could entertain with a straight face. Yet once again, Robert does not merely assert this claim as flowery poesy for a forlorn lover, as words of metaphor devoid of literal meaning. In fact, Robert says, "who is to say that [this] is not true. I certainly will not say that it is not true" (466). This then means that he in saying something quite at odds with an annihilationist and ultimately nihilistic reading of the meaning of both his life and his death.

If Robert's assertions to Maria are not idle words unintended for serious reflection, but rather are words of profound meaning, it seems that we would have grounds for questioning the nihilism of the concluding chapter. And indeed, an array of new possibilities would emerge. With this understanding in mind I propose a more complex assessment than is usual of Robert Jordan's final hours on the forest floor. I focus on one critical line in the concluding chapter, namely when Robert Jordan says: "I have fought for what I believed in for a year now. If we win here we will win everywhere. The world is a fine place and well worth the fighting for and I hate very much to leave it. And you had a lot of luck, to have had such a good life. You had just as good a life as grandfather's though not as long. You've had as good a life as anyone because of these last days" (467).

This line, which can be construed as a culminating line of the work, indicates, I assert, that the novel can be read as expressing a firm rejection of nihilism. It can be read as attesting to a rejection of nihilism for two reasons. First, an existentialist orientation toward the world, as evidenced by the thought of the classical Continental existentialist philosophers, does not hold that its position is qualitatively *better* or even qualitatively *as good* as earlier modes of life—the exact point maintained by Robert Jordan. Existentialism acknowledges loss and deprivation relative to earlier and traditional modes of being. It is for this reason that *dread* is such a profound concept for existentialists. Robert Jordan's words supply a repudiation of the existentialist worldview by asserting no grounds for viewing the world and his life with dread. For once again a genuinely existentialist viewpoint does not claim that its assessment of the world—where life is devoid of meaning, where a senseless death is the only fate for forgettable man—is better or even as good as the earlier and more traditional modes of living, ways of being in the world where man abides in enchanted spaces made especially for him, spaces replete with life-affirming significance. Though, for the proponent of existentialism, its narrative is truer than these traditional accounts, existentialism cannot by its adherents be called qualitatively better. For if that were so, dread would not be the characteristic existentialist phenomenon: Its message would be a new evangel, a writ of joy—happy tidings to which hungry humanity would flock for nourishment. Men would cry, as of old: "he appeared and the soul felt its worth. A thrill of hope, the weary world rejoices, for yonder breaks a new and glorious morn."[6] That such is not the case can be seen by just how mightily the existentialists have to *defend* life.

By claiming that he has had "a life as good as grandfather's" and one as good as "anyone," Robert Jordan is rejecting existentialist nihilism. To appreciate this fully we must establish several points. First, we need to establish that the life that he claims his has been as good as is the life of the adherent of traditional moral values. Second, we need to appreciate just how fully existentialism, as evidenced by its chief proponents, never asserts itself to be as good a way of life as that lived by earlier traditional believers in an ordered view of life.

First, is the life Robert Jordan is claiming his life has been as good as a life of an adherent of traditional values? It seems that it must be. One way to see this is to appreciate how complex the reference is to those whose lives Jordan's has been as good as: It includes his grandfather's, but also all other people's: "You've had as good a life as *anyone* because of these last days." This then must necessarily include the life of the traditional believer uncontaminated by an inkling of existentialism, a man alive in his enchanted space, alive with hope in the triumphant of traditional values.

Moreover, another way to appreciate how Jordan is claiming an equivalence with the lives of traditional believers in a moral universe can be established by appreciating the context in which he advances his claim: His thought is expressed in a spoken environment saturated with older English usage, which envelops the scene with an aura of traditionalism. Disarmingly, his colleagues have spoken throughout the novel in Archaic English, with "thee" and "thou" in rich abundance. This locution takes on a new meaning in the context of Robert's thoughts in the moments before his death. It is as if Hemingway is invoking at this critical juncture the King James Bible or the traditional Anglican Prayer book, further driving the reader to think that Jordan is uttering an equivalence with those men of old who sung, prayed, and confessed in the tongue of the ancient faith (Baker 1952, 298).[7]

Lastly, Hemingway can be read as having a traditional reference in mind for Robert Jordan's words when we keep open the very real possibility that the passage requires an autobiographical reading. We may be permitted and even required to view these lines as references to Hemingway's own grandfathers. The critic Q. I. Janjua, among others, has noted that *For Whom the Bell Tolls* contains liberal touches of autobiography.[8] The plausibility of autobiographical elements being cast among the lines of the last chapter is displayed when we recall that Robert Jordan revered the courage of his grandfather, whom he calls an American Civil War hero, and that Robert summons the courage to act like his grandfather and does not give in to the temptation of suicide, as his father disgracefully had. This tableau evokes parallels with Hemingway's own family background. Hemingway's maternal grandfather was Earnest Hall, after whom he was named. He was a veteran of the Civil War. His paternal grandfather was also a veteran of the Civil War. As Kristy Lobe notes, "the [Hemingway] family was proud of its military traditions"[9] What is more, Hemingway's father had committed suicide, and Hemingway saw that suicide as a grave failure on the part of his father. In all, that the last hours of Robert Jordan's life may reflect important elements in Hemingway's own life seems compelling.

If we accept such a reading new vistas of meaning open up. Hemingway's maternal grandfather was certainly a moral traditionalist. He settled in Oak Park and built the family's position there—in large part because Oak Park was such a thoroughly religious part of the Chicago metro area. His paternal grandfather was also a fervent adherent of traditional moral values. He was a "serious, and deeply religious man."[10] So by Robert Jordan's life being as good as his grandfather's, Hemingway could mean that it is a life as good as that of a sincere moral traditionalist, that is, as good as his own traditionally moral maternal and paternal grandfathers.

For these reasons, we can read Robert Jordan as indeed saying that his life has been as good as the life of a believer in moral truth. It is as good because he himself has come to affirm these values and so to live in a world which upholds and affirms human dignity and meaning. Yet this must mean therefore that Hemingway is not articulating a nihilistic existentialism, a point we can underscore by developing just how deleting, just how draining existentialism is, a point the existentialists themselves acknowledge.

We can see the depleting and diminishing character of existentialism in the thought of Albert Camus, one of the great French exponents of existentialist thought. In *The Myth of Sisyphus*, one of the most powerful manifestos of existentialism, Camus asserts that life is absurd and meaning impossible. Camus states that for those who acknowledge this bitter truth, "the key thing that matters is not to live *as well* as possible but to life *as much* as possible" (Camus 1983, 84).[11] For what Camus, now awoken the realities of the world, wants is "to know if one can live a life—merely survive—without appeal," that is, without hope. "This is all that interests me" (Camus 1983, 84).[12] To do so is precisely the meaning of existentialist defiance. Defiance, then, is not to live *well*—defiance is free of qualitative assessment—it is merely to live as such in a world defined by absurdity. Defiance therefore is abstinence from suicide. Indeed, Camus starkly remarks that "there is but one truly serious philosophical question"—and for the existentialists philosophical questions are precisely *not* arid questions of logical analysis, but are the vital questions of life—"and that is suicide" (Dienstag 2001, 935).[13]

Camus may well be guilty of incoherence—claiming as he does that life has no meaning yet firmly rejecting the option of suicide; a decision not to kill oneself is an expression of a value preference, and so demands that one accept the minimally qualitative claim that mere human life possesses value and so is not a sheer absurdity. That mere life itself has a residual value is why at the end of the *Myth of Sisyphus* Camus can voice some words of approbation for that man whose "refusal to hope is persistent evidence of a life led without consolation," a man, inconsolable though he be, who decides to roll the wheel of "heart-rending" fate perpetually. That that man can be applauded only follows if mere life has value. Indeed, that mere life does have some value seems to be why Sartre, so influenced by Camus, can say that Existentialism is indeed a Humanism. This reading of existentialism, however, still positions Hemingway squarely outside an existentialist orbit. Jordan asserts not merely that life has some scintilla of redeeming merit but that his life is "as good as the life of his grandfather"—that is, the life of those who lived in the presence of traditional and transcendent truths (Dienstag 934, 936).[14]

Not nihilism, therefore, but an openness to traditional values is affirmed by Robert Jordan on the piney hilltop. If this is so, the further question arises whether we can see the thread of a specifically religious or theistic traditionalism in Hemingway's work. Moral realism, or the acceptance of moral values as objectively and universally true, might not demand by logical necessity the affirmation of theism. In the booming trade of publishing apologias for atheism, a growing number of atheist scholars have produced impassioned defenses of their creed, defending their worldview in part by developing a host of arguments attempting to establish the very point that one can be "good without God" (Martin 2007).[15] They might be right. Can we say therefore not only that Hemingway espoused moral values, but that he also embraced a religious understanding of these values? I argue that we can, and that we can do so by first appreciating the profound

Hemingway, Religion, and Masculine Virtue 113

admiration expressed in at least part of Hemingway's work for the person of Jesus of Nazareth.

2. "Today is Friday" and the Importance of Jesus

"Today is Friday" is one of Hemingway's most underappreciated works of short fiction. The work's spiritual depth however merits for it a place of acclaim in the Hemingway corpus. The story articulates, I argue, a message of profound spiritual significance. Written in May 1926, and published as a pamphlet (1926)[16] in the same year, Hemingway demanded that the piece be included in the first collection of his short stories published by Charles Scribner's Sons in 1938, and in subsequent editions of his collected short fiction. The playlet paints a scene of three Roman soldiers being served wine in a bar owned by a Jewish merchant. The soldiers have just finished their shift. They recount their work that day: crucifying Jesus.

Several lines haunt this story and lend the work its profound significance. The third soldier has clearly been sickened by the affair. This sets up what I think is the primary theme of work—the specialness of the person of Jesus. The sickness of the third soldier after crucifying Jesus is an expression of the uniqueness of Jesus, for why else would a Roman soldier, an expert at killing, a veteran of the grizzly enterprise of crucifixion, be sickened by the death of this man, among all his tormented victims? It must be that there is something special about *this* execution, of all the others this soldier must surely have inflicted in his bloody billet.

The first soldier also seems to have been struck in some way by the specialness of Jesus. He repeats the reverberating line, "He was pretty good in there" four times (Hemingway 1953, 356–359). By repeating the line so many times the soldier seems clearly to think that Jesus is somehow special, that he is distinct in some significant way, somehow, above others.

The second soldier appears to understand that the third and first soldiers are in their own way saying that Jesus is unique. The second soldier responds to his two colleagues by saying, in effect, both that there is nothing truly special about Jesus, but also that any such specialness could only be a crude kind of specialness, as he denies the possibility of there being anything *truly* special about anyone.

To the third soldier, the second soldier says his "gut-ache" must be the result merely of drinking the local water; it's nothing more than a purely physical reaction to water his body can't handle. His sickness is not in any way attributable to the killing of the man Jesus. With respect to the first soldier, the second soldier clearly recognizes that the first soldier is seeing something distinctive in Jesus. For he asks, why did Jesus not come down from the cross? To ask that very question only makes sense if one is responding to someone who thinks that special things are possible for such a condemned person. One would never ask of an ordinary prisoner on death row, why didn't he break free from his executioners? Such a question would only make sense as a response to the thought that the person on death row is somehow unlike other men.

So the second soldier recognizes clearly that the first is saying that Jesus is special. Yet he rejects such a view. What is especially fascinating though is that he denies that Jesus is special while simultaneously having a very impoverished understanding of what it could mean for any person to be special. The second soldier can only understand specialness in terms of physical power—the power to do great deeds of physical strength, like freeing oneself from executioners. The soldier is saying in his own way, if Jesus were special, that would certainly mean he would have especially strong physical powers, and that he could have come down from the cross. For this soldier, specialness is only physical and quantitative. The only sense of specialness the second soldier can entertain is a merely physical extraordinariness, which is nothing beyond a heavy weight on the scales of human power. There is nothing *truly*, or qualitatively, special in this world at all.

The first soldier makes it clear that the second soldier is not understanding him, and that he is seeing in Jesus a more fundamental form of specialness beyond great physical power—that Jesus is special in some much more radical sense. Jesus' way of being and his will and heart are qualitatively different for the first soldier. For to the question, "why didn't he come down from the cross?", the first soldier says, "he didn't want to do that." "It is not his play" (359).

The second soldier cannot understand such a view. The specialness of Jesus, in his mind, could only be that of physical strength, nothing more. Hence he responds to the radical words of the first soldier with a firm denial, saying that no one—whether of superhuman physical strength or not—would not *want* to come down from a cross, down from such torment.

The first soldier though has detected something truly different in Jesus. That truly distinct specialness consists in his heart, and the impact his heart has on others. By not *wanting* to come down Jesus shows himself to have a strangely mysterious heart. Moreover his heart impacts people *to see the world differently*, a point evidenced by the way the first soldier has now come to see the world around him.

For the first soldier, now at the bar after seeing Jesus die, does indeed seem to respond to the world in a different way than Roman soldiers typically do. How is this so? He sees, we are told, the Jewish merchant at the end of the night as a "nice fella." The words of the second soldier, on the contrary, make it clear that he—a Roman soldier—despises this Jew: "he is a kike, like all the rest of them," says the soldier (359). He is disgusting and low, a man only after the money of the soldiers, a point that is made clear from how the second soldier erupts when the merchant asks for but a little payment toward the debts accumulated by the crew.

The first soldier has said that George is a "nice fella." Incredulous to this claim, the second soldier says, in effect, that if you think *he's* a nice fella, you must think *everyone* is a nice fella—*everyone*. So he says, "everybody's a nice fella to you tonight" (359). For this second soldier, to have such a charity of vision could be nothing more than cock-eyed crazy talk.

The story, therefore, seems powerfully to communicate the message that Jesus *is* special, special in how he transforms people's way of seeing and relating to others; He has a transformational power to change one's view of those one has always seen as beneath oneself, a transformative power of broadening sympathy, solidarity, and fellow feeling.

"Today is Friday" affirms Jesus as a man of a special stature. Yet of course one can affirm Jesus as having transformative powers, yet still see him as a mere human. One could affirm that this man had a major impact on others and not be a religious believer. This remarkable man could by some special charisma have had the power to turn people's hearts, yet that does not require one to entertain any element of traditional religious transcendence. Remarkable things just might happen within nature. Is a genuinely transcendent and religious understanding of the world endorsed in Hemingway's writing?

3. *The Old Man and The Sea* and Christian Transcendence Affirmed

Written in Cuba in 1951, and published in 1952, *The Old Man and the Sea* earned Hemingway a Noble Prize for Literature in 1954—the medallion for which, in that same year, he dedicated to La Virgen de la Caridad, the Virgin of Charity, the patroness of Cuba. The epic work tells the tale of an old physically weakened widower who struggles to find an adequate catch off the shores of his meager home. He has lost the friendship and support of his companion the young Manolin, and he is desperate to prove himself once again an able fisherman, and to supply food for his table. He goes out far in the waters—farther than he has ever gone—and wrestles a great Marlin, which after hours of laborious effort he finally captures, only to see it devoured by a shiver of ravenous sharks. Walking home after his exhausting ordeal, he carries his gear as a cross and arrives to see that his dear friend the boy Manolin will remain with him. He regains his strength, dreaming serenely of playful lions on a distant beach.

Inspired in part by Stoneback's general perspective on Hemingway, and also by Melvin Backman's important work, "Hemingway: The Matador and the Crucified," and the work of Delbert Wylder, I argue that this piece is an epochal statement of a religious, and specifically Catholic, worldview.[17] The work can support a reading that views the tale as a masterwork of spiritual redemption, a story defined in characteristically Catholic soteriological terms. Specifically, I shall argue that the story is a *felix culpa* narrative: A tale of how misdeeds and human pride—the fall—form the essential components of ultimate happiness, a classically Catholic story of ultimate redemption.

At the start of the story we are told that the old man has fallen away from his faith. He describes himself as not being a religious man, although he prays sometimes, but only in a mechanical fashion, unable to remember the lines of the most common prayers. Moreover, he is a man who throughout his life has been full of boastful pride in his powers. He was at one time a champion hand wrestler, who gave up the sport since no one, in his estimation, could provide competition for his own prowess. He was also at one time a champion fisherman. Hence as Delbert Wylder remarks, "it [is] clear that Santiago feels himself superior to other men" (203). As a character, he is conceived in pride, the sin of Adam.[18]

His pride expands as the story continues, culminating in Wylder's words in "the choice to extend himself beyond the human" (205). He does so by going far out beyond the horizon, farther than he knows he can safely operate. There, in the waters beyond his control, he meets his prey. An overweening pride now consumes him. He goes "beyond human limits" to hook his quarry (211). After hours of effort, having hold of the great fish through excruciating toil, he thinks himself capable of finally hoisting the great beast in his meager sloop. Exerting all his powers he overcomes the fish, killing it. In seeming victory, he recognizes now the driving force behind his action and the true source of his motivation: "You did not kill the fish only to keep alive and to sell for food, he thought. You killed him for pride" (1952, 105).

At this point, however, such a recognition by Santiago of his pride carries no clear sense of self-condemnation. It is only when the sharks appear that Santiago's pride comes to be seen as a problem. The sharks attack treacherously (Wylder, 211). He first responds with resolution and some measure of hope that he can prevail. Eventually, as Wylder notes, the treachery of the sharks' persistent attack makes Santiago "aware of his own treachery (Wylder 211)"—of his own overweening pride, now recognized as a scar on his character (Wylder 211). He abandons hope—seeing his quest as now beyond redemption. In a forlorn state he strikes at the sharks with sheer "malignancy" (Hemingway 1952, 102). He comes to commit the ultimate sin of despair—the sin against the Holy Spirit which is unpardonable if not expiated, wrestling the piscine mammoth with a blackened heart. When the sharks finally devour the massive fish, his life has come to nadir.

It is at this point that Santiago yells aloud, "I wish it were a dream and that I never hooked him. I'm sorry about it, fish . . . I'm sorry, fish . . . half fish . . . fish that you were. I am sorry that I went out too far. I ruined us both." Hemingway clearly wants the old man to represent humanity as a whole. As critic Clinton Burhans remarks, "In his realization that in going out alone and too far he has ruined both himself and also the great fish, the old man reflects Hemingway's feeling that in his individualism and his pride . . . , man inevitably goes beyond his true place in the world and so brings violence and destruction on himself and others" (Burhans 1960 quoted in Baker 1962, 154).[19]

However as Robert W. Lewis recounts, "[Santiago] must be completely humiliated before he can emerge from the sea as a new man" (Burhans 1960 quoted in Baker 1962, 154). Yet in this way precisely does he emerge. The story therefore is not a tragedy; it is instead, a story of redemption, of hope, of transcendence. It is so because it seems exactly to express the concept of the *felix culpa*. It is precisely by going out too far and on his own and not giving in to the fish—by *culpa* or blameworthy action—that Santiago and so mankind is put on the track to ultimate redemption, to fullness of life. Man's fall is a happy fall—a *felix culpa*.

Santiago's fall is the essential precondition for his spiritual awakening—an awakening Hemingway conveys through the dreams in Santiago's rest, and which is confirmed by the leadership of the child Manolin. Together the dream and the child can signify the reality of the Kingdom of Heaven. *Culpa* is also *felix*: Blameworthy deeds are inseparable from ultimate felicity. Dreaming of the lions at play, and with the boy now leading the old man, the final section of the work very plausibly can be interpreted as a reference to ultimate religious redemption.

The dream is a reverie of playful lions on beaches of a distant shore. The lions we are told "play like cats." That Santiago sees lions at play expresses a message of enormous depth. A lion is the master of his territory, the lord of his pack, the avenger of all who challenge him. When accompanied by lionesses beneath him, the assemblage is known by that name which alone captures the essence of so fearsome a troop: A pride of lions await. The lion can be seen as the incarnation of animal pride, and, thus, the quintessence of fallen nature. Yet the vision Santiago has is of lions at play—at peace, innocent. The vision then can be seen to fulfill the promises of Saint Paul and the prophet Isaiah.

Paul in his Letter to the Romans says that the natural world has been scarred; for the natural world itself is marked by pride, and the conflict and frustration that follow from it. The natural order, cast into frustration, into unfulfillment caused by the natural drive for self-exertion found in all of the created world following the fall, is marked with futility, the futility of constant savagery. St. Paul then asserts that the natural order, suffering from futile, prideful butchery, "groans for its salvation" (Romans 8:22). A vision of salvation therefore will for St. Paul be a vision of nature healed. The vision will be of the fulfillment of the words of the Prophet Isaiah: "The wolf will live with the lamb, the leopard will lie down with the goat, the calf and the lion and the yearling together" (Isaiah 11:6). The lion and the lamb will live in brotherhood—the lion, therefore, free to rest, and free to play. The dream of lions at play can be seen as a dream and a prophetic foretaste of a reality yet to come, a dream of a world made innocent—the scars of pride and strife and anguish removed: a new heaven and a new earth.

Yet the vision of nature healed is not the only element of the redemption pointed to at the end of Hemingway's story. Manolin will now lead the Old Man—the child will lead the former man of pride. We must remember that Manolin gets his master food upon his return from the ocean; he plans the next sail; and he now has the spear wielded by his older friend. He is the guiding one. "It becomes clear that Manolin will supersede Santiago ... Manolin is going to take the lead," notes Wylder (215, 216). Indeed it must be so as Santiago is so drained that his friend the young boy must be a leader of this physically decrepit old man. All this then can be seen to fulfill a further promise in the prophet Isaiah: "The wolf will live with the lamb, the leopard will lie down with the goat, the calf and the lion and the yearling together; *and a little child will lead them*" (Sylvester 1999, 180).[20] The leadership of the boy can be read as a vision of the prophetic promise of the Kingdom of Heaven.

The Old Man and the Sea then does appear to be a *felix culpa* story. Moreover, a *felix culpa* story is at root a story of pilgrimage, when pilgrimage is properly understood. For pilgrimages are not always or necessarily travails of the already converted undertaken to achieve a higher plane of spiritual devotion. Instead, throughout Christian history the pilgrimage has very often been a punishment for a sin: "a sentence for some crimes indeed required pilgrimage," Stoneback notes (2003, 57). The pilgrim does not necessarily start from a position of faith, but can start from criminality or loss (2003, 57). The *felix culpa* expresses the logic of pilgrimage, understood in this way. As many Christian philosophers have remarked, there is a tragic aspect to divine love—it involves loss at first. And so the true pilgrim—like in the *felix culpa*—has *both* anguish and joy. He is "tragic and sublime" (Hartshorne 1953, 168).[21] Indeed, pilgrimages can bring forth what Stoneback calls "the spiritual anguish and joy of the true pilgrim" (2003, 52).[22]

Seeing pilgrimage, properly understood, as just another term for the *felix culpa* story can give us additional confidence in the interpretation I have presented. It is known that Hemingway did indeed view *The Old Man and the Sea as* a pilgrimage tale. In 1954 Hemingway wrote to a Catholic priest, Father Brown, that "You know about Santiago and you know the name is no accident" (Stoneback 2003, 53).[23] On the basis of this exchange Stoneback argues convincingly that Santiago is named after Santiago the patron pilgrim of Europe, after whom the classic European pilgrimage route, the Route of Santiago de Compostella, is named (Stoneback 2003, 53).[24]

The old protagonist then seems to be a pilgrim. Yet the very logic of pilgrimage is the logic of the *felix culpa*. Saints of old might not have expressed so ancient a message with greater or more heart rending passion.

II. THE OUTLINE OF THE CATHOLIC HEMINGWAY HERO

I have argued that Hemingway's body of work does have a religious component. It is not perhaps the only undercurrent, but it is one that we cannot neglect. This undercurrent can be seen to assume the character of a specific hero-type: a Hemingway Catholic Hero. A summary of this view of religious heroism would look as follows.

The hero is Christian and, it would seem, especially Catholic in his worldview. As James Brodman argues, Catholicism has encouraged men to view their work on earth as "that of Christ, difficult to accomplish, an example to the broader community—a divinely approved active life" (Brodman 2009, 275).[25] Catholic Hemingway Hero recognizes the harshness of the fallen world, the bitter constancy of injustice, betrayal, and bad luck, and the power of the physical world to crush man. Yet through this recognition he comes to be self-reflective. And he comes to show great strength and perseverance.

This perseverance is deeply informed by his capacity to appreciate the goodness which does exist in the world, and to sense that everything that exists has value. As Robert Jordan remarks in his final moments: "Down out of the gray rocks and the pines, the heather and the gorse, across the yellow high plateau you see it rising white and beautiful. That is just as true as Pilar's old women drinking the blood down at the slaughterhouse. There's no *one* thing that's true. It's all true. The way the planes are beautiful whether they are ours or theirs" (Hemingway *For Whom the Bell Tolls* 1940, 467)—it is all beautiful. He experiences the world with a great generosity of seeing and feeling. For "the world is a very good place and worth the fighting for." Note it is "the world" that is worth fighting for and a very good place, says Robert, not just any one part of the world, evidencing once again a capacious sympathy with all that exists, a point further echoed in the way the first soldier sees the Jew—the classic "other"—as a "good fella." All has value.

This sympathy is confirmed by his openness to transcendence, yet an openness which he sees as a gift, and one not defined by escapism or triumphalism or overestimation of human ability to secure God's grace or master creation. The road on earth is hard and final salvation for the world beyond, a world he holds to out of appreciation for the wonders of God that defy our imagining and control.

This frame of mind makes the Catholic Hemingway Hero a possessor of important and meaningful traits including the following. His reflectiveness means that he does not adhere to mass movements and abstract ideologies. Robert Jordan comes to spurn the abstractions and appeals to political mass movements made by the Republican ideologues. His sense of the tragic element in this life means he has no naïve sense of progress or easy faith that is unchallenging or simple.

His recognition of imperfection, along with his affirmation of value in life in general, allows him not to demand perfection, and certainly not physical perfection. Pilar for example is ugly, yet the real leader of her troops; the old man is decrepit, yet saved. The openness to what is ugly or strange or worn out allows him to recognize strength and honor in so much that is "other," including, simply, ordinary women and their daily travails. Indeed, in "Today is Friday" the fact that Mary Magdalene, not an idealized woman, stayed with Jesus, and not the men, is reiterated three times.

His confidence in transcendent values, recognition of human imperfection, and appreciation of otherness, permit him to avoid the glorification of revenge. Robert Jordan, for example, does not kill to return death with death; he has grown weary of war and the abstractions of the Republican cause; he fights out of love for friends and a sense of duty. So there is no burning resentment in the Catholic Hemingway Hero. The Catholic Hemingway Hero has that same sentiment expressed by the Angelic evangel Matthew, who recounts Christ saying of the Father, He "makes his sun rise on the evil and on the good, and sends rain on the righteous and the unrighteous" (Matthew 5:45). There is no room for vengeance for one who so believes, as all are valuable to God: He "makes his sun rise" and "sends rain" to all in the created order.

III. IMPLICATIONS FOR TODAY

Hemingway's writings support an interpretation that provides a foundation for a certain way of being in the world, a distinctive view of life and one's response to existence. Moreover, this way of life can be shown to have a genuine application to pressing social and political concerns. Specifically, the Hemingway Catholic Hero can supply an understanding of masculinity that should be considered in the growing number of debates surrounding masculine virtue in the contemporary world.

The topic of masculinity is an issue drawing increasing theoretical reflection. As Harvey Mansfield has recently taken great pains to demonstrate, manliness is a topic that has attracted and deserves serious study (Mansfield 2006). In a world that seems ever more to aspire to fashion a gender-neutral understanding of social and political affairs, the question of what manliness is and whether manliness should be affirmed has assumed pressing significance. I believe that the type of character to be found in the Catholic Hemingway Hero represents a form of masculinity that is credible in the contemporary age, and which is all the more so when viewed in comparison to rival views of religiously grounded masculine revivalism.

The Hemingway Catholic Hero supplies a plausible account of masculinity for the modern world, a world that has been deeply shaped by the rise of the Women's Movement. Feminism has affirmed the value of female strength, and the inclusion of women in traditionally masculine roles in social, cultural, economic, and political life. The Catholic Hero can affirm this power and inclusiveness. He is not prone to resentment or to seek revenge for lost privilege. He can affirm the spectacle of feminine power as part of the world he loves. In fact, he is inclined to recognize in ordinary women a capacity for great strength. Yet at the same time he himself remains strong, while arresting the rise of any arrogance; he knows all shall perish and not achieve their mortal desires. Further, his inner strength allows him to see the value of life in all its complexity, without reducing that very complexity to simplified doctrine or dogma. In all, his is a way of life that would appear to be quite relevant to modern times.

Yet this view of masculinity is just one in a growing marketplace of ideas on masculine virtue. The terrain has been claimed by at least two other versions of manly virtue, views that have proven remarkably popular: The understanding of masculine virtue found in Mel Gibson's *The Passion of the Christ*, and the masculine revivalism of the Promise Keepers Movement. I shall juxtapose these two views of male virtue with that of the Hemingway Hero I have outlined. If these views are seen as essentially or fundamentally inconsistent with Hemingway view's then it would seem, given the suitability of his understanding to contemporary life, that these are likely false paths, and we can have considerable confidence in Hemingway's path for modern man.

1. Hemingway's Catholic Hero, Gibson's Christ, and Masculine Revivalism

In 2004 actor Mel Gibson directed and co-produced a major blockbuster film, *The Passion of the Christ*. Written by Gibson along with Benedict Fitzgerld,[26] the movie was remarkably popular, grossing nearly $400 million in the United States alone. The movie was popular among many conservative Catholics, and also among a great number of Protestants. James Martin, S.J. has documented the intensity of support for this movie (made by a Catholic) among Protestants, and especially conservative Protestants (Martin 2004).[27] One of the key components in the popularity of the movie—in addition to the publicity generated by its critics, which always aids sales—is the fact that the movie has been seen by many to convey a statement on masculine virtue, a point recently made by Lisa Tyler (2007, 155–169). The work's popularity in part comes from the way it portrays the masculinity of Jesus and serves as an inspiration for many men to live newly invigorated lives. The movie portrays the sheer stamina and physical prowess of Christ in bearing his torment, while also conveying the loving tenderness of Christ, especially toward his mother. Furthermore, the final scene of the movie shows a Christ Triumphant, a resurrected man walking boldly to martial drums to reclaim the world. As Tyler argues, the movie communicates the message that these are attributes appropriate to men, and so the film serves as a role model for men today (Tyler 155, 158).[28] The movie is therefore in part Gibson's own version of *An Imitation of Christ*.

As Tyler argues, the Christ depicted in the *Passion* bears many similarities to the Christ conveyed in "Today is Friday." For one thing, both are seen to have extraordinary physical strength, striking to all who behold it. However Hemingway's religious values, I argue, deviate considerably from those of Gibson's Christ, and for not less than four reasons.

First, the closing shots of the *Passion* seem ominous: *Christus Victor* marches from the grave, as Jim Wallis relates, to the low thundering sounds of war drums (Wallis 2004, 123). It seems to Gibson that Jesus is ushering in not a kingdom of the spirit and a godspell of transcendent salvation, but a pronouncement of physical victory for the faith-filled on earth, the reconquest of fallen spaces—the redemption *in* and *of* the here and now. Such a view is absent from Hemingway's Catholic Hero. He does not give us victory in this life on the plane of the body. The Catholic Hero remains strong in this world, knowing he will fail, as the body would define victory, yet retaining confidence in enduring values, and hope in a world to come.

Secondly, and related to the first, the Hemingway Catholic Hero does not seek revenge against his wrongdoers or those who challenge him. Yet the martial drumbeats seem indeed to evoke a sense of vengeance in *The Passion*. As does the severe damage that Gibson's post-crucifixion earthquake exacts on the Jewish Temple. And perhaps most clearly, *The Passion* evokes a profound sense of vengeance in the "the troubling scene of the black crow pecking out the eyes of the unrepentant criminal"—a scene that can only be understood to "carry [the] message [of] revenge" (Wallis 2004, 123). As Jim Wallis asks, "Is this the message of the gospels, that unjust violence leads 'just' to payback" (Wallis 2004, 123)? Hemingway's Hero says no.

Third and related to what we have said before, in the *Passion* the resurrected Christ is overflowing in physical beauty and perfection. For Gibson goodness is associated with the physically beautiful. The bodily and physically perfect are associated with the believer, and the physically deformed are associated with unbelief and evil. As Monica Migliorino Miller remarks, "one of the most disturbing and even perplexing images in the movie occurs during the scourging of Christ at the pillar. It occurs when the beating becomes most intense—when the soldiers switch from beating Christ with rods to beating him with cat-o-nine-tails." At this point Satan appears for a second time. "As she [Satan] slides across the screen the viewer sees that she is carrying a child. He is a very large child. His arms and back have hair and he has a large, squarish [i.e., ugly], almost adult-sized head" (Migliorino 2004, 5). "He looks at Christ being mercilessly beaten and smiles grotesquely and hideously" (Migliorino 2004, 6). As Miller states, "The Devil is there with her demon child as the reverse and opposite image of Mary and Christ" (Migliorino 2004, 7). Gibson is equating therefore the physically beautiful with the redeemed—and the physically deformed with the realm of unbelief and loss of salvation, and even manifest evil. Yet this juxtaposition is deeply opposed to the Catholic Hemingway Hero. He is not himself a man of physical perfection—he is, in the epoch novella, a decrepit old man with torn hands. He is an admirer of how the downcast stay loyal to Jesus in "Today is Friday." And he is willing to be led by a strikingly ugly woman in *For Whom the Bell Tolls*.

Fourth, Gibson's man keeps women on the sideline. The *Passion* has great emphasis on the mother of God, yet almost no portrayal of Mary Magdalene—that is, no reference to ordinary and not extraordinary womanhood. As Gaye Ortiz remarks, "Gibson gives little away regarding ... Mary Magdalene. He certainly does never hints at her starring role in the resurrection, as witness to the empty tomb" (Ortiz 2004, 113). Gibson's Magdalene is but a constant companion to Jesus' mother throughout the film, following her in "cowering, quivering awe" (Ortiz 2004, 113). In all, as the movie critic for the *New York Times* remarks, "In Gibson's treatment ... Mary Magdalene is so passive as to be almost invisible" (Ortiz 2004, 112). For the Hemingway Catholic Hero on the other hand, ordinary women can be seen as powerful forces. Hence Pilar is described as brave and industrious. And when she argues that the mission to destroy the bridge is a sound one, the band follows. And she takes on the important role of guarding the explosives at night. And she leads the attack on the saw mill. She, the simple, ugly woman, is a very powerful force.

Seen in its totality, what I am calling the Hemingway Catholic Hero is quite distinct from Gibson's muscular portrayal of Christ and its implicit cataloging of a set of male values. Gibson's view however is not the only or even the most popular expression of a religiously grounded masculine revivalism to find expression of late. A mass movement explicitly based on the revival of male virtues has arisen that seeks nothing short of a renaissance of manly virtue, a movement to which I now turn.

2. Hemingway's Catholic Hero, The Promise Keepers Movement and Masculine Revival

The Promise Keepers movement is another popular expression of masculine revivalism. As Dane Claussen remarks, the movement is self-consciously aiming at the revival of manhood in the modern world (Claussen 1999). The movement is a mass one seeking to inspire a newly invigorated Christian maleness, a revival of manhood based on conservative Protestantism (Bartowski 2004, 4–7).[29] There are many good things about this movement, and many of the criticisms of it appear to be quite misguided. Yet I argue that there are at least three major points at which the Promise Keepers' understanding of manhood diverges significantly from that of the Catholic Hemingway Hero.

First, the Promise Keepers is in fact a mass movement, and one grounded in a rigid understanding of doctrine. The movement seeks to congregate and inspire tens of thousands of men at rallies across the country. Also it holds to a literal exegesis of the Bible, with little interpretive flexibility. The Hemingway Hero however does not seek power in numbers and mass causes. Hence Robert Jordan has come to be suspicious of the Republican cause and the Republican military force. Moreover, he fights out of duty and not loyalty to a doctrinaire and inflexible cause.

Second, Promise Keepers appear to be driven by a sense of resentment. Its appeal as a mass movement is born of resentment in at least two senses. First, it rebels against general cultural developments (Hardisty 1999, 93–6).

As Michael Chrasta notes, "Theirs is a classic reform movement, the kind that develops when revived men try to remedy a perceived social problem, in this case, a pervasive and destructive cultural malaise" (Chrasta 2000, 25). It is also a movement driven by resentment in the sense of being impelled often by personal failures. As Brian Brickner notes, a very high percentage of Promise Keepers members have been divorced or experienced strain: "one cannot spend extensive time with Promise Keepers without witnessing the wounds of life, the discomforts, anxieties, and burdens of the camel" (Brickner 1999, 119). So many are "tormented and pained" (Brickner 1999, 120). For these reasons it is often resentment that drives men into this mass movement. On the contrary, for Hemingway's Catholic Hero the tragedies in life do not lead to resentment but to a focus on individual inner strength, followed by a recognition of triumph in final transcendence.

Moreover, the Promise Keepers movement strives to find power in this life by in effect conjuring the supernatural, which in turn elevates the sense of human capacity in this world. Promise Keepers is a movement based on signs and wonders. According to the thought of its founders, the primary method of gaining power is through alleged supernatural works and wonders (Dager 1998). However as Al Dager notes, "The problem with the charisma approach [of the Promise Keepers] is not the desire for revival but the belief that revival can come through a methodology of oppressive worship and praise—by holding one's hands up and demonstrating. Such attempts to conjure the presence of God, or to attempt to get him to move on one's behalf are akin to witchcraft" (Dager 1998).

This conjuring of divine power, certified by supernatural signs, is thought to empower men to be, in effect, a kind of conqueror over the world. Hence members look for signs and wonders and then feel empowered to act, possibly without real restraint, once the divine favor is felt sufficiently powerfully. So Promise Keepers can breed a triumphalism over the world of the here and now. (Bright 2002). As Al Dager notes, this can lead to a charismatic arrogance (Al Dager 1998). Such a view is deeply inconsistent with the Catholic Hemingway Hero. His emphasis is on the hard journey, the recognition of long voyages, not the sudden or persisting transformation. He does not see this world transformed yet persists in the face of it.

If what I have identified as a Hemingway-drawn religious hero is in fact plausible for our time, and if these alternatives are inconsistent with such a Hemingway view, we would indeed have good grounds for questioning such efforts to reaffirm masculinity; perhaps these other views are false paths.

IV. CONCLUSION

It bears repeating that by speaking of a Hemingway religious Hero I only mean to suggest that such a view is one coherent element in Hemingway's oeuvre. It is certainly not the only way to read Hemingway. My point is rather that there are strong grounds for holding that Hemingway may well be much more subtle than he is traditionally seen to be. And this very real possibility of a much more differentiated hero form has relevance for political thought today: The view that we can plausibly ascribe to at least part of Hemingway's corpus appears to have instructive things to tell us about the pressing question of masculinity in the post-feminist world, and the role of religion in inspiring a masculinity that is not shorn of all traditional masculine attributes, yet which can flourish in our present complex world.

NOTES

1. And G. R. Wilson, Jr. accurately describes the code as a "dark vista." G. R. Wilson, Jr., "Incarnation and Redemption," in *Ernest Hemingway's* Old Man and the Sea, ed. Harold Bloom (Philadelphia: Chelsea House, 1999), 123.
2. As Killinger notes, existentialism is first and foremost a debunking philosophy, debunking older concepts of value and the meaning and purpose of life. Michael Aeschliman in the same vein notes that existentialists "loot and ruin our 'res publica,' that body of beliefs, truths, behaviors, traditions, and achievements which is [our] patrimony . . . " Michael Aeschliman, *The Restitution of Man: C. S. Lewis and the Case Against Scientism* (Grand Rapids: Eerdmans, 1998), 85.
3. Killinger, *Hemingway and the Dead Gods*, 98. Additional defenses of Hemingway as an existentialist nihilist include Richard Lehan's essay on Sartre and Camus in *A Dangerous Crossing: French literary Existentialism and the Modern American Novel* (Carbondale: Southern Illinois University Press, 1973), 46–56. Scott Donaldson remarks how widely held the interpretation of Hemingway as an existentialist nihilist is, adding only that if Hemingway can be relieved of the charge it is only because he fails to adopt the philosophical locution of the existentialists, using his craft to artistically describe and not to theorize the facts of human life. Donaldson, *By Force of Will*, 234.
4. Lisa Tylor, "He was Pretty Good in There Today: Reviving the Macho Christ in 'Today is Friday' and Mel Gibson's *The Passion of the* Christ," *Journal of Men, Masculinities and Spirituality* 1, no. 2 (June 2007), 156. Stoneback strongly counsels readers to be "aware of the depth of Hemingway's writerly iceberg." H. R. Stoneback, "Pilgrimage Variations: Hemingway's Sacred Landscapes," *Religion and Literature* 35, no. 2/3 (Summer 2003), 53.
5. The literature on this is voluminous. For a representative sample see Leo Gurko, *Ernest Hemingway and the Pursuit of Heroism* (New York: Crowell Co., 1968).
6. The first translation into English of the traditional carol 'O Holy Night' dates from at least 1855.
7. And that Anglican prayer book, Carlos Baker famously asserted, was seldom out of Hemingway's reach. Carlos Baker, *Hemingway: The Writer as Artist* (Princeton: Princeton University Press, 1952), 298.
8. Qaisar Iqbal Janjua, "Earnest Hemingway's *For Whom The Bell Tolls*: A Critical Analysis," available at www.scribd.com.
9. Kristy Lobe, http://www.Ernest-Hemingway/25428.
10. Ibid.
11. Albert Camus, *The Myth of Sisyphus* (New York: Random House, 1983), 84. Emphasis added.
12. Ibid.

13. Joshua Foa Dienstag, "Nietzsche's Dionysian Pessimism," *American Political Science Review* 95, No. 4 (Dec 2001), 935. Moreover further evidence of how existentialism can be viewed as a harbinger of dread and not an evangel of life can be seen by the way in which Camus himself addresses the potential consequences of existentialism: As Michael Aeschliman notes, "Camus attributed the rise of Nazism to the [growing] sense of the metaphysical absurdity of life." Aeschliman, *The Restitution of Man*, 75.
14. Joshua Foa Dienstag has taken the lead in articulating a perspective, which he sees emanating from the works of Nietzsche, that might come close to affirming the idea that life for an existentialist can be *as good* and *as happy* as it had been for those who lived according to older values. He develops an interpretation that holds that Nietzsche embraced Dionysian pessimism, or a pessimism of strength: a recognition that the world has no meaning or value but a recognition accompanied by "cheerfulness" and the assertion that this very recognition can be "good for one's health." (p. 936) Even if we accept such a construction of Nietzsche, it is not at all clear that the life of the Dionysian pessimist—the new morn *this* man heeds—is as good or as happy as that in earlier modes of living. Indeed, Dienstag notes that Nietzsche's thought "does not mean that happiness must disappear from human life . . . but if happiness is to be found it can only be on . . . new terms"—which are clearly *diminished* terms, though still genuine terms of happiness. (p. 934) Hence, "Nietzsche neither appeals to nor promises . . . happiness." (p. 936) Assuming this view to be Nietzsche's, the life of a Dionysian pessimist may not be devoid of happiness, but it is indeed diminished—it is merely the best one can construct in the world of eternal becoming. Dienstag, "Nietzsche's Dionysian Pessimism."
15. Among this vast, and one might suspect faddish literature, see Michael Martin, *Cambridge Companion to Atheism* (Cambridge: New York, 2007), and especially David O. Brink's essay, "The Autonomy of Ethics."
16. Englewood, New Jersey: The As Stable Publications, 1926.
17. For Stoneback see below. For Melvin Blackman see "Hemingway: The Matador and the Crucified," in *Hemingway and His Critics; an International Anthology*, ed. Carlos Baker (New York: Hill and Wang, 1961), 245–258. Delbert Wylder provides an excellent interpretation of the work that has some parallels with my own view in his chapter The Hero as Saint and Sinner. Delbert E. Wylder, *Hemingway's Heroes* (Albuquerque: The University of New Mexico Press, 1969). He also alludes, as scholars I believe must, to the multiform character of Hemingway's masterwork by quoting favorably critic Earl Rovitt's understanding of *The Old Man and the Sea*: "Within the frame of the general interpretation of this story, there are many possible special readings; for Hemingway has so successfully narrated [the story] that . . . the travail can be seen as a religious one, an introspective one, or an aesthetic one," its meaning in some real sense being "almost incommunicable" in its profundity. Earl Rovitt, *Ernest Hemingway*. New York: Twayne Publishers, 1963, 90. Quoted in Wylder, *Hemingway's Heroes*, 201.
18. The great church father Augustine, quoting Ecclesiasticus 10:12–13, states clearly in Ch. 13, Book 16 of *The City of God*, "pride is the commencement of all sin."
19. Clinton S. Burhans, Jr., "*The Old Man and the Sea*: Hemingway's Tragic Vision of Man," *American Literature* 13 (January 1960), quoted in *Ernest Hemingway: Critiques of Four Major Novels*, ed. Carlos Baker (New York: Charles Scribner's Sons, 1962), 154.
20. Isaiah 11:6. Important is also the fact, noted by Bickford Sylvester, that Manolin is the diminutive of Manuel, the Spanish name for Savior or Redeemer,

which further serves to underscore a prophetic reference. "The Cuban Context of *The Old Man and the Sea*" in *Ernest Hemingway's* The Old Man and the Sea," 180.
21. Charles Hartshorne, *Reality as Social Process: Studies in Metaphysics and Religion* (Boston: Free Press, 1953), ch. 8, p. 168.
22. Stoneback, "Pilgrimage Variations," 52. Gabriel Marcel defines the Christian as essentially a sinful being who is also a person on pilgrimage. Recognizing man as sinful, and so not minimizing the brutality of which human nature is capable, yet also seeing man as *homo viator*—as a person conducting a pilgrimage—constitutes the core of a metaphysics of hope. See Gabriel Marcel, Homo Viator: *Introduction to a Metaphysics of Hope* trans. Emma Craufurd (New York: Harper and Row, 1965).
23. Quoted in Stoneback, "Pilgrimage Variations," 53.
24. Stoneback, "Pilgrimage Variations," 53.
25. James William Brodman, *Charity and Religion in Medieval Europe* (Washington, DC: Catholic University of America Press, 2009), 275. This is not to say that one could not construe this Hemingway Hero as expressing a Christian spirituality consonant with elements of Protestantism or Orthodoxy. However, in line with Hemingway's own religious journey as an adult, which as Stoneback demonstrates was precisely a journey in and through the Catholic Church, the religious character of the hero form seems best expressed as Catholic.
26. Much of the theology comes from Anne Catherine Emmerich's (1774–1824) *The Dolorous Passion of Our Lord*, also called by Brentano "The Lowly Life and Bitter Passion of Our Lord Jesus Christ and His Blessed Mother."
27. James Martin, "The Last Station: Catholic Reflections on *The Passion*," in *Perspectives on* The Passion of the Christ: *Religious Thinkers and Writers Explore the Issues Raised by the Controversial Movie.* (New York: Miramax Book, 2004).
28. Tyler, 56, 158. Tyler outlines as well the ways in which Gibson's portrayal of Christ follows in the tradition of "Muscular Christianity." Institutionalized in such organizations as the YMCA, Muscular Christianity in the nineteenth and early twentieth centuries sought to inspire men to a manly faith in imitation of the robust and rugged savior.
29. The movement is also not a dead one. See John Bartowski, *The Promise Keepers: Servants, Soldiers, and Godly Men* (New Brunswick, NJ: Rutgers University Press, 2004), 4–7 describing recent efforts to revive its mass appeal. And moreover, the same work indicates that the values of the movement remain—the massive rallies have indeed faded, yet simply because of a lack of novelty concerning the mass football stadium rally; the ideas and meetings, though on a lesser scale, still continue. Bartkowski, *The Promise Keepers*, 150.

WORKS CITED

Aeschliman, Michael. *The Restitution of Man: C. S. Lewis and the Case Against Scientism*. Grand Rapids: Ferdmans, 1998.

Baker, Carlos. *Hemingway: The Writer as Artist*. Princeton: Princeton University Press, 1952.

Barrett, William. *Time of Need: Forms of Imagination in the Twentieth Century.* New York: Harper, 1972.

Bartowski, John. *The Promise Keepers: Servants Soldiers, and Godly Men*. New Brunswick, NJ: Rutgers University Press, 2004.

Blackman, Melvin. "Hemingway: The Matador Crucified." In *Hemingway and His Critics: An International Anthology*. New York: Hill and Wang, 1961.
Brickner, Bryan. *The Promise Keepers: Politics and Promises*. Lanham, MD: Lexington Books, 1999.
Bright, Bill. *Promises: Daily Devotion for Supernatural Living*. Peachtree City, GA: New Life Publications, 2002.
Brodman, James. *Charity and Religion in Medieval Europe*. Washington, DC: Catholic University, 2009.
Burhans, Clinton Jr. "The Old Man and the Sea: Hemingway's Tragic Vision of Man." *American Literature* 13 (1960: 446–55).
Camus, Albert. *The Myth of Sisyphus*. New York: Random House, 1983.
Chrasta, Michael. "The Religious Roots of the Promise Keepers." In *The Promise Keepers: Essays on Masculinity and Christianity*, edited by Dane Claussen, 20–28. Jefferson, NC: McFarland and Co., 2000.
Claussen, Dane. *Standing on Promises: The Promise Keepers and the Revival of Manhood*. Cleveland: Pilgrim Press, 1999.
Dager, Albert J. "Promise Keepers: Claims Mandate to Unite all Christians." *Media Spotlight* 21 (2): 1998. Available at www.geocities.com/hebrews928/pdx398.html?200923.
Dienstag, Joshua. "Nietzsche's Dionysian Pessimism." *American Political Science Review* 95 (4) 2001: 81–101.
Donaldson, Scott. *By Force of Will: The Life of Ernest Hemingway*. New York: Viking Press, 1977.
Emmerich, Catherine. (1774–1824) *The Dolorous Passion of Our Lord*, also called by Brentano "The Lowly Life and Bitter Passion of Our Lord Jesus Christ and His Blessed Mother." Rockford, IL: Tan Books and Publishers, 1976.
Gurko, Leo. *Ernest Hemingway and the Pursuit of Heroism*. New York: Ciowell Company, 1968.
Hardisty, Jean. *Mobilizing Resentment: Conservative Resurgence from the John Birch Society to the Promise Keepers*. Boston: Beacon Press, 1999.
Hartshorne, Charles. *Reality as Social Process: Studies in Metaphysics and Religion*. Boston: Free Press, 1953.
Hemingway, Ernest. *For Whom the Bell Tolls*. New York: Scribner, 1940.
———. *The Old Man and the Sea*. New York: Scribner, 1952.
———. *The Short Stories of Ernest Hemingway*. New York: Scribner, 1953.
Hoffman, Steven. "Nada and the Clean-Lighted Place: The Unity of Hemingway's Short Fiction." In *New Critical Approaches to the Short Stories of Ernest Hemingway*, edited by Jackson B. Benson, 172–191. Durham: Duke University Press, 1990.
Janjua, Quaiser Iqbal. "Ernest Hemingway For Whom the Bell Tolls: A Critical Analysis" at www.scribd.com.
Killinger, John. *Hemingway and the Dead Gods: A Study in Existentialism*. Lexington: University of Kentucky Press, 1960.
Lehan, Richard. *A Dangerous Crossing: French Literary Existentialism and the American Novel*. Carbonale, Il. Southern Illinois Press, 1973.
Lobe, Kristy. http://www.Ernest-Hemingway25428.
Lynn, Kenneth S. *Hemingway*. New York: Simon and Schuster, 1987.
Mansfield, Harvey. *Manliness*. New Haven: Yale University Press, 2006.
Marcel, Gabriel. *Homo Viator: Introduction to a Metaphysics of Hope*. Translated by Emma Crauturd. New York: Harper and Row, 1965.
Martin, James. "The Last Station: Catholic Reflections on The Passion." In *Perspectives on The Passion of the Christ: Religious Thinkers and Writers Explore the Issues Raised by the Controversial Movie*, 95–110. New York: Miramax Books, 2004.

Meyers, Jeffrey. *Hemingway: A Biography*. New York: Simon and Schuster, 1985.

Miller, Monica Migliorino. *The Theology of The Passion of the Christ*. New York: Palgrave MacMillan, 2004.

Ortiz, Gaye W. "Passion-ate Women: The Female Presence in The Passion of The Christ." In *Re-Viewing The Passion: Mel Gibson's Film and its Critics*, edited by S. Brent Plate, 109–120. New York: Palgrave Macmillan, 2004.

Rovitt, Earl. *Ernest Hemingway*. New York: Twayne Publishers, 1963.

Stoneback, H. R. "Pilgrimage Variations: Hemingway's Sacred Landscapes." *Religion and Literature* 35 (2003): 49–65.

———. "In the Nominal Country of the Bogus: Hemingway's Catholicism and the Biographies." In *Hemingway: Essays of Reassessment*, edited by Frank Scafella, 105–140. New York: Oxford University Press, 1991.

Sylvester, Bickford. "The Cuban Context of the Old Man and the Sea." In *Ernest Hemingway's The Old Man and the Sea*, edited by Harold Bloom, 165–184. Philadelphia: Chelsea House, 1999.

Tylor, Lisa. "He was Pretty Good in There Today: Reviving the Macho Christ in 'Today is Friday' and Mel Gibson's The Passion of the Christ." *Journal of Men, Masculinities and Spirituality* 2 (2007): 155–169.

Wallis, Jim. "The Passion and the Message." In *Perspectives on The Passion of the Christ: Religious Thinkers and Writers Explore the Issues Raised by the Controversial Movie*, 111–126. New York: Miramax Books, 2004.

Wilson, G. R. "Incarnation and Redemption." In *Ernest Hemingway's Old Man and the Sea*, edited by Harold Bloom, 119–124. Philadelphia: Chelsea House, 1999.

Wylder, Delbert E. *Hemingway's Heroes*. Alberquerque: The University of New Mexico Press, 1969.

Part IV
The Impossibility of Politics

7 Hemingway's *For Whom the Bell Tolls*
Rebellion and the Meaning of Politics in the Spanish Civil War

Kerstin Hamann[1]

Scholars identify *For Whom the Bell Tolls* as "Hemingway's most overtly political novel" (Nakjavani 1988, 144), or, in the words of Meyers (1990, 104), it is "the greatest political novel in American literature." First published in 1940, it is set during the Spanish civil war. Hemingway himself was an active participant in the war, and MacDonald (1997, 327) states that Hemingway takes a "definite ... political attitude" towards the war. Yet in sharply contrasting analysis, Cooper (1987, 109) notes that several critics assert that the novel is not political, or misses the main issues in the war, because it refrains from propagandizing. The discrepancy between these two interpretations of the work as a political novel hinges on the definition of "political" or politics. Within a political science framework, if "political" tends to focus on a specific set of political institutions or specific party politics, the novel appears less political because in the book, neither Hemingway nor his protagonist profess support for a certain type of democratic institutions or political parties. In terms of ideology, the novel clearly adopts an anti-Fascist stance, yet it reveals no obvious preference for the type of society that would be desirable if the Republican Loyalists won the war. The protagonist Robert Jordan maintains a commitment to the "Republic" in terms of an electoral, democratic republic rather than specifying concrete institutions that might reveal attachment to a more transparent and coherent ideology. Hemingway portrays support for the Republican cause, but surprisingly, he also exposes the brutality on the part of the Republican fighters. Similarly, the novel does not present uncritical and enthusiastic support for the Communist leaders of the Republican war effort. Thus, rather than offering support for a specific type of polity, or defending a specific political ideology, the political aspect of the novel is more nuanced. It describes the Republican struggle during the war and profoundly depicts the impact of politics in defining people's lives. Watson (1992b, 103) observes that "*For Whom the Bell Tolls* may not be a novel about the politics of the Spanish Civil War, but the politics of that war permeate the novel at almost every level of thought and action." While our social science lens focuses attention on institutions and institutional change through well-defined interests and more formal organizations, *For Whom the Bell Tolls* probes the more intimate and individualistic defining process of those interests. In particular, the novel focuses our attention on the meaning of rebellion as a political act of self-realization, best exemplified in the actions of the novel's rebel protagonist, Robert Jordan.

Hemingway addresses this topic through Jordan's multi-faceted and complex rebellion. Jordan opposes the Fascists attempting to take over Republican Spain. At the same time, he cannot wholeheartedly support the Communists that dominated much of the fight against Fascism. Once committed in practice to fighting the Fascists he is caught in a web of seeping doubt and ambivalence to the Communist cause. This simultaneous and opposing rebellion against established ideologies has been alluded to as "anarchism" (Waldhorn 2002, 168). In the end, it is the commitment and action of the individual against Fascism rather than adherence to a particular ideology that gives Jordan's life meaning when he muses, "I have fought for what I believed for a year now" (Hemingway 2003, 467; Waldhorn 2002, 168). It is through *participation* in politics in the context of war that individuals find meaning, camaraderie, and love.

Yet, while *For Whom the Bell Tolls* tells a story about an individual finding meaning in his life through rebellion, it is also a story about a specific political event, the Spanish civil war that waged for three years (1936–1939). Like the protagonist, Hemingway himself was involved in the war and taking sides, attempting to defend the Republic against the insurgents. As such, this chapter refers to the way Hemingway portrays the war in his novel, and analyzes the description of the Spanish civil war to evaluate the extent to which his interpretation is congruent with those provided by some of the leading scholars on the civil war. While political scientists aptly identify the competing goals and strategic decision making, they fail to capture politics as a catalyst for individual transformation. Through the novel, the story of the characters offers a dimension of politics that is often missed in tightly constructed social science explanations.

The remainder of this chapter explores different dimensions of rebellion in *For Whom the Bell Tolls*. The next section outlines the war against Fascism in the historical context of the civil war. I then analyze the fight against Fascism as well as Jordan's rebellion against Communists and other Republicans as demonstrated in the novel. Finally, I conclude with the novel's ideas on a transformative and individual meaning of the politics of civil war. War provides a brutal set of experiences but also opportunities, bringing meaning to the life of the individual especially with respect to love and death, as portrayed in the novel.

I. THE CIVIL WAR AND THE REBELLION AGAINST FASCISM

1. The Significance of the Spanish Civil War

The story is set during the Spanish civil war, during which Nationalist insurgents fought against the defendants of the Second Republic, the first meaningful—though deeply polarized and unstable—democratic experience in Spain's history. As noted by scholars of Spanish history and politics: "For the first time, under the Republic, a democratic system functioned; elections were genuine elections fought by mass parties" (Carr and Fusi 1981, 2). The Republic collapsed just five years after it was pronounced although it officially continued to exist until the end of the war in 1939; its short history was one of politicization and polarization as well as fragmentation on both the left and the right. The main issues concerned reforms in three areas, which proved profoundly conflictual: religion, land reform, and regional issues (Beevor 1982, 27). While the left and the right became more polarized, fragmentation within the left and right camps also increased (see e.g., Beevor 1982, ch. 3; Payne 1987, chs. 3 and 4). Yet, popular support for the extreme right remained low, even towards the end of the Republic. In the Republic's last election in February 1936, the Fascist Falange gained just 0.7% of the popular vote, "probably the weakest showing of Fascism in electoral competition in any European country where a national Fascist party contested elections" (Payne 1987, 65). Nonetheless, the Republic became increasingly ungovernable and the government lost control in the midst of revolutionary movements and chaos. The final straw leading to the civil war was provided by the assassination of Calvo Sotelo, a prominent leader of the rightist opposition, by the state police forces (Payne 1987, 50).

Much like the main conflicts during the Second Republic, the reasons for its fall were thus numerous and complex.[2] However, with the beginning of the civil war, these complex issues were simplified: The two warring sides comprised on the one hand the insurgents, fighting to overthrow the Republic (located on the right of the political spectrum), and on the other the defenders of the Republic (situated on the political left). Both sides suffered from internal fragmentation. At the most general level, and certainly from an international perspective, the civil war assumed international relevance beyond the Iberian peninsula as it constituted "the defense of democracy against the spread of Fascism" (Balfour 2001, 254). Fascism threatened to dominate Europe, Hitler was in power in Germany, and Mussolini had firmly consolidated his power in Italy. Both Germany and Italy supported the Nationalist insurgents; the Fascist powers also used Spain as a testing ground in their own military build-up, perhaps best illustrated by the bombing of the Basque town La Guernica by German and Italian warplanes in April 1937 (Beevor 1982, 166–167; Payne 1987, 139–140). Thus, the stakes in the Spanish civil war appeared high as the defeat of Fascism here would send an important signal to other Fascist leaders in Europe.

The historian Hugh Thomas (2001, 449) states that the war "would be more even than a European civil war: It would be a world war in miniature;" similarly, Preston (2006, 7) explains that the war "was above all a Spanish war . . . yet it was also the great international battleground of Fascism and Communism." In this context, the meaning of individual action becomes significant. In the novel, individuals are willing to risk their lives for a seemingly insignificant and likely futile military attack, which only gains meaning when it is placed in the larger context of the fight against Fascism on a European scale.

Hemingway himself "had long believed that war was evil"; yet, in the case of the Spanish civil war, he "found a war that he could justify in moral and political terms, and his writing reflects this change. Although at times he was critical of the way the Republican leadership was conducting the war, he never questioned the validity of their cause" (Cooper 1987, 89). Thus, Hemingway was a staunch supporter of the Republic without defining particular goals and institutions for the future: "I . . . belonged to none. . . . I had no party but a deep interest in and love for the Republic" (cited in Baker 1962, 111). He abhorred Fascism, in part for its restrictions on individual freedom, which related directly to his role as a writer. In a 1937 speech, Hemingway declared: "There is only one form of government that cannot produce good writers, and that system is Fascism. For Fascism is a lie told by bullies. A writer who will not lie cannot live or work under Fascism" (cited in Cooper 1987, 84). Hemingway was personally involved in the civil war as a "propagandist, polemicist, public spokesman, and fund raiser" (Watson 1992b, 104). As such, he raised money to fund ambulances for Spain, and took part in producing a film[3] about the war that was shown in the U.S. and raised funding and support for the Republican side (Meyers 1985, ch. 15). During the war, he cooperated with the international Communists and supported their campaigns internationally (Watson 1992a). Evidently, Hemingway's concern for and involvement in the Spanish war was certainly motivated by his love for Spain, which was well known and had been the subject of some of his earlier writings, including *Death in the Afternoon*. But the civil war was an important subject to write about not just because it took place in Spain, but because the relevance of fighting Fascism went beyond the Spanish setting and instead was important on an international level. To the extent that Fascism threatened humanity across Europe, *For Whom The Bell Tolls* provides a context for a universal understanding that individuals are inevitably impacted by politics; individuals, in turn, can respond to politics so that they gain identity and meaning through political battles.

2. Jordan's Rebellion Against Fascism

Lines of opposition are easily drawn in the battle for the Republic and against Fascism. The Republicans fought against the Nationalist insurgents, who were united by their desire to restore order over the "chaos" of democracy

(Balfour 2001, 253–254). The Nationalists supported the Catholic Church, planned to repress demands for regional autonomy, and to strengthen the central state. Jordan joins the Republican side against the Nationalists, attempting to quell the rise of Fascism in Spain as part of a larger battle against Fascism on an international scale. Jordan was keenly aware of the rise of Fascism in Europe and therefore of the significance of the civil war in Spain; thus, he states, "If we win here we will win everywhere" (Hemingway 2003, 467). Similarly, he reasons, "The first thing was to win the war. If we did not win the war, everything was lost" (Hemingway 2003, 136). Even if the war was not won, Jordan tells himself, it would hold up the Fascists enough so they would not be able to attack other countries (Hemingway 2003, 432), thus fulfilling a strategic mission. As Molesworth (1992, 88) puts it, "The 'cause' was the belief that Fascism, and its love of death, could be beaten." Jordan himself states explicitly, "I'm an anti-Fascist" (Hemingway 2003, 66). The story and its protagonist's actions are thus primarily motivated by the fight against Fascism, which threatened to overpower democracy in Spain, but also in other countries, especially Germany and Italy. To beat Fascism in Spain was to send an important signal internationally in an attempt to save humanity not just in Spain, but also elsewhere.

Robert Jordan is an American college professor specializing in Spanish culture and literature. In his quest to prevail over the Fascist insurgents, he is not part of the regular troops of the International Brigades, but instead works by himself under the orders of the Russian leaders of the Republican war effort. He is assisted by a partisan guerrilla group organized behind the enemy lines. Jordan has become an expert in dynamiting, and his mission is to blow up a bridge of strategic importance to the Fascists in an attack planned by the Communists. He is supposed to go behind the enemy lines and detonate the bridge once the Republican attack has begun in order to stop the Fascists from receiving reinforcements. Jordan's mission, and by extension the role of the guerrilla groups supporting him, is thus of strategic importance for the success of Republican war effort. The role of the guerrillas behind Nationalist lines, organized by the Soviets, in the war was generally minimal and presented "rarely a problem" for the Nationalists, in part because they lacked civilian support in the areas they occupied (Payne 1987, 137). In the novel, too, the guerrillas primarily busy themselves with hiding out in the mountains and staying safe; their last notable involvement in the war had been an attack on a train three months earlier, and they have to be careful when they go to town to get food and information to make sure they are not identified and betrayed. Thus, blowing up the bridge is a major operation that some guerrillas strongly support for its significance in winning the war, while others are more skeptical (El Sordo) or openly opposed (Pablo) due to the strategic problems of the plan, especially concerning the logistics of the retreat of the guerrillas upon completion of the attack.

Despite the strategic importance of the mission, Jordan is uncomfortable with the plan from the moment he receives the order from the Russian

General Golz—"I understand it," he says, "I do not say I like it very much" (Hemingway 2003, 6). He is preoccupied with and almost worried about the details of the plan, he has a bad feeling about the planned logistics of the attack, and he receives multiple negative vibes in the days preceding the attack. Pilar, a leading member of the guerrilla group assisting him, refuses to tell him what she reads in his palm on their first encounter—presumably his death (Hemingway 2003, 33). He realizes that the technicalities of blowing up the bridge would be easy and straightforward, yet the logistical conditions under which he must do so make it difficult and dangerous—"They were bad orders all right for those who would have to carry them out" (Hemingway 2003, 43); the situation is aggravated by the snow that falls before the attack and that allows the Nationalists to follow the tracks and wipe out one of the guerrilla bands supporting the attack; and one of his own band members sabotages the mission by stealing and destroying part of his equipment necessary to blow up the bridge. To Jordan, this is the worst situation he has found himself in during his involvement in the war—"'I have been in many things. And worse than this,' he lied" (Hemingway 2003, 342). However, he knows that in war one has to follow orders even when in disagreement; he muses, "You are instruments to do your duty. There are necessary orders . . . You have only one thing to do and you must do it" (Hemingway 2003, 43). The bridge has more significance than just supporting one individual attack because "that bridge can be the point on which the future of the human race can turn" (Hemingway 2003, 43). Therefore, Jordan's individual action acquires meaning and importance, making it impossible for him to abandon the plan even in face of adversity. The importance of the battle against Fascism in a general sense is sufficiently significant to overcome skepticism with the details and logistics concerning the orders to detonate the bridge. It is the act of the rebellion, then, rather than the consequence of the action for either the battle or for himself that matters. In fact, even when Jordan is convinced that he will not survive the attack and that it will be impossible to carry the mission out successfully, he nonetheless proceeds with his preparations (Hemingway 2003, 385). Jordan is also aware that the Republicans might lose the war; yet, his loyalty and commitment do not falter. "What if they were killed tomorrow? What did it matter as long as they did the bridge properly?", he reflects (Hemingway 2003, 355). His own life gains meaning and his identity evolves particularly in relation to his role in the war against Fascism. To echo Cooper (1987, 115), "Jordan is a 'success' not because he blew up the bridge, but because he is true to himself and his commitments even if it means death."

Jordan declares himself an anti-Fascist. The Fascists are considered a threat to humanity, and their brutality is pictured explicitly in several scenes throughout the book even though the goals and institutions of Fascism are not articulated. For instance, María's tale of how her parents got murdered and how she herself got abused by Fascist soldiers, or the slaughter of El Sordo's guerrilla group, depict Fascists as the enemy to humanity.

They appear to take pleasure in killing other human beings. Yet, at other times, Jordan also humanizes Fascist soldiers (see Waldhorn 2002, 170). For example, when one of the Republican guerrilla bands supporting Jordan is eliminated by the insurgents, the Nationalist Lieutenant in charge of the troops finds one of the guerrillas still alive and "shot him in the back of the head, as quickly and as gently, if such an abrupt movement can be gentle. . . .". The same person thinks, "What a bad thing war is" (Hemingway 2003, 322), and he considers some of his own actions and orders as "barbarous" (Hemingway 2003, 326). One of Jordan's most devoted helpers, the old man Anselmo, reflects that the men he will help kill are "the same men that we are. . . . It is only orders that come between us. Those men are not Fascists. . . . They are poor men as we are" (Hemingway 2003, 193). As Sherwood (1997, 325) phrases it, Hemingway "wrote with aching sympathy for all the victims of Fascism, including the Fascists themselves." Jordan recognizes the humanity behind some of the enemy forces without humanizing Fascism itself as an ideology. He is keenly aware of the divisions within the Nationalist camp, for example, when he distinguishes the actions of the Falangists from others Nationalists (Hemingway 2003, 353). The process of rebellion, independent of victory or any particular collective political outcome, can rescue even those individuals within the enemy side from the pervasive grab of Fascism.

3. Jordan's Rebellion Against Republicans

Hemingway's participation in the war on the Loyalist side unsurprisingly coincides with the novel's support of the Republicans. Given his "side" of the cause, it was perhaps more surprising that much of Hemingway's writing in the book "was critical of the Loyalists and their leftwing allies, the very side he had supported during the war" (Watson 1992b, 104). Thus, Jordan's committed fight against Fascism does not mean that he was fighting *for* the ideals of the Communists, who dominated much of the Republican struggle and led the international efforts (Watson 1992a, 38), or that he supported their strategies and conduct. He was fighting for the Republic as a form of government, but not for a specific party, faction, or ideology among the Republicans. Jordan answers the question of whether he is a Communist with "No I am an anti-Fascist" (Hemingway 2003, 66); on another occasion he tells himself: "You're not a real Marxist and you know it" (Hemingway 2003, 305). As Baker (1962, 12) phrases it so aptly, he "is with, but not of, the Communists." Clearly disagreeing with much of what the Communists did and stood for, but yet understanding the need to follow Communist leadership as the only means to win against the Fascists, Jordan reflects on his own politics: "What were his politics then? He had none now, he told himself" (Hemingway 2003, 66). Given the behavioral evidence that Jordan sacrificed his life in the battle for the Republic, this is an odd statement. However, if Jordan locates his self-defining process by politics other than packaged ideology or partisanship, his abnegation may be consistent.

Jordan's ambivalence as to his own ideological beliefs or political goals is in some ways reflective of the divisions within the Republican side, which "was fighting for objectives that were not always compatible with each other" (Balfour 2001, 254). This was true for the role of the left not just during the civil war, but had already become evident during the Second Republic. For example, the leftist Republican-Socialist coalition (1931–1933) was characterized by divisions and disagreements, concerning "both the principles and pace of socioeconomic reform" (Payne 1987, 38), and collapsed due to "internal division" (Payne 1987, 40). Leftist groups outside of the ruling coalition also opposed the government, and in some cases the Republic itself: The Communist Party (PCE), for instance, controlled by the Soviet Union, aimed at overthrowing the Republic, as did other parts of the extreme left, including the Leninist BOC (Worker-Peasant Bloc), and the anarcho-syndicalist trade union CNT. In fact, the CNT had staged several insurrection attempts as early as 1932 to 1933, destabilizing the ruling Republican-Socialist coalition (Payne 1987, 39). During the civil war, divisions within the Republican front over strategy and ideology were extensive and stretched to a "civil war within the civil war" when, in May 1937, the Communists engaged in armed battle against parts of the revolutionary CNT and the POUM, a revolutionary Marxist party in the streets of Barcelona (Balfour 2001, 258–259; Carr and Fusi 1981, 6).

The splits during the existence of the Republic indicated that despite agreement on a democratic process, disagreement on issues was widespread, with a "potentially savage conflict over the scale of the social and economic reform it should pursue, or . . . over what the 'content' of the Republic should be" (Preston 2006, 38). The Republic itself contained a wide variety of political ideologies, including moderate Catholicism, revolutionary leftism, and extreme conservatism. The leftist leadership of the Second Republic was known for its antagonism to the Catholic Church, which in turn continued to be the "unifying force" among the insurgents (Balfour 2001, 254). The Republic itself, for much of its existence, was ruled under some kind of state of exception, which included limits to freedom of expression;[4] governments did not always include those parties that had won the most votes; several of the leftist parties were not loyal to Republican democracy and refused to take on governing responsibilities—for instance, the Socialists "refused to participate in a 'bourgeois' regime," making it impossible for the Popular Front to form a majority government after the 1936 election (Payne 1987, 45). Thus, the supporters of the Republic were mostly united by their opposition to Fascism rather than by their vision of Republican politics and a postwar society.

Given this lack of a cohesive ideology and agreement on policies, support for the "Republic" as an alternative system of government rather than a particular political leaning within the Republic is perhaps the best Jordan can come up with. His ambiguity and uncertainty identify a more general condition of complexity as the Republic oriented around a multitude of things and represented different things to different people. Certainly, there is a shared consensus around citizens' self-determination through competitive elections. Jordan explains, "I believe in the people and their right to govern themselves as they wish" (Hemingway 2003, 304). Yet, apart from the affirmation of a democratic process, *For Whom the Bell Tolls* reflects the divisions on some of these issues. Religion serves as an illustration that stands out for the ambiguity among the Republicans. The Nationalist soldiers pray a lot, while the guerrillas discuss the absence of religion quite frequently and generally emphatically—for example, María wonders whether marriage still carried any importance "since we no longer have the church" (Hemingway 2003, 344). At the same time, several of the Republicans bemoan the loss of religion: Anselmo "missed the prayers but he thought it would be unfair and hypocritical to say them" (Hemingway 2003, 197), but after the death of Sordo and his band, he overcomes his fears of disloyalty to the Republic and prays for their souls and to find strength for the next day (Hemingway 2003, 327). Similarly, the boy Joaquín, a member of El Sordo's band, begins to pray when he is dying. These examples illustrate that governmental policies do not necessarily change individuals' beliefs or fill their emotional and spiritual needs, in this case regarding religion, despite the fact that the Republican forces murdered over 4,000 priests and over 2,600 monks and nuns in addition to 13 bishops, primarily at the outset of the war (Balfour 2001, 257). Thus, particular policies and politics of the Republic were not without critics among its own supporters. Yet in Hemingway's book, even those characters that do not conform or who disregard some of the politics undertaken during the leftist leadership of the Republic are committed to fight for the Republic.

What did the Republic mean then to the supporters portrayed in the novel? For one, Jordan thinks it is crucial that the Republic win because otherwise "it would be impossible for those who believed in it to live in Spain . . . he knew that it would be from the things that happened in the parts the Fascists had already taken" (Hemingway 2003, 163). He wants the Republic to win so that Spain would be a safe place and a "good place to live in" (Hemingway 2003, 162). Anselmo realizes that if he ever wanted to return to his house, the war had to be won (Hemingway 2003, 194). Hoping for a more just society, he wants victory so that "we should govern justly and that all should participate in the benefits according as they have striven for them" (Hemingway 2003, 285). But the guerrillas themselves disagree on what should happen after the war: One of them worries whether they might win the war but "lose the revolution" and suggests to shoot "the anarchists and the Communists and all this *canalla* except the good Repbulicans," without specifying who would qualify as such (Hemingway 2003, 285); Pilar declares that "I believe firmly in the Republic and I have faith" (Hemingway 2003, 90). These examples illustrate that the Republic meant different things to different characters in the novel, but for all of them it represents the defense against Fascism with its denial of freedom and self-determination.

While Jordan confesses to believe in the value of the Republic as a form of government (Hemingway 2003, 304), he profoundly disagrees with much of the Communist leadership. His dealings with and attitudes toward the Communists were more complex and ambivalent than his rejection of Fascism precisely because the Communists dominated the international efforts of the fight against Fascism in Spain. Hemingway himself was aware that "the Communists had effectively turned the war effort into something like a police state, jailing and executing, and often torturing, other leftist leaders" (Molesworth 1992, 90). Yet, the battle against Fascism was impossible without subjecting to Communist leadership. Carr and Fusi (1981, 5) state that the Nationalists succeeded in winning the war primarily due to their "superior equipment and superior discipline in the army and . . . a unified wartime government." Historians tend to agree that the Nationalists won the war in part because of the superiority of their army, including weapons, but also due to a higher degree of unity and discipline among the Nationalist troops. In contrast, the forces fighting for the survival of the Republic "had to be forged out of politically divided fighting units . . . Republican fronts collapsed because of the lack of co-ordination or through political division" (Balfour 2001, 263). This was aggravated by a lack of ammunition, poor weapons, and the lack of international support, especially from Britain and France, which followed a policy of non-intervention (Balfour 2001, 263–264).[5] Hence, while the Nationalists had the support of Germany and Italy, the Republicans had to rely on the International Brigades—and the Soviets. Graham (2005, 41) observes that "Soviet aid saved the Spanish Republic from almost certain military defeat in November 1936," due to the tanks, staff, training, and planes and pilots the Soviets provided throughout the winter of 1936, especially during the battle for Madrid.

Perhaps unsurprisingly, then, Hemingway, together with other writers, such as André Malraux, looked "to the Communists for effective leadership . . . Although these men did not adhere to the party line, they thought the Communists offered the best organization and discipline and thus the best chance to defeat Fascism" (Cooper 1987, 93). Hemingway put himself under the command of the Communist leadership in aiding the Republican side and his "belief in the Loyalist cause also led him to work with political figures he had earlier despised and to accept actions he had earlier condemned. To . . . win the war, he was willing to support Communist leadership . . . and to condone the repression of anyone who might hinder the war effort" (Cooper 1987, 92). His pragmatic attitude is summed up in a letter he wrote to his mother-in-law: "There is only one thing to do when you have a war and that is to win it" (cited in Cooper 1987, 93). In this situation, the responsibility of defending the Republic, and potentially all of humanity, fell on the individual. Hemingway's novel shows that it is perhaps especially under adverse circumstances that individuals make choices that give meaning to their life. Perhaps it is through the drive and process of individual self-realization rather than shared ideology that very powerful collective political action takes place.

Molesworth (1992, 92) concludes that the novel is poised between support for the Republicans and defeated individualism. This position, it could be argued, is best exemplified in Robert Jordan, who is fighting as an individual rather than as part of the regular troops of the International Brigades. By supporting the cause of the Republicans but disagreeing with many of the methods and logistics employed by the Communist leaders in the defense of the Spanish Republic, Jordan embodies rebellion not just against Fascist supremacy, but also Communists, even though the cause of defeating Fascism overrides his critical attitudes against the Communists. However, it is notable that Jordan does not reflect on his feelings towards Communism as an ideology or as a political system. His goal is to win the war, not to support Communism. In thinking what might happen if the Republicans won the war, he wonders: "And what about a planned society and the rest of it? That was for the others to do. He had something else to do after this war" (Hemingway 2003, 163), thereby disassociating himself with the policies of the Communists, and while he submits himself to working under the Communists during the war, he assures himself that "afterwards you can discard what you don't believe in" (Hemingway 2003, 305). His explicit rejection of Communism is limited to the faults he finds with the Communists' behavior in the Civil War—while acknowledging their contribution to the Republican struggle: "He accepted their discipline because, in the conduct of the war, they were the only party whose program and whose discipline he could respect" (Hemingway 2003, 163).

Therefore, even though his commitment to fighting for the Republic never falters, his criticism of the Communist leadership spearheading the battle is profound. What were Jordan's qualms with the Communists then? Jordan recognizes the disregard for human life in some of the Communist leaders. Watson (1992b) identified several individuals in history that provided the model on which some of Hemingway's Communist characters are based. Each had an important role in the war and had a reputation for brutality, perhaps best exemplified in the Commissar Marty (Hemingway 1993, 418–419; see also Martin 1992). Molesworth (1992, 85) observes that the "only person who takes unstinting pleasure in killing is the commissar, Marty." Watson (1992b, 117) concludes with respect to the role of the Communist leadership that the "signs of totalitarian power were all there in the novel because they were there in Spain . . . In Spain one could see for the first time, and see up close, the true face of the totalitarian state imported into Spain by the Soviets . . . ". The behavior of the Communists in Spain, then, was in some ways reflective of Soviet politics, and perhaps of the future of Spain itself if the Republican forces under Communist leadership were to win the war. Furthermore, Hemingway takes issue with the Communist leadership style and bureaucracy. Criticism in the novel extended to the

Commissar system introduced by the Communists, which was corrupting their leaders (Watson 1992b, 107), and to military decisions made for political, not military, rationales. Military leaders are often unqualified; the Commissar Marty, for instance, has problems reading and interpreting a map (Hemingway 2003, 422).[6] Hemingway (2003, Ch. 18) also portrays the cynicism present in the Soviet leaders in their Madrid headquarters, the hotel Gaylord, in a section in the book the historian Thomas (2001, 381n2) calls "brilliant." Watson (1992b, 110) concludes on Hemingway's critique of the Communist leaders that their "catalogue of crimes against the values of a free and democratic society constitutes an unmistakable indictment of the totalitarian Soviet state and of the unscrupulous instruments the Soviets and Communists were willing to use in Spain to achieve their goals."

Furthermore, even though the Communists in the novel provide the most effective leadership for the Republicans during the war, their bureaucracy also renders them inefficient. It is, after all, the Communist command chain that is eventually responsible for Jordan's death. As mentioned earlier, Jordan is wary from the beginning about the way the demolition of the bridge was planned by the Communist leadership. Furthermore, when he sends a member of the guerrilla band as a messenger to the Communists to warn them about problems with the attack and urging them to cancel the offensive, the command chain delays the receipt of the note so long that it is too late to cancel the offensive, and with it the blowing of the bridge. Thus, the inefficient bureaucracy and the divisions within the Republican left produce the delay that leads Jones (1997, 316) to conclude that "the war on the Republican side is so badly conducted that the hero is killed in futilely blowing up a bridge." In fact, Jordan dies "because of the stupidity and treachery on his own side" (Jones 1997, 319). But Jordan also understands in hindsight that the entire operation was doomed to fail from the outset—as he is dying, he realizes that "You were bitched when they gave Golz those orders. That was what you knew . . . " (Hemingway 2003, 469). His premonitions about the attack turned out to be true; the plan leads to the protagonist's death. Hemingway's criticism of the attack that was doomed to fail had a historic reference, as it was based on a real offensive that had failed due to leadership problems and poor decisions within the Republican ranks (Thomas 2001, 668–669). The inclusion of the failed offensive thus presents a scathing critique of the problems of Communist leadership in the war.

Hemingway's criticism of the Republican side does not just pertain to the Communist foreigners, though, but also extends to Spaniards fighting on the Loyalist side. One of the prominent criticisms in the book concerns the brutality used, and enjoyed, by the Republicans. For example, as Anselmo, Jordan's guide, explains to him, there "are many of those who enjoy" killing among the guerrillas (Hemingway 2003, 42). Jordan is clearly disturbed by that image and declares that as far as "liking" to kill men, "Nobody does except those who are disturbed in the head" (Hemingway 2003, 39).

However, the point is most explicitly and powerfully made in the depiction of the brutality of the massacre conducted by Republicans, as recounted by Pilar (Hemingway 2003, Ch. 10; for an interpretation of the tale, see Gajdusek 1992). In fact, Stoneback (1992, 109) concludes that the "overwhelming dramatic force of Pilar's tale, . . . far outstrip[s] in its horror any account of Fascist brutality." Leading historians of the Spanish civil war have identified a similar massacre in the Andalusian town Ronda during the first month of the war, resulting in the murdering of 512 people, as the historic event that provided the basis for Hemingway's account (Thomas 2001, 263; see also Buckley 1997). Yet, the brutality of the massacre, and Jordan's recognition of and familiarity with the violence employed by the Republican side, does not stop him from continuing to commit to the Republican struggle. Despite his admitted disillusionment, the rebellion retains powerful relevance for Jordan's process of self-realization.

Furthermore, Jordan also disagrees with Pablo, the leader of the guerrilla band, who opposes the mission. There is distrust, cowardice, and betrayal among the guerrillas supporting the Republicans: Some would prefer inaction to action so that their location will remain safe and they will not need to move. There is greed. Pablo, the band leader, has "gone bad" and steals some of Jordan's equipment needed for the attack. Jordan and other band members actually contemplate, but eventually refrain from, killing Pablo, whom they consider a threat to the success of the attack on the bridge. Pablo also expresses resentment against the foreigners fighting with the International Brigades (Hemingway 2003, 54). The Republicans, then, lack unity and agreement, and face sizeable obstacles for a successful fight against the Fascists within their own rank, a theme that also permeates George Orwell's depiction of the Spanish Civil War in *Homage to Catalonia*.

Thus, Hemingway "has not omitted the drunkenness, the disorder, the cruelty, the selfishness, the confusion" on the Republican side (Jones 1997, 319). Many Republican characters—e.g., Pablo and Pilar—understand the futility of the violence. Pablo "recognizes the evil, and, of the people he has killed, he later says: 'I would restore them all to life'" (Stoneback 1992, 109). Pilar, for her part, sees the limitations of the "pleasure" of killing others (see Molesworth 1992, 85). Despite Jordan's unfailing commitment to the Republicans, however, the story of the massacre "evoked the wrath of the Communists and other leftists and earned Hemingway the stigma of betrayal of the cause" (Stoneback 1992, 106).

The war brings out the worst in everyone, regardless of political leanings and loyalties. As Frederking states in the Introduction to this volume, "Hemingway's characters discover their best and worst selves through the act of confrontation" (18). The Loyalists are not exempt from this rule: While they find—and demonstrate—loyalty, friendship, courage, and love during battle, they also engage in treachery and brutality. War brings to the fore all the complexities of the individuals' characters. In uncovering the complexity of political experience, the individual is not driven to support political causes without circumspect reflection and caution. In fact, the political victory or new regime can be more of a side benefit of the central meaningful purpose of self-realization. Devoid of partisanship and ideology, the individual's participation in political rebellion constitutes a meaningful act with relevant collective political consequences. Politics becomes the defeat of Fascism and Jordan is defining himself through this formidable strife to rescue humanity, a goal that transcends politics narrowly defined as party politics or ideology. Thus, without an explicit ideological framework as the goal of the rebellion, it is the act of rebellion itself that constitutes a meaningful political act.

II. THE MEANING OF REBELLION FOR LOVE AND DEATH

For Jordan, rebellion means more than the fight against Fascism and for humanity. Instead, it is in rebellion in the context of war that he confronts love and death, and realizes his potential dimensions of self.

1. Rebellion and Love

It is during the rebellion that the protagonist finds love, and it is the rebellion that gives the love meaning. At the beginning of the novel, Jordan claims that his job in the war leaves him no time for women. Yet, when preparing the attack with the guerrilla band, Jordan falls in love with María, a member of the band, almost as soon as he first meets her. Falling in love, he feels "happier than he had ever been" (Hemingway 2003, 72). María, in turn, admits that she also loved him from the first time she met him—in fact, she had loved him "always" even before they had met (Hemingway 2003, 73). Love, a stranger to both of them before, becomes possible and urgent despite the unlikely prospect of happiness, and in fact despite the unlikely possibility of their love even happening. As one critic of the book points out, the behavior of María, a village girl, is not credible: A young Spanish woman from her background would have never offered herself to a man she just met without being asked by the man (Barea 1997, 357). Yet, in the novel, established cultural norms are overcome by the intensity and urgency of the life of the rebels. It is in the context of the rebellion that norms of behavior change, making the love between Jordan and María possible for the war "compounds the urgency of the passion of María and Robert . . . there is no such thing as appropriate behavior" when love and war coincide (Josephs 1994, 93). Hemingway once stated that war "speeds up the action and brings out all sorts of stuff that normally you have to wait a lifetime to get" (cited in Josephs 1994, 93). Jordan acts accordingly and is aware of the fact that in times of war, cultural norms become irrelevant and meaningless. He realizes that in approaching María, he had broken one of the two rules necessary to get along with Spanish people: Leave the women alone. But "he realized, very suddenly, that he did not care. There were so many things that he had not to care about, why should he care about that?" (Hemingway 2003, 24).

Thus, in the novel, love at first sight and almost immediate romance are possible during times of war and rebellion when norms of behavior would have made this impossible in the absence of war. The lovers' behavior itself is a rebellion against established norms of behavior, necessitated and made possible by the context of war. Nonetheless, in the end, rebellion, political action, is more important to Jordan than love, and he is willing to sacrifice his love (and María's future) for the rebellious act of blowing up the bridge, even though he understands that he is likely to die in the event.

2. Rebellion, Death, and the Meaning of Life

Having been aware of the logistical complications of his mission from the outset, Jordan nonetheless carries on with its execution, even when additional complications and ominous events occur, including the snowfall and the subsequent elimination of El Sordo's band and Pablo's betrayal. Being fully aware not just that the mission might fail, but that he himself might die in the effort, Jordan nonetheless thinks that the attack is worth it as it is an important piece in the fight to save humanity. This significance of the bridge gives his own action meaning, even as it leads to his death. "Jordan's growing defeatism" (Molesworth 1992, 93) pinpoints the fact that rebellion in itself is the act that gives meaning to individual action. As he is dying, he reflects: "I have fought for what I believe in for a year now. . . . The world is a fine place and worth fighting for" (Hemingway 2003, 467).

The civil war, then, is more than a battle between two fronts. It is a stage on which complex patterns play out and on which the individual has to figure out the right thing to do. Individual responsibility cannot be simplified to the question of which side is right and which side is wrong—the novel contains enough criticism of the "right" side to show that choosing to fight in its support is not necessarily a foregone conclusion. Yet, Jordan makes that conscious choice to suppress his criticism and to support what he thought was ultimately the only thing that could save humanity.

It is not only Jordan, however, who finds meaning in rebellion. In fact, he is following a tradition in his family. Jordan's late grandfather (and spiritual guide in tough times) had fought in the American Civil War, or "War of the Rebellion," as his grandfather refers to it (Hemingway 2003, 337; see also Nakjavani 1988, 140). Furthermore, Jordan continues the family tradition of Republicans, as his father was a "Republican" all his life, as was his grandfather. Rebellion for a just cause is thus something that lends meaning to individuals' lives, and that ties generations together and creates family bonds. For Jordan, his grandfather's actions still have meaning and have a profound impact on his own thinking as he converses with him in his mind, looking for guidance. Stoltzfus (2003, 45) concludes of *For Whom the Bell*

Tolls that "those who are willing to die for the general good affirm a value that transcends them as individuals," thus stressing the value of rebellion and the dignity of the individual. The story of Jordan's grandfather shows that this truth does not just apply to the context of the Spanish Civil War, but that this truth holds generally for all those who rebel in their pursuit for the right thing and just cause. The novel thus focuses on the setting of the war in Spain, but the central message goes beyond the fight between the Republicans and the Fascists. To quote Schorer (1997, 340), "Indeed, the individual vanishes in the political whole, but vanishes precisely to defend his dignity, his freedom, his virtue." This defense of dignity, freedom, and virtue is made possible by Jordan's commitment to rebellion, even in the face of death, even when it means the sacrifice of his love. The only thing left to do for the individual "In the midst of all this political turmoil and self-destructive feuding in the Republic . . . [is to] press forward, do what he can, and never give up. Within the chaos of the war, individual actions and beliefs still have meaning" (Cooper 1987, 114). Without a deeply held ideological commitment other than the opposition to Fascism, Jordan can focus on meaning beyond particular political outcomes. Through his focus on the process of rebellion, Jordan defines his individual life's meaning.

III. CONCLUSION

Hemingway wrote a novel that is based on the fight against Fascism, a movement that threatened not just Spain, but had much wider international implications. Yet, the novel does not condemn all those fighting on the side of the Nationalist insurgents; nor does it glorify the politics of the supporters of the Republic. It is within this complex context, simplified to two sides—Republicans vs. Fascists—that individuals have to make difficult decisions, and that these decisions attain meaning. French (1967, 90) observes, "Those who wished for a rebel victory in Spain to satisfy their personal lust for power defamed the Loyalist cause by equating it with Communism. Hemingway attempted to get behind the labels that oversimplified the world's concept of the struggle and to force the isolated individual to recognize his own demanding responsibilities." For Jordan, the three days prior to the attack on the bridge condense a lifetime: "You've had as good a life as any one because of these last days" (Hemingway 2003, 467). On another occasion, he muses, "You have it *now* and that is all your whole life is; now" (Hemingway 2003, 169). Rebellion takes many forms in the novel: the military rebellion against the insurgents attempting to take over the country; the internal rebellion against the Communist leadership of the Republicans; the rebellion against norms of behavior. Life becomes meaningful and individual actions lead to political change in spite of their unwillingness to embrace blueprint institutions and rigid ideology. In this more nuanced sense, *For Whom the Bell Tolls* is a profoundly political novel.

NOTES

1. Many thanks to Angelina Lander and Kerri Milita for valuable research assistance and to Lauretta Frederking, Bruce Wilson, and Anna Lillios for helpful comments on earlier drafts.
2. Referring to the breakdown of the Second Republic, Payne (1987, 34) notes that "Even professional historians do not agree how this came about."
3. Hemingway helped produce and narrated *The Spanish Earth*, directed by Joris Ivens in 1937 (Meyers 1985, ch. 15).
4. Between 1933 and 1936, the Second Republic was ruled under one of three levels of suspension of constitutional rights "on a national or regional basis almost continuously," of which a state of exception was one, the others being a state of alarm and a state of war (Payne 1987, 40).
5. On the international dimension of the war, see e.g., Preston (2006, Ch. 5); Thomas (2001, Book Three).
6. This inability to use maps was apparently present among several Republican military leaders during the war; Beevor (1982, 167) comments on "Colonel Yartz, who appears to have been incapable of reading a map."

WORKS CITED

Baker, Carlos. "The Spanish Tragedy." In *Ernest Hemingway: A Critique of Four Major Novels*, edited by Martin Steinmann, Jr., 108–130. New York: Charles Scribner's Sons, 1962.

Balfour, Sebastian. "Spain from 1931 to the Present." In *Spain: A History*, edited by Raymond Carr, 243–282. Oxford: Oxford University Press, 2001 [2000].

Barea, Arturo. "*For Whom the Bell Tolls*." Reprinted in *Ernest Hemingway: The Critical Heritage*, edited by Jeffrey Meyers, 350–361. London and New York: Routledge, 1997 [1982]. Originally published in *Horizon* 3 (May 1941): 350–361.

Beevor, Antony. *The Spanish Civil War.* New York: Penguin, 1982.

Buckley, Ramon. "Revolution in Ronda: The Facts in Hemingway's For Whom the Bell Tolls." *The Hemingway Review* 17 (1): 49–57, 1997.

Carr, Raymond and Juan Pablo Fusi. *Spain: Dictatorship to Democracy.* 2nd ed. London: Unwick Hyman, 1981 [1979].

Cooper, Stephen. *The Politics of Ernest Hemingway.* Ann Arbor, MI: University of Michigan Press, 1987.

French, Warren. *The Social Novel at the End of an Era.* Carbondale, IL: Southern Illinois University Press, 1967.

Gajdusek, Robert E. "Pilar's Tale: the Myth and the Message." In *Blowing the Bridge: Essays on Hemingway and For Whom the Bell Tolls*, edited by Rena Sanderson, 113–130. New York: Greenwood Press, 1992.

Graham, Helen. *The Spanish Civil War: A Very Short Introduction.* Oxford: Oxford University Press, 2005.

Hemingway, Ernest. *For Whom the Bell Tolls.* New York: Scribner, 2003 [1940].

Jones, Howard Mumford. "*For Whom the Bell Tolls*." Reprinted in *Ernest Hemingway: The Critical Heritage*, edited by Jeffrey Meyers, 316–319. London and New York: Routledge, 1997 [1982]. Originally published in *Saturday Review of Literature* 23 (26 October 1940): 15–19.

Josephs, Allen. *For Whom the Bell Tolls: Ernest Hemingway's Undiscovered Country.* New York: Twayne Publishers, 1994.

MacDonald, Dwight. "*For Whom the Bell Tolls.*" Reprinted in *Ernest Hemingway: The Critical Heritage*, edited by Jeffrey Meyers, 326–331. London and New York: Routledge, 1997 [1941]. Originally published in *Partisan Review* 8 (January 1941): 24–28.

Martin, Robert A. "Hemingway's For Whom the Bell Tolls: Fact into Fiction." In *Blowing the Bridge: Essays on Hemingway and For Whom the Bell Tolls*, edited by Rena Sanderson, 59–66. New York: Greenwood Press, 1992.

Meyers, Jeffrey. *Hemingway: A Biography.* New York: Harper and Row, 1985.

———. "For Whom the Bell Tolls as Contemporary History." In *The Spanish Civil War in Literature*, edited by Janet Pérez and Wendell Aycock, 85–107. Lubbock, TX: Texas Tech University Press, 1990.

Molesworth, Charles. "Hemingway's Code: The Spanish Civil War and World Power." In *Blowing the Bridge: Essays on Hemingway and For Whom the Bell Tolls*, edited by Rena Sanderson, 83–98. New York: Greenwood Press, 1992.

Nakjavani, Erik. "Knowledge as Power: Robert Jordan as an Intellectual Hero." *The Hemingway Review* 7 (2) (1988): 131–146.

Payne, Stanley. *The Franco Regime 1936–1975.* Madison, WI: The University of Wisconsin Press, 1987.

Preston, Paul. *The Spanish Civil War: Reaction, Revolution and Revenge.* New York: W. W. Norton, 2006.

Schorer, Mark. "The Background of a Style." In *Ernest Hemingway: a Critique of Four Major Novels*, edited by Martin Steinmann, Jr., 87–89. New York: Charles Scribner's Sons, 1962.

Shorer, Mark. "*For Whom the Bell Tolls.*" Reprinted in Ernest Hemingway: The Critical Heritage, edited by Jeffrey Meyers, 337–341. London and New York: Routledge, 1997 [1982]. Originally published in *Kenyon Review* 3 (Winter 1941): 101–105.

Sherwood, Robert. "*For Whom the Bell Tolls.*" Reprinted in *Ernest Hemingway: The Critical Heritage*, edited by Jeffrey Meyers, 324–325. London and New York: Routledge, 1997 [1982]. Originally published in *Atlantic* 166 (November 1940): front section.

Stoltzfus, Ben. "Camus and Hemingway: The Solidarity of Rebellion." *International Fiction Review* 30 (January) (2003): 42–49.

Stoneback, H. R. "The Priest Did Not Answer: Hemingway, the Church, the Party, and For Whom the Bell Tolls." In *Blowing the Bridge: Essays on Hemingway and For Whom the Bell Tolls*, edited by Rena Sanderson, 99–112. New York: Greenwood Press, 1992.

Thomas, Hugh. *The Spanish Civil War.* New York: Random House/The Modern Library 2001 [1961].

Waldhorn, Arthur. *A Reader's Guide to Ernest Hemingway.* New York: Syracuse University Press, 2002.

Watson, William Braasch. "Joris Ivens and the Communists: Bringing Hemingway into the Spanish Civil War." In *Blowing the Bridge: Essays on Hemingway and For Whom the Bell Tolls*, edited by Rena Sanderson, 37–58. New York: Greenwood Press, 1992a.

———. "Hemingway's Attacks on the Soviets and the Communists in *For Whom the Bell Tolls.*" *The North Dakota Quarterly* 60 (1992b): 103–118.

8 "The Revolutionist"

David Winston Conklin

I. HEMINGWAY'S CONTRIBUTION TO THEORIES OF REVOLUTION

Political theories about the causes of revolution include macro and micro level explanations. At the macro level, structural conditions and ideologies are critical factors in understanding the emergence of rebellion and revolution. Prevailing ideologies can drive collective mobilization. Weber (1930) and Tawney (1920) discussed the role of religious reformation in transforming a society's attitudes towards personal property and material acquisition. In recent decades, some revolutionary activity in the Middle East has been linked with certain adherents to the Muslim religion and with particular Islamic sects. Individual beliefs that one is risking one's life for a supernatural power may give strength to a revolutionary movement. Many revolutionary movements cultivated nationalism to overthrow foreign political and economic domination. The American Revolution can be seen in this context, as can the twentieth-century revolutions against colonialism. In each case, basic changes in the political system follow as a result of ideologies including those rooted in religion, equality, and liberty.

Many uprisings and wars have involved the attempt by one geographic region to impose its political system on a different geographic region, or the attempt by one region to revolt against the domination by another. In some wars, the differences in political system reveal more basic differences in culture, language, and religion. Hence, many factors emphasizing political conflict may play a role in the revolution by one region against another. While ideology can be a driving factor, ideology cannot explain the micro level processes of the revolutionists who participate. Macro theories share an orientation around conditions and the opportunities and constraints of those conditions for individual action, but apart from assuming an ideology, they do not explain an individual's embrace of ideology as a justification for action. Nor can these macro level theories explain an individual who participates in the violence of a revolution without embracing its ideology.

Micro level theories emphasize individual calculation in understanding rebellion. Leadership can be critical to explain cascades of individual actions driving forward fundamental political, economic, or social change at the collective level. Through the articulation of intellectual criticisms of an existing order and the presentation of new ideals and particular philosophical concepts, leaders convince the public that political change is necessary. A revolutionary leader must espouse a cause and must persuade the masses that this cause is just and deserves their support. Through charisma and propaganda, a leader can emphasize the alteration of traditional relationships—for whatever reasons—thereby creating anxiety and the willingness to revolt. A widespread change in social status can lead people to question their political system.

Often, ambiguity and uncertainty exist in terms of the relative importance of various elements that underlie a revolution. Often, there can be a wide range of explanations for similar actions within any particular revolution. The weights that political analysts assign to different macro level and micro level motivating forces may vary from one revolution to another, but also vary according to perspective or selected focus.

Underneath these analyses the question remains, "Why do people become revolutionaries and risk death?" In "The Revolutionist" (2003 [1925]), Hemingway presents a young man who fought for the Hungarian Communist movement, was tortured by the Whites in Budapest, and escaped to Italy. His only passport and funding are a piece of oilcloth from party headquarters, saying that he is a comrade and requesting that comrades aid him. The story ends in a Swiss jail. With Hemingway's stark narrative the reader asks: What motivates the revolutionist to inflict violence and to risk his life repeatedly in hopes of overturning incumbent political systems? Many of Hemingway's writings provide insights into the mind of the potential revolutionist, and in today's political context, they add to our understanding of terrorism. For Hemingway, certain men—and even some women—have a seemingly simple and natural desire to fight, to face personal danger, and to conquer physical hazards. For Hemingway, certain men—and even some women—want to kill, whether this involves taking the lives of other humans or the lives of animals. Inherent in such persons is a desire to struggle. There may be a goal in the military victory or the trophies from bull-fighting or big-game hunting, but a much stronger statement emphasizes the constitution of a killer with a politically relevant target perhaps, but not necessarily driven by a political or economic outcome. These persons serve as an everpresent pool from which political leaders can draw supporters who will fight and die for a cause. Perseverance is a crucial attribute, leading characters to their own deaths as well as the death of others. Hemingway brings us to respect and to feel affection for the raw passion of the warrior, undeterred by strategic thinking, whether or not we share his or her objectives. In this process, Hemingway gives us a more intimate understanding of the revolutionist than we acquire from traditional political academic analyses.

Hemingway's stories remind us that certain men and women have been eager to fight and risk death, and he provides us with insights into those rebels who are critical for understanding revolution. He provides characters who appear to be rebels independent of macro level conditions and apart from micro level strategic calculation. For Hemingway, there are born warriors and there are those who become warriors through internal transformation. A person can become a 'born again warrior,' and Francis Macomber ("The Short Happy Life of Francis Macomber" in Hemingway 2003 [1921]) illustrates this process. Equally dramatic is the process through which a revolutionist can give up on the particular target or revolution. In *For Whom the Bell Tolls* (2003 [1946]), Pablo struggles with his emotional commitment to the Communist side in the Spanish civil war. Hemingway adds to the poignancy of Pablo's struggles by describing the steadfast loyalty to the cause of Pablo's 'mujer'. In Hemingway's stories we gain entry to a wide range of thought processes within the mind of the revolutionist. In this way, Hemingway highlights the limits of our theories. As prominent political scientist, Timur Kuran acknowledges, "identifying the limits of knowledge is not a declaration of failure. It is itself a contribution to the pool of useful knowledge as well as a necessary step toward charting a realistic scientific agenda" (Kuran 1995, 331).

Hemingway's contribution to social science theories about revolution includes these outliers who play critical roles in driving forward rebellion. In addition to understanding the role of the rebel and the character of the rebel, which is often non-calculating and not attentive to structural opportunities and constraints, Hemingway uncovers the impact of the process of revolution, the rebellion, and the fight on the individual. Hemingway's soldiers, matadors, and hunters rebel without calculation but become transformed by the experience. It is the process of rebellion that develops their sensitivities to opportunities and raises consciousness to structural inequalities.

II. MACRO LEVEL THEORIES

Macro level theories of revolution emphasize different aspects of structure to explain mobilization of individuals in opposition. For Marx, it is the conditions of capital and labor. For Lenin, it is the organization of the party and the skilful use of the media and force. More recent interpretations of a structuralist type of argument include emphasis on the solidarity around nationalism that comes from political and economic conditions (Connor 1990; Gellner 1994; Tarrow 1994; Hechter 2000; Smith 2003). Skocpol's seminal study (1979) of revolution considers the macro conditions but also focuses on the strategic opportunities provided by the structure of political institutions. In so far as they share the emphasis on structure to explain rebellion, they also share an inability to identify timing and individual decisions to rise up in confrontation. Why any particular individual abandons the norm in order to fight against the status quo, usually at great risk, is relatively unattended by these theories.

1. Marx and Economic Determinism

Marx interprets history from the perspective of revolutionary struggles and he describes the nature and causes of these struggles. The focus of Marx's analysis is not history, but rather the prediction of future revolution and the description of its causes, its nature, and its outcome. Marx presents an economic determinism: economic forces shape social and political relationships. In capitalism, Marx sees that economic forces will lead inevitably to Communist revolution. In capitalist societies, some people own the means of production while others do not. Marx believes that modern technology makes large-scale production less costly than small-scale production. Hence, ownership will increasingly be concentrated in fewer hands. An ever-larger portion of the population will have to work as wage earners for this ever-diminishing capitalist class. "Society as a whole is more and more splitting up into two great hostile camps, into two great classes directly facing each other: Bourgeoisie and Proletariat" (Marx in Eastman, 1932, 322). In his works entitled *Capital*, Marx analyzes the process of wage and price determination. He believes that capitalists will pay their workers less than the value that the workers create. Marx examines the exploitation process scientifically rather than emotionally, and predicts that this exploitation leads inevitably to political and economic and social transformation.

Ultimately, particular types of ideology as well as political and economic conditions cannot explain comprehensively why individuals rebel. If you are a Communist you fight bourgeois capitalism, if you are a social democrat you defend rebellion in the face of relative deprivation and if you are a Fascist you defend rebellion in order to realize the particular brand of institutions and ideas. Hemingway's stories share insight into the process of struggle and decision-making to participate in spite of very different political or economic outcomes. In *To Have and Have Not* the juxtaposition of Communist revolutionaries, and Harry Morgan raging against the system of democratic capitalism that leaves him outside potential privilege, emphasizes the arbitrariness of ideology for the revolutionist. Macro theories present conditions and the potential opportunities and constraints of those conditions for individual action, but apart from assuming ideology, they do not explain an individual's embrace of ideology as a justification for action. Very contrasting ideologies seem capable of invoking the passion of a revolutionist, and the diversity of Hemingway heroes confronting very different regime types as well as a wide range of more indirect political targets suggests the limits of social science explanation from a macro perspective.

2. Oberschall: The Macro Causes and Micro Processes of Revolution

Oberschall discusses the competition between established interests and the revolutionaries as they each seek the support of the masses. He examines significant and widespread emotional and nonrational elements as well as the conscious calculations by individuals of their risks and rewards.

> Both sides lack full and accurate information about each other; they have misconceptions about each other's strengths and weaknesses; and they respond to concrete problems and choices in complex ways, with a mixture of outrage, anger, puzzlement, and shrewd informed calculation (Oberschall 1973: 25).

Oberschall discusses the individual's calculation of the benefits he or she may gain from a successful revolution and the losses that he or she may suffer if the revolution fails. Each individual weighs these risks and rewards in deciding whether to join the revolutionaries or the reactionaries. Oberschall sees the interaction of these individual decisions as a kind of game. Each individual wants to be on the winning side, and so each is influenced by the decisions of the others.

Policy change inevitably hurts some individuals while helping others, and so any change can cause individuals to contemplate revolution. From this perspective, disparity even within economic progress can become a structural cause of a revolution. Rising incomes may lead to more discontent rather than satisfaction. Oberschall points to additional types of structural change as sources of insecurity, including population change, migration, the growth of cities, and the introduction of new technologies and new employment skills. Even while some groups advance, reaping unheard of profits for example, they push institutionalization of new policies to defend their gains against newer claimants. "Existing institutions and social arrangements are no longer suited to solve new problems of an altogether different order of magnitude. Dissatisfaction mounts; impatience, cramp, hatreds accumulate. Reforms lag behind new needs . . . . Change and conflict are intricately linked" (Oberschall 1973: 34–35). Oberschall emphasizes that the revolutionary forces will grow if the governing elite is unresponsive, prevents protests, and refuses to make concessions. However, De Toqueville argues that at some point reform cannot dissuade the discontented from demanding not just reform but control of the administration (1980, 226). Indeed, the process of granting reforms may itself cause greater discontent, particularly if the process is erratic, half-hearted, and subject to retractions. Oberschall focuses on the potential economic gains that revolutionaries can achieve under a new order, but he does not explain how the risk of death enters into the individual's calculation of risks and rewards. Hemingway's heroes from Harry Morgan, Santiago, Nick Adams, to Robert Jordan all suspend a reasonable calculation of risk. Whether conscious or not, these protagonists defy strategic decisions connecting potential action or inaction to a perceived goal.

III. HEMINGWAY'S CONTRIBUTION TO MACRO THEORIES

To a significant degree, Hemingway turns macro theories on their head. Instead of ideology driving revolution, he unpacks the importance of the revolution, or rebellion, for creating beliefs and ideology. The individual rebel acts without so much study of the collective conditions around him as much as the very private conditions moving within him. The connection between Hemingway's characters and the macro level theories of rebellion is that the process of rebellion reveals the problems of society—the conditions of inequality; the lack of honorable men (*Across the River and Into the Trees* Hemingway: 170); and the emptiness of political rhetoric. Rather than the structural conditions driving rebellion, as seminal thinkers like Marx and Oberschall discuss as well as more recent scholars like Skocpol and Tilly, rebellion becomes the starting point for the process of discovering political and economic conditions. The act of rebellion becomes a call to consciousness transforming beliefs and awakening the revolutionist to his or her solidarity, enemies, and potential to participate in the collective action of change.

As described by a conversation between the American Colonel and his Italian countess in *Across the River and Into the Trees*, the evaluation of personal goodness relative to the cause is forged through actions and relationships rather than through the adoption of an ideology.

> "Why do you hate cavalry? Almost all the good boys I know were in the three good regiments of cavalry, or in the navy."
>
> "I don't hate anything, Daughter," the Colonel said, and drank a little of the light, dry, red wine which was as friendly as the house of your brother, if you and your brother are good friends. "I only have a point of view, arrived at after careful consideration, and an estimate of their capabilities."
>
> "Are they not really good?"
>
> "They are worthless," the Colonel said. Then, remembering to be kind, added, "In our time."
>
> "Every day is a disillusion."
>
> "No. Every day is a new and fine illusion. But you can cut out everything phony about the illusion as though you would cut it with a straight-edge razor" (Hemingway: 213).

Through rebellion, beliefs can be nurtured and life's meaning is clarified by conscious realization of right and wrong, comrade and enemy. Interestingly, often the clarity of belief reveals the limits, constraints, and misguided propaganda surrounding ideology. From *In Our Time*, after being injured in battle, Nick Adams turns to the Italian soldier and states "you and me, we've made a separate peace". Ideology may be a motivation for many, but for the individual who has experienced battle, ideology remains an illusionist's game of politics. Beliefs are cultivated around relationships and certainties develop about what makes a man a good man, and what makes character worthy of admiration.

IV. MICRO-LEVEL THEORIES

Some authors emphasize the role of particular leaders in the process of violent political change. Lenin believed that a small elite of determined leaders could play a decisive role and that skills and techniques were essential to winning the revolution. The abdication of an existing leader can be a major step in some revolutions. In the case of the Shah of Iran, Duvalier in Haiti, or Marcos in the Philippines, the personal decision to flee rather than fight directed the course of events significantly. Rational choice theories of political change focus on descriptions of political entrepreneurs. These individuals are frontrunners of change. They evaluate the costs and benefits of change and invest in the rallying effort to change public opinion. In this way, seemingly warrior-like behavior fits into rationality assumptions in so far as it is an investment in changing group behavior toward dramatic political change. At the same time, through the free rider concept, rational choice also explains much more comfortably why we don't see revolutions and leaders of revolutions very often.

Leaders in any institutionalized political process confront rebels who seek to advance a subversive political cause through violence. Many authors have discussed revolutions pointing to particular issues around which an opposition has coalesced. Authors have also examined the basis for social movements that have struggled against the established regime. Marx presents the conditions for economic determinism and inevitable revolution. Oberschall, and more recently Kuran, focused on both the macro and micro conditions that underlie a successful overturning of the political establishment. Hemingway offers an additional perspective from dominant macro and micro level theories of revolution, providing an understanding of the psychological and emotional transformation within an individual that underlies a willingness to kill and be killed.

1. Ted Gurr: Why Men Rebel

Micro level theories of revolution can include macro level conditions but focus on the individual decision-making as the essential factor in understanding revolution. Ted Gurr's seminal book *Why Men Rebel* emphasizes the concept of *relative deprivation*. Each person has a set of expectations about the material possessions and lifestyle to which he or she is rightfully entitled. At the same time, each person sees the capabilities he or she has to achieve or to maintain these rightful expectations. Discontent and rebellion are caused by the individual's estimation of the gap between capabilities and expectations. "Societal conditions that increase the average level or intensity of expectations without increasing capabilities increase the intensity of discontent" (Gurr 1970, 13) People look at the success of others with whom they identify and feel that they should be similarly rewarded. People listen to the promises of new opportunities and feel that they should be able to participate. "Deprivation-induced discontent is a general spur to action. Psychological theory and group conflict both suggest that the greater the intensity of discontent, the more likely is violence" (Gurr 1970, 13)

Relative deprivation causes a deep and enduring frustration which expresses itself in anger and violence. The phrase "relative deprivation" suggests that people compare their current condition with their own past condition as well as with the experiences of others. A number of factors can cause a shift in one's condition, leading to frustration, anger, and violence and this is the problem for generalization. It is impossible to predict or even explain why one set of conditions causes someone to rebel while the same set of conditions continues with a status quo for others.

Revolutionary movements include distinct cascades of public opinion change. However, the initial tipping points of change can include individuals who are not entrenched politically at all and who do not engage in strategic calculations connecting their interests and potential actions with well defined outcomes. Varshney captures a meaningful distinction between instrumental rationality and value rationality that is more compatible with Hemingway's potential revolutionist.

> Instrumental rationality entails a strict cost-benefit calculus with respect to goals, necessitating the abandonment or adjustment of goals if the costs of realizing them are too high. Value-rational behavior is produced by a conscious "ethical, aesthetic, religious or other" belief, "independently of its prospects of success." Behavior, when driven by such values, can consciously embrace great personal sacrifices (quoted in Bloom 2005, 85).

Hemingway's heroes begin to fight without or independent of reasonable calculations of risk (*To Have and Have Not*), continue to fight beyond reasonableness (*Old Man and the Sea*, *For Whom the Bell Tolls*), and embrace a glorious death (*Death in the Afternoon*).

2. Timur Kuran

More recent work by Timur Kuran (1995) incorporates the idea of preference falsification into a rational choice model to make sense of the apparent suddenness of revolutions. We all have revolutionary thresholds and as long as a small critical mass emerges in terms of these declining revolutionary thresholds, often in response to very small events, there can be dramatic changes in political behavior outcomes. While focused on the individual,

Kuran explains an individual's decision making calculus on costs and benefits in terms of existing and future conditions. Individuals have goals and unique calculations so that when conditions are right for the individual, he or she will step forward to participate as frontrunners of change. Within the battles, whether against nature or against animal, or man against man, Hemingway's characters are strategic, often vigilant in terms of rational calculation, but the decision to fight is never part of that calculation. Timing, location, and process are weighed carefully and fit comfortably within the rational choice paradigm. However, the choice to fight, and the explanation why one individual fights and another does not cannot be captured by these models.

Rational choice explanations present compelling descriptions of the costs and benefit calculation confronting a potential warrior. We have a concrete comparative statics analysis of the contrasting decisions and outcomes, and therefore assumptions underlying these decisions and outcomes, but we have no sense of the individual character and psychological disposition driving the decision. The debate about rational choice is familiar to social scientists and does not need to be repeated here, but it is the story behind the individual interpretation of costs and benefits that is absent from these types of explanations.

V. HEMINGWAY'S CONTRIBUTION TO MICRO THEORIES

Hemingway does not emphasize the randomness of rebellion as much as he draws attention to the irrelevance of a particularized set of structural conditions or objective determinants for the emergence of a rebel and the violence of a rebel's opposition. *To Have and Have Not* juxtaposes the ideological vacuum of the 'revolutionary terrorists' from Cuba with the ideological vacuum of Harry Morgan, a capitalist willing to kill to protect his smuggling profits. The particularities of structural inequalities seem incidental to the sometimes hard wiring, but sometimes spontaneous emergence of these types of individuals to manifest the rebellion. In this novel, the reader senses the arbitrariness of ideology and the extent to which ideology is incidental to the violence and the rebellion. Certainly, rebels may find an ideology to support his or her rebellion but it is the rebel that emerges and exists prior to and beyond any political ideology.

Hemingway does not move deeply into psychological explanations. He tells us about these characters but he does not guide us through the thick layers of experience and emotion that have led to the rebel identity. Through his characters we find both "born warriors" and "born again" warriors. For some there is a moment of bickering in a marriage, for others it is a gun to one's head, for some it is seemingly nothing at all. As described by De Toqueville, these unknowable outlier behaviors can precipitate a wave of support. "So long as no one thinks of resisting, you can lead him on a thread, but once a revolutionary movement is afoot, nothing can restrain him from taking part in it" (1980, 241). Whether born or born again, these varied stories fit with Kuran's description of different revolutionary thresholds as an essential dimension for understanding sweeping political change. Neither move beyond the description of certain individuals as frontrunners and necessary pieces of dramatic political change.

Arguably, it is Hemingway's refusal to provide extensive biographies of explanation for his individual warriors that leaves them accessible to everyman. Of course, their behavior connotes outlier status, but the triggers that turn individuals from conformists to revolutionists are often fairly pedestrian. In this way, the potential revolutionist is everywhere and everyman. This sentiment echoes a claim by De Toqueville as we are reminded that the thresholds for revolution loom in ubiquitous shadows: "That is why our rulers are so often taken by surprise; they fear the nation either too much or not enough, for though it is never so free that the possibility of enslaving it is ruled out, its spirit can never be broken so completely as to prevent its shaking off the yoke of an oppressive government" (1980, 241). By avoiding a probing psychological profile we are open to possibilities of identification with the characters. If public opinion is so vulnerable to sweeping change, our revolutionists become critically important. According to Pape (2005), "surveys of Palestinians living in the West Bank and Gaza have shown levels of popular support for suicide terrorist attacks against Israel rising from roughly a third of respondents in 1994 to 1999 to more than two-thirds since the start of the second intifada in 2001 . . . A poll of Saudis taken after September 11, 2001, found that over 95 percent of respondents agreed with Osama bin laden's objection to American forces in the region" (82). Their actions, independent of supporting ideologies or apart from the absence of intellectual claims, can propel societal change. Hemingway's spartan writing style emphasizes the potential generalization of the warrior condition and shifts emphasis from the uniqueness of the character, and so the revolutionist, to the immediacy and relevance of this character for the reader.

What really separates Hemingway's descriptions from rational choice explanations then is the portrayed disconnection between the protagonist's interests, actions, and goals. Secondly, Hemingway's stories move away from social science orientation around the cause of particular outcomes to emphasize the impact of change for the individual. Where rational choice explanations focus on the political outcomes, Hemingway's interest is the impact of political action and rebellion on the individual. Through battle in war, through a bullfight, or on a hunting safari, man discovers his potential and realizes his capacity for power. The power described by Hemingway is far removed from political outcomes and consequences. The power that follows from rebellion is internalized and celebrated as man's best self—at last potentially realized. Whether matador, solider, or hunter, he takes the challenge with little consideration of calculated risk for a particular outcome, and emerges triumphant from conquering his former self and embracing a new self—a better self for the discovery, the battle, and the victory.

Dennis Chong's (1991) comprehensive analysis of theories of rebellion refutes the prevailing assumption that individuals are consistent in their characters and therefore decisions. Instead, he presents individuals as malleable and relatively unfixed in terms of their potential personalities, characters, and therefore future decisions. Hemingway also draws the picture of internal change both in terms of the potential spontaneous emergence of a rebel, like Francis Macomber, but also in terms of the emotional and ideological consequences of rebellion. What makes Hemingway unique and his literature a contribution to the theoretical discussion is the focus on the outcome of rebellion for the individual. Hemingway's characters do not always begin with courage but the stories of rebellion contain the defining act that cements courage as character. Not all individuals are rebels, but for those who are there is the moment of transformation often coming from the very first act of rebellion, and it is through an act of rebellion that the individual becomes defined, and becomes oriented around the fight against a status quo.

In *For Whom the Bell Tolls*, Pablo and Pilar speak about slayings in the town and share conversation about the importance of a good death. They discuss the death of the town priest at the hands of the mob;

> He died very badly, Pablo said. "he had very little dignity."
>
> "How did you want him to have dignity when he was being chased by the mob?' I said. "I thought he had much dignity all the time before.
>
> All the dignity that one could have."
>
> Yes, Pablo said. "But in the last minute he was frightened."
>
> "Who wouldn't be?' I said "Did you see what they were chasing him with?"
>
> "Why would I not see? Pablo said. "But I find he died badly."
>
> "In such circumstances any one dies badly,' I told him. "What do you want for your money? Everything that happened in the Ayuntamiento was scabrous'
>
> "Yes, said Pablo. "There was little organization. But a priest. He has an example to set."
>
> "I thought you hated priests."
>
> "Yes, said Pablo and cut some more bread. 'But a Spanish priest. A Spanish priest should die very well."
>
> "I think he died well enough," I said. "Being deprived of all formality."
>
> "No, Pablo said. "To me he was a great disillusionment."

Further, the authenticity of the outcome for the individual depends largely on the good battle, and the good battle depends critically upon the valiance of winner and loser both. This is most powerfully conveyed in *Death in the Afternoon*. "All of bull-fighting is founded on the bravery of the bull, his simplicity and his lack of experience. There are ways to fight cowardly bulls, experienced bulls, and intelligent bulls, but the principle of the bullfight, the ideal bullfight, supposes bravery in the bull and a brain clear of any remembrance of previous work in the ring" (145).

Similarly, however, the heroic bullfighter is portrayed to bring truth and feeling to the death in our own lives. Hemingway offers the possibility of the fighter, the rebel, in everyman. Following his own commentary about bullfighting, Hemingway recreates the ideal rebel for his reader: If a fighter is too good then we can't relate, and if he is too weak then we can't admire him. It is ideal for our own transformations as spectators if he is just better than our own selves, or just a little different in his willingness to risk in this way. This is the moment and the opportunity for anyone to move beyond the experience of awe to embrace the possibility of becoming a hero—a revolutionary. These are the moments for leaders' actions to rally together the masses. For our understanding of revolution, this can be the precipitating moment for collective change.

> The nearest you come to that combination (grace and capability) Joselito, his brother, and his only fault was that everything in bullfighting was so easy for him to do that it was difficult for him to give it the emotion that was always supplied by Belmonte's evident physical inferiority, not only to the animal he was facing but to every one who was working with him and most of those who were watching him. Watching Joselito was like reading about D'Artagnan when you were a boy. You did not worry about him finally because he had too much ability. He was too good, too talented. He had to be killed before the danger ever really showed. Now the essence of the greatest emotional appeal of bullfighting is the feeling of immortality that the bullfighter feels in the middle of a great faena and that he gives to the spectators. He is performing a work of art and he is playing with death, bringing it closer, closer, closer to himself, a death that you know is in the horns because YOU have the canvas-covered bodies of the horses on the sand to prove it. He gives the feeling of his immortality, and, as you watch it, it becomes yours. Then when it belongs to both of you, he proves it with the sword (213).

Through the image of the bullfighter, in the delicate balance of a moment with very real pending death and bravery, we find Hemingway's hero who is willing not only to confront death but play with it. This is the rebel who dares to challenge and reveals his willingness to surrender all of himself not for a cause, or outcome, as much as a moment of exquisite connection between an individual and himself or herself, an individual and the opponent, an individual and his or her possibilities. The experience brings winner and loser together in this moment of individual and collective transformation.

VI. HEMINGWAY'S "BORN WARRIORS" AND "BORN AGAIN WARRIORS"

A central attribute of Hemingway heroes is a desire to confront serious personal dangers in hopes of achieving some cause or purpose. For Hemingway's bullfighters, there is an internal drive to push the limits of personal safety to gain the crowd's approval. Among the bullfighters, there is an ongoing contest to perform the most risky manoeuvres and to win the most ears and tails as marks of conquest. Winning trophies is also important for Hemingway's big game hunters. Placing oneself at risk is at the core of the sport. A lion or elephant may be the victor. For Hemingway's soldiers, danger is exhilarating, and courage in the face of danger is thrilling. Hemingway's heroes are not concerned about their own death and dying, or about killing other people or animals. These are born warriors.

Hemingway introduces warriors as general types of personality or character. Some, like the bullfighter are distinctly different from the rest of humanity. Some, like Hemingway's born again warriors are characters with whom the reader can associate personally, recognizing certain features in himself or herself. Born warriors, but also born-again warriors can be a crucial element of success for revolutions. Beyond or apart from rational calculations, Hemingway brings a perspective how a political movement can gain the dedicated support of people who are willing to kill and to die for the cause. Warriors are waiting, and searching, for a cause to fight for and even to die for. Political theorists may focus on the causes of revolutions, but it is Hemingway who explains how the rebel, through the experience of rebellion and the consciousness that follows, becomes a revolutionist.

"The Short Happy Life of Francis Macomber" has become one of Hemingway's best-known stories. Here he describes the average man's fears in the form of Francis Macomber, an American who has hired Robert Wilson to guide a hunting safari. Wilson is the archetypical big game hunter, having no personal concerns about this deadly contest. However, Francis is terrified in the safari's first serious encounter with danger. Hemingway describes this fear in detail. Francis wants to shoot from the car to avoid the risk of being attacked. "He only knew his hands were shaking and as he walked away from the car it was almost impossible for him to make his legs move. They were stiff in the thighs, but he could feel the muscles fluttering" (15). He forgets to turn the safety catch off. When he does shoot, he fails to kill, but seriously maims the lion. Francis and Robert Wilson finally enter the grass where the lion is hiding, but when the wounded and angry lion charges, Francis turns and runs. Here Hemingway presents a reasonable response for what is likely an average person.

The focus of the story is the transformation of Francis into a warrior. Confronting a wounded buffalo, Francis suddenly has a rebirth.

> I'm really not afraid of them now. After all, what can they do to you?
> ... That's it, said Wilson, Worst one can do is kill you.

Hemingway tells us Wilson's thoughts:

> "You know I don't think I'd ever be afraid of anything again," Macomber said to Wilson. "Something happened in me after we first saw the buff and started after him. Like a dam bursting. It was pure excitement."
> "Cleans out your liver," said Wilson. "Damn funny things happen to people."
> Macomber's face was shining. "you know something did happen to me," he said. "I feel absolutely different."
> His wife said nothing and eyed him strangely. She was sitting far back in the seat and Macomber was sitting forward talking to Wilson who turned sideways over the back of the front seat.
> "You know, I'd like to try another lion," Macomber said. "I'm really not afraid of them now. After all, what can they do to you?"
> "That's it," said Wilson. "Worst one can do is kill you. How does it go? Shakespeare. Damned good. See if I can remember. Oh, damned good. Used to quote it to myself at one time. Let's see. 'By my troth, I care not; a man can die but once; we owe God a death and let it go which way it will he that dies this year is quit for the next.' Damned fine, eh?"
> He was very embarrassed, having brought out this thing he had lived by, but he had seen men come of age before and it always moved him. It was not a matter of their twenty-first birthday.
> It had taken a strange chance of hunting, a sudden precipitation into action without opportunity for worrying beforehand, to bring this about with Macomber, but regardless of how it had happened it had most certainly happened. Look at the beggar now, Wilson thought. It's that some of them stay little boys so long, Wilson thought. Sometimes all their lives. Their figures stay boyish when they're fifty. The great American boy-men. Damned strange people. But he liked this Macomber now. Damned strange fellow. Probably meant the end of cuckoldry too. Well, that would be a damned good thing. Damned good thing. Beggar had probably been afraid all his life. Don't know what started it. But over now. Hadn't had time to be afraid with the buff. That and being angry too. Motor car too. Motor cars made it

familiar. Be a damn fire eater now. He'd seen it in the war work the same way. More of a change than any loss of virginity. Fear gone like an operation. Something else grew in its place (32–33).

Francis's story represents the spontaneous emergence of a born-again warrior. He shifts from the overwhelming frustration with the unhappiness of his marriage, to realize the hypocrisy of his relationship through a moment of crisis. A defining moment of cowardice pushes him toward a new place of consciousness and ultimate rebellion. Through the act of rebellion, Francis defines a better a version of himself and his bravery grows with his increasing consciousness of oppression.

1. Hemingway's Matadors

The matador exhibits dramatic and uncommon characteristics. The matador's objective is to come as close to death as possible, as often as possible, with as much courage and grace as possible. At the end of the fight, the matador kills the bull. A president or judge evaluates the matador's performance and may award prizes. The spectators wave white handkerchiefs to indicate their judgement that the matador deserves a prize. This responsiveness of the crowd influences the president's decision. In order of prestige, the "trophies" include one ear, two ears, the tail, and a hoof. For a perfect performance, the matador may be awarded "Todos de los trofeos": two ears, the tail, and a hoof. A successful recipient can then make several complete circuits of the arena, to the applause of the crowd, leaving the arena triumphantly on the shoulders of spectators.

During the "corrida" or an afternoon of fights, three matadors may each face two or three bulls. Hence, a competition exists between the matadors, each trying to outdo the others in the risks he takes and the skill with which he can control the bulls and avoid personal injury and death. Bulls are bred to achieve maximum desire to charge, and their bravery and speed are important aspects of the contest. When a bull enters the ring, he is greeted by "picadors" on horseback who seek to aggravate the bull with their long sharply-pointed poles. "Banderilleros" stick their short, sharp gaily-festooned "banderilleras" into the bull's back in order to further enliven the bull. By the time the matador faces the bull, the enraged animal is truly dangerous.

Hemingway has written extensively about matadors. He describes the development of his personal friendship with leading matadors, and these portrayals assure us that he is unfolding the intimate mind and emotion of the matador. He visits the wounded matador in the hospital, and he describes the woundings and the wounds in detail. In "The Dangerous Summer," Hemingway takes us through a long series of "corridas" in which two rival matadors engage in a "mano a mano" ongoing duel in the famous bull rings of Spain. The rivalry is deeply personal as each matador repeatedly challenges death. Excitement is shared by everyone.

From his personal experiences, in *Death in the Afternoon* Hemingway outlines the differences between the good killer and the bad killer:

> a killing is judged by the place in which the sword is put in and by the manner in which the man goes in to kill rather than by the immediate results. . . . I have seen a matador applauded enthusiastically because he killed his bull with a single entry when the killing was no more than a riskless assassination; the man having never exposed himself at all, but merely slipped the sword into an unprotected and vulnerable spot. . . . The great killer must be able to do this with security and with style and if, as he goes in left shoulder first, the sword strikes bone and refuses to penetrate, or if it strikes ribs or the edge of the vertebrae and is deviated so that it goes in only a third of the way, the merit of the attempt at killing is as great as though the sword had gone all the way in and killed, since the man has taken the risk and the result has only been falsified by chance . . . since the beauty of the moment of killing is that flash when man and bull form one figure as the sword goes all the way in, the man leaning after it, death united the two figures in the emotional, aesthetic and artistic climax of the fight (245–247).

Here is the mind and emotion of the revolutionist capable of transforming the collective—the born warrior who happens to have become a matador. In the process of confrontation, he discovers meaning in the fight and that intense passion becomes generalized for the spectators.

2. Hemingway's Big Game Hunters

Many of Hemingway's short stories describe big-game hunters, often in the setting of Africa. The hunters face complex challenges. They must first track the animals who roam freely over a vast expanse, and who can run quickly when approached. Their prey can hide in the grass, or brush, or forest, and can attack them without warning. A wounded animal becomes particularly dangerous as it prepares to fight its assailants, crouching until it makes a final charge. The hunter risks his or her life in this violent duel. The risks of personal danger are exhilarating. The hunter's objective is to achieve victory with skill and grace. The prize is a head or skin to be mounted on the wall. In these stories, the reader likely cannot see himself or herself as the hunter. Yet the stories are fascinating in their revelation of the mind of the hunter.

In *"The Old Man and the Sea"* we witness the ultimate big-game hunter. He has failed to catch a significant fish for many months, but he has persevered. When he does hook the big one, he confronts the worst weather that nature can throw at him, and predator fish eat away at his mammoth catch. Yet he perseveres. Finally, he brings the remaining skeleton to the beach, leaving it as his trophy for victory at last. The trophy asserts the process only, and all that really exists to affirm his victory is his inner transformation. There is no concrete outcome for celebration. The change is revolutionary but not in terms of political, economic, or social outcomes but through transformation of the self.

3. Hemingway's Soldiers

Hemingway uses war scenes to convey the attributes of the warrior. These scenes are rarely the typical day in a war. Rather, the various scenes are created so as to demonstrate particular attributes. As Sean Hemingway, the author's grandson explained:

> In Hemingway's "*Men at War*," his anthology of the best war stories of all time, he divided the stories into sections taken from Clausewitz's magnum opus "On War" that defined what Hemingway believed were the salient elements of war: Danger, courage, physical exertion, suffering, uncertainty, chance, friction, resolution, firmness, and staunchness. To Clausewitz's observations, Hemingway added, "War is fought by human beings" (Sean Hemingway ed. 2003: xix).

For Hemingway, the warrior repeatedly puts his or her life at risk even when deeply in love. Romance makes death an even greater sacrifice, and yet the warrior perseveres. In *For Whom the Bell Tolls*, an American, Robert Jordan, has joined the Communist forces fighting Fascism in Spain, bringing skills in designing explosions. Maria has become a prisoner at Valladolid. A train taking her and other prisoners has been blown up by a Communist group, and Maria escapes with them. Roberto and Maria struggle through the mission of destroying a bridge. Both warriors persevere until Roberto, severely wounded, sends Maria to safety while he uses his final moments of life to delay the pursuers.

In his last major war novel, *Across the River and Into the Trees*, Hemingway places love at the center of the story, with dialogue that presents any two people in love and their terms of endearment. Hemingway devotes little space to discussions of the causes for which his soldiers are fighting. It is for historians and political theorists to philosophize about Communism, or Fascism, or world wars. Hemingway's focus is the evolving mind of the soldier transformed from experience:

> Cowardice, as distinguished from panic is almost always simply a lack of ability to suspend the functioning of the imagination. Learning to suspend your imagination and live completely in the very second of the present minute with no before and after is the greatest gift a soldier can acquire (Hemingway 1942)

Hemingway also explores the revolutionist's shift towards cowardice, and so the rejection of the revolution. In *For Whom the Bell Tolls*, the leader of the guerrilla group struggles with his commitment to destroy the bridge, knowing that the enemy will wage a relentless pursuit. This equivocation broadens and deepens as Pablo questions his support for the cause itself. In sharp contrast with Pablo's thought processes, Hemingway presents the thinking of Anselmo as he justifies the deaths he has caused, and of Pablo's 'mujer' as she contemplates the need for Robert Jordan to kill her vacillating partner. Pilar explains the courage and dedication that once were Pablo's; "In the first days of the movement and before too, he was something. Something serious. But now he is finished. The plug has been drawn and the wine has all run out of the skin (89)". Earlier Hemingway tells us that "the woman of Pablo could feel her rage changing to sorrow and to a feeling of the thwarting of all hope and promise (58)". A revolutionist can be an individual that is hard-wired to kill, like the matador or big game hunter, but it is also true that there can be individuals transformed into revolutionists by seemingly small acts of injustice, cumulative oppression, or participation in violent conflict. Like the born again Francis Macomber or soldier Pablo, a revolutionist can emerge spontaneously and quite possibly recede as well.

VII. TODAY'S REVOLUTIONIST

Political analysts may write about suicide bombers and terrorists in terms of Islamic fundamentalism or the charisma of Osama bin Laden. They may describe the Tiananmen Square massacre and its image of a solitary young person standing in the path of a tank as a popular desire to achieve democracy. They define the fighting by the Taliban in Afghanistan as a patriotic and religious response to foreign troops. Yet something is missing in these cerebral analyses oriented around the political or economic outcome. Hemingway gives us this missing component—an understanding that in any time there are warriors eager to fight and risk death—for a cause, perhaps, but the cause may not be so meaningful for our understanding of their actions. Ultimately, a good death may be more important than a good life. In describing the early kamikaze, Scott Atran states:

> The kamikaze ("divine wine") first used in the battle of the Philippines (November 1944) were young, fairly well educated pilots who understood that pursuing conventional warfare would likely end in defeat. . . . Few believed they were dying for the emperor as a war leader or for military purposes. Rather, the state was apparently able . . . to convince the pilots that it was their honor to "die like beautiful falling cherry petals." (Atran quoted in Bloom 2005, 86)

By Hemingway's novels, we see enough diversity in age, beliefs, and life experiences to absorb that there are always potential revolutions waiting to happen because there are always potential revolutionists. Robert A. Pape's comprehensive study of suicide terrorism confirms the relative ordinariness of the suicide terrorists (2005). He includes data for 462 suicide terrorists, and more detailed survey data for a total of 278 suicide terrorists. Contrary to common and scholarly perceptions, the majority are not unusually young teenage boys. Although there is significant variation across groups, the average age is 22.7 years (208). Among the more selected group of 77 Arab suicide terrorists, they are better educated compared to the non-terrorist peer group (213), and they are more typically members of working-class or middle-class rather than the common presentation of unemployment or economic interests as a driving factor of desperation (214). Quite strikingly, the data reveal the absence of documented mental illness and the absence of previous criminal behavior. Also surprising, of 384 suicide attackers with known religious information, only 43% are religious (210).

Through Hemingway we see the varied paths of experience leading up to the rebel, and transforming the rebel. Through Hemingway's stories, therefore, we confront the very ordinariness of the potential revolutionist and subsequent limits of our social sciences to explain why and when the revolutionist will emerge.

WORKS CITED

Atran, Scott. "Genesis of Suicide Terrorism," *Science* 299 (March 7, 2003): 1535.
Bloom, Mia. *Dying to Kill: The Allure of Suicide Terror.* New York: Columbia University Press, 2005.
Chong, Dennis. *Collective Action and the Civil Rights Movement*, Chicago: The University of Chicago Press, 1991.
Connor, Walker. "When is a nation?" *Ethnic and Racial Studies* 13 (1) (1990): 92–103.
De Toqueville, Alexis. Edited by John Stone and Stephen Mennell. *Alexis De Toqueville on Democracy, Revolution, and Society.* Chicago: University of Chicago Press, 1980.
Eastman, Max, ed. *Capital and Other Writings of Karl Marx.* New York: Random House, 1932.
Gellner, Ernest. *Encounters with Nationalism.* Cambridge: Blackwell, 1994.
Gurr, Ted. *Why Men Rebel.* Princeton: Princeton University Press, 1970.
Hechter, Michael. *Containing Nationalism*, New York: Oxford University Press, 2000.
Hemingway, Ernest. *Across the River and Into the Trees.* New York: Scribner, 2003 [1950].
———. *Death in the Afternoon,.*New York: Charles Scribner's Sons, 1960.
———. *For Whom the Bell Tolls.* New York: Scribner, 2003 [1946].
———. *The Dangerous Summer.* New York: Charles Scribner's Sons, 1985.
———. *The Old Man and the Sea.* New York: Charles Scribner's Sons, 1950.
———. "The Revolutionist." In *Short Stories,* New York: Scribner, 2003 [1925].
———. "The Short Happy Life of Francis Macomber." In *The Short Stories,* New York: Scribner, 2003 [1936].
———. *Hemingway on War.* Edited by Sean Hemmingway. New York: Scribner, 2003.

Hemingway, Ernest, ed. *Men at War: The Best War Stories of All Time.* New York: Crown Publishers, 1942.
Kuran, Timur. *Private Truths, Public Lies: The Social Consequences of Preference Falsification.* Cambridge: Harvard University Press, 1995.
Oberschall, Anthony. *Social Conflict and Social Movements.* New Jersey: Prentice-Hall, 1973.
Pape, Robert. *Dying to Win: The Strategic Logic of Suicide Terrorism.* New York: Random House, 2005.
Skocpol, Theda. *States and Social Revolutions: A Comparative Analysis of France, Russia, and China.* Cambridge: Cambridge University Press, 1979.
Smith, Anthony. "Adrian Hasting's on Nations and Nationalism." *Nations and Nationalism,* Vol. 9 (1) (2003): 25–28.
Tawney, Richard Henry. *The Acquisitive Society.* New York: Harcourt, Brace, and Howe, 1920.
Tarrow, Sidney. *Power in Movement.* Cambridge: Cambridge University Press, 1994.
Tilly, Charles. *From Mobilization to Revolution.* Reading: Addison-Wesley, 1978.
Varshney, Ashutosh. "Nationalism, Ethnic Conflict and Rationality." *Perspectives on Politics.* 1 No. 1 (March 2003): 85–86.
Weber, Max. *The Protestant Ethic and the Spirit of Capitalism.* Translated by Talcott Parsons. Los Angeles: Roxbury Publications, 1930.

9 *To Have and Have Not*
Hemingway Through the Lens of Theodor Adorno[1]

Lauretta Conklin Frederking

To Have and Have Not centers on the life of Harry Morgan. Morgan's life and death is defined by his participation in the informal economy of smuggling, and through his travel between Miami and Havana, we capture a stark analysis of the political and economic systems of capitalism juxtaposed against Communist revolutionaries. As much as we are offered some gratuitous observations about the differences, the penetrating insights come from weaving stories that ultimately settle upon a picture of much more similarity. Hemingway dwells on power and myth as the underlying thread of his critique of political systems more generally. The contribution of this particular novel is a meditation on the meaning of political activity and participation given the context of all political systems plagued by these broader realities of power and myth. Regardless of ideology, democratic capitalism or Communism, power and myth dominate both systems and create an individual sense of meaninglessness around political activities and goals.

Given the dilemmas and discontent presented by both Communism and capitalism, what are the possibilities for change? Hemingway's novel includes a scathing portrayal of revolutionaries denouncing this particular path for political change. The juxtaposition of Harry Morgan and the revolutionaries in *To Have and Have Not* creates an interesting contrast between revolutionaries and rebels. Especially in terms of political activities there are differences that emerge from attitude and intention with behavioral consequences for organization, process, goals, and political outcomes. Insofar as a revolutionary is tied to an ideology, even if the ideology opposes the current system, he or she is confined to a power structure. By refusing to surrender to ideology, a rebel removes himself or herself as much as possible from the constraints of judgment and expectation. And while a revolutionary is caught in justifying behavior with particular goals, the rebel is conscious of every action as a defining action for his or her identity. This conceptual distinction between the rebel and revolutionary has not been developed in political science, but with Hemingway's novels we experience the part of political behavior that addresses individual intentions as much as action (See Conklin in this volume). Obviously, as social scientists we gravitate to observable outcomes where we can identify a well defined and transparent causal connection. Hemingway uncovers those intentions which sometimes manifest in actions, but just as likely can be followed by inaction. We know that critical turning points in war and political outcomes often hinge upon the highly contingent response and the decision not to act. Through Hemingway's portrayals of political events the contingency of each outcome is often apparent as well as the emotional complexity underlying behavior. For some, this complexity may suggest that Hemingway cannot be digested easily into existing social science frameworks for analysis.

However, studying Hemingway's novel through the lens of Theodor Adorno's philosophy, suggests a conceptually important and shared perspective that sharply distinguishes the rebel from the revolutionary. Through his novels and short stories, Hemingway's rebel characters represent many of the ideas articulated in Adorno's writings. In particular, Adorno emphasizes autonomy, authenticity, and reflectivity as ideal characteristics of an individual struggling within a political and economic system that celebrates institutionalized power and stifles individualism. Adorno's description of the struggle as well as the ideals of resistance parallel the backdrop of many of Hemingway's stories and define many of his characters. *To Have and Have Not* is not unique, but this novel successfully crystallizes many of these ideas shared between the two writers.

In many ways, both the revolutionary and the rebel present a challenge to the stability of democratic capitalism but Hemingway distinguishes between the power intentions and actions of the revolutionary compared to the intention of authenticity which characterizes the rebel. Because of his or her concrete opposition to an existing political and economic system, the rebel can be misunderstood as a participant in a coherent ideological cause rather than merely participating in his or her own process and meaning from rebellion. Throughout the novel, Hemingway casts support for the rebel insofar as authenticity includes awareness and opposition without the revolutionary's inevitable delusion of systemic change. Hemingway's rebel instigates immediate and tangible opposition without cultivating long run plans dependent upon others or dependent upon significant financial capital. In terms of political mobilization, and within political science, we study revolutions through organized groups and formal leadership; there is an underlying assumption connecting participation with defined goals. *To Have and Have Not* provides insight into the relevance of the rebel who may fight without political intention but whose actions nonetheless carry political consequences.

I. HEMINGWAY AND ADORNO: INTELLECTUAL REBELS

As I addressed in the introduction to this volume, Hemingway has been assigned political labels as diverse as Communist sympathizer, individualist, and elitist. Ultimately, most literary critics have settled upon a statement that Hemingway is apolitical and most political scientists avoid his literature altogether. This chapter challenges the apolitical designation by approaching Hemingway's political complexity through the lens of Theodor Adorno's political philosophy. There was significant confusion around interpreting Adorno's vision, including the label of "unpolitical aesthete" (Berman 2002, 111), and he also emphasized many ideas similar to Hemingway. Like Hemingway, Adorno has been boxed into political designations by some scholars and then brought out of those particular boxes by other scholars who focus on evidence of some other defining attribute. Within political philosophy, Adorno's ideas have been linked quite closely with Kant (Freyenhagen 2008, 105; O'Connor 2004, 99–126), Hegel (Gibson and Rubin 2002, 23), Marcuse (Claussen 2008) Horkheimer (Bowie 2004, 248–278; Claussen 2008) and Nietzsche (Adorno 2000 [1963]) and at the same time his voice is clearly distinct from each of these other scholars, as well as the Frankfurt school with whom he is most closely associated (Rubin 2002).[2] Ideologically, the diverse analysis of his philosophy is captured appropriately by Nigel Gibson and Andrew Rubin:

> Adorno's politics has always been a contested terrain. The right wing views him as a Marxist critic of capitalism; the Old Left finds him too close to American foreign policy; and the New Left is split between finding inspiration in his critique of a capitalist culture and being disenchanted by his dismissal of practice.... Adorno's own attitude to Marx remains problematic.... seen in instrumental rather than revolutionary humanist terms.... can also be read as a retreat from a dialectical critique of capitalism. (Gibson and Rubin 2002, 17–18)

Rather than fitting Adorno and Hemingway into established ideologies, both belong outside of our compact delineations. One of the elements that bring cohesion to their complex and seemingly contradictory positions is their shared opposition to all institutionalized power. In *To Have and Have Not*, Hemingway's juxtaposition of characters living in, or struggling for, very different regimes reveals a disdain for dictatorship, democratic capitalism, and Communism. About Adorno, Edward Said stated that he "was a quintessential intellectual hating *all* systems, whether on our side or theirs, with equal distaste" (1994a, 55 quoted in Gibson and Rubin, 1). Formalized power inherent in political systems tends to wreak corruption as well as the myths that perpetuate corruption and alienate the individual within these systems. However, in spite of their support for an ongoing and universalized opposition, neither Adorno nor Hemingway settles on nihilism as the thread of legitimacy. Autonomy, authenticity, and reflection are central to Adorno's philosophy and provide a lens for studying Hemingway's novel, as well as many of Hemingway's broader themes throughout his work. In many ways, autonomy, authenticity, and reflection are the characteristics that move Adorno away from the socialist and collectivist political agenda but also provide substance beyond destruction so that he remains removed from the nihilists. *To Have and Have Not* is a rich novel that presents Harry Morgan as the embodiment of autonomy, authenticity, and reflection. Most particularly, Morgan's autonomy, authenticity, and reflection contrast sharply with so many of the other characters and the economic and political systems within which he lives and dies. *To Have and Have Not* brings life to Adorno's ideas and Adorno's perspective brings a framework to study Hemingway's political relevance more generally.

II. POWER, CORRUPTION, AND MYTH

For Adorno, the political system of democratic capitalism, as much as the political system of dictatorship, was an assault on individual autonomy. As Russell Berman points out, Adorno's

> *Dialectic of Enlightenment* is replete with these elisions between the United States and Nazi Germany. The political substance of the analogy is a profound critique of the transformation in the United States regarding the expansion of the state administration, standardization of life practices, the proliferation of the commercial culture industry, and the transformation of individual personality type increasingly incapable of maintaining an autonomy, individual integrity, in the face of overarching structures of power (Berman 2002, 119).

Similarly, Hemingway describes his characters in terms of their experiences with the brutality and systemic inequality nurtured by capitalism: "Conch town, where all was starched, well-shuttered, virtue, failure, grits and boiled grunts, under-nourishment, prejudice, righteousness, interbreeding and the comforts of religion" (Hemingway 2003 [1937], 193). For Hemingway, it is important to convey the seductiveness of the socio-economic foundation as much as the despair. However, those who *have* all the material assets in Hemingway's novel are empty in many more ways than those who *have not*. Whereas those who *have not* articulate powerlessness as a source for discontent, those who *have* seem unconscious to their own powerlessness within a system that binds and terrorizes both the *haves* and *have nots*. In the final vignettes of the novel describing the wealthy on their yachts, the rich and privileged desperately maintain their appearances—of contentment, of having, and of winning. Any truth that begins to gnaw through their unconsciousness, frothy selves is nipped by their discernible urgent need to maintain status.

Protecting their superficial lives requires a web of lies and corruption. Cheating is systemic and Hemingway's characters of social and economic privilege remain aloof to their crimes of exploitation. Life becomes a game to negotiate individuals' livelihoods with strategies for domination over others. From the perspective of the privileged class, the world is indeed divided by those who have and those who have not, and remaining in the former arena demands full attention to asserting all economic and political and social power over others.

In one of the vignettes, a wealthy grain broker laments the investigation by the Internal Revenue Bureau. His protected world is collapsing but he continues to perceive the dynamic in terms of those with power who 'necessarily' exert power over those without. Despite his own fraudulent and criminal behavior, pushed forward by greed and protected by false egoism, he refused to acknowledge any personal responsibility,

> and wondered what the department had, what they had found and what they would twist, what they would accept as normal and what they would insist was evasion; and he was not afraid of them, but only hated them and the power they would use so insolently that all his own hard, small, tough and lasting insolence . . . would be drilled through, and, if he were ever made afraid, shattered (234).

Individuals are relevant in terms of the perpetual fear of domination by others or the potential to dominate others. The power structure becomes the defining foundation for interactions and the barometer for measuring one's position in life. Adorno described this type of systemic corruption: "individuals relate to one another as mere "agents and bearers of exchange value" (Adorno 1969–1970, 148–149 quoted in Cook 2008, 14). At the same time, they are isolated and alienated from one another precisely because their interpersonal relations are often cemented by nothing more substantive than exchange" (Cook 2008, 14). The lack of emotional connection reinforces the transactional society which in turn reinforces the stark interpretation of individuals in terms of their exchange value. In this description Adorno and Hemingway share a perspective that capitalism breeds human interactions without intimacy and inequality without collective solidarity.

Within the novel, there is more expressed empathy (perhaps romantic) for the *have nots*. Initially, we might perceive that Hemingway shares Adorno's overwhelming accusation that humanity has degraded itself to exchange value. However, the seeds of genuine solidarity and intimacy come through his novel as well. These flickers of thick human exchange take the form of loyalty and trust and emerge from the shared dependency for survival among those who are more obviously deprived. When Harry returns from a rum-smuggling run with a wounded mate they are trying to dump all the liquor before the inspectors catch them. A fellow fisher happens to have taken a boat trip with a couple of zealous government men who sense the trouble around Harry Morgan's boat and want to be a part of heroically catching him. They order their Captain Willie to head in that direction:

> "Now will you take us over to that boat," he said smiling. He had a smile which was reserved for such occasions.
>
> "No, sir."
>
> "Listen, you half-witted fisherman. I'll make life so miserable for you—"
>
> "Yes," said Captain Willie.
>
> "You don't know who I am."
>
> "None of it don't mean anything to me," said Captain Willie.
>
> "That man is a bootlegger, isn't he?"
>
> "What do *you* think?"
>
> "There's probably a reward for him."
>
> "I doubt that."
>
> "He's a lawbreaker."
>
> "He's got a family and he's got to eat and feed them. Who the hell do you eat off of with people working here in Key West for the government for six dollars dollars and a half a week?" (80–81)

Ultimately, Captain Willie saves Morgan from arrest by continuing further out to sea rather than turning around to allow the men to report their suspicions back in town. Bonds of solidarity appear spontaneously and define sides in terms of the larger macro issues of the political economy. In the hostile exchange between the government men and Captain Willie the latter states:

> I thought you'd be interested in these things as a government man. Ain't you mixed up in the prices of things that we eat or something? Ain't that it? Making them more costly or something. Making the grits cost more and the grunts less? (84)

While there is a meaningful possibility for rich human connection, it is often fleeting. One of the crewmen identifies Morgan's brutality and reveals the sharp limits of solidarity: "You ain't human . . . You ain't got human feelings" (86). Hemingway also carves a sacred space for the solidarity and authenticity of soldiers. In juxtaposing the few who escape the transaction society, he poses the critical question in his novel through a bar conversation among soliders: "War is a purifying and ennobling force. The question is whether only people like ourselves here are fitted to be soldiers or whether the different services have formed us" (205). If power and transaction values dominate interpersonal relations then change depends upon either the belief that some individuals are hard-wired differently or perhaps there can be hope around the belief that some institutions remain immune to the typical struggle of society more generally. Hemingway provides some optimism in these moments of individual clarity and solidarity. Whereas Adorno is most certain that solidarity has become an ideal only (Freyenhagen 2008, 108), Hemingway offers moments of meaningful connection that penetrate far beyond transaction and realize bonds of solidarity. But if one recognizes this connection potential as part of human nature, then where can these individuals push for change within the existing institutions that seem to constrain human connection?

Both Adorno and Hemingway address pessimism around the formalized political route for change. Adorno in particular defines the limits of the political realm for individual development:

> What propaganda has done to the concept of politics is undergoing. In the past, politics meant the conscious, independent, and critical effort, in thought and deed, to replace bad social conditions with better ones. Today politics is generally merely a façade. It no longer means the realization of humanity but only inter-state power struggles (Kraushaar 1998 II, 52 in Berman 2002, 121).

Further, Adorno feared that the route for opposition was far beyond formalized politics. Pushing for reform within the system, through National Socialism for example, was much more dangerous than rejecting the whole. At the time, as is true today as well, there was pretense that reform, where revolution seemed impossible, could lead to eventual political transformation. For Adorno, as with others in the Frankfurt school perhaps most notably Herbert Marcuse, the illusion of potential transformation through reform surrenders individual autonomy and integrity and perpetuates existing structures of power (Berman 2002, 124). Because participation in the existing structures of power undermines solidarity as well as autonomy, it becomes inevitable that any opposition through participation undermines the very possibility of more comprehensive opposition in the future (Cook 2008, 14). Indeed, for Adorno, participation even if it is oriented around transforming the system, if it is "deciding within their coercive structure" (Adorno 1973, 226n quoted in Tettlebaum 2008, 145) then it is the foundation for the most heinous political outcomes—most especially addressed in Adorno's writings is the looming possibility of repeating Auschwitz (Adorno 1978, 68 in Berman 2002, 130).

Given the impossibility of change from within the political system, revolution as a route for the fundamental transformation of all existing social, economic, and political relations seems necessary. However, neither Adorno nor Hemingway finds relief in this route of opposition. Hemingway gives a portrait of the revolutionary as someone who ultimately wants to switch places with those in power, rather than someone who seeks transformation of power relations more generally. Propaganda aside, all political regimes share a structure of illusion, rigidity, and domination. From Harry's perspective "One bunch of Cuban government bastards cost me my arm shooting at me with a load when they had no need to and another bunch of U.S. ones took my boat" (148). Here, governments share the corruption that perpetuates power over others.

Similarly, Adorno doesn't surrender to the attractiveness of political action around the goals of an ideological revolution. For him, ideology invades the individual with myth and surrenders the individual to a power structure that can be as debilitating as the existing formal economic and political structures. Even worse, revolutionary ideologies justify new but parallel power conditions with well articulated critiques of the current relations. Previous cynicisms, which had protected individuals from opting in to existing power relations and institutions, are now suspended by the optimism for change through adhering to a new ideology and through concrete action. Adorno and Hemingway remind us that the seduction of ideological critique is not the path to comprehensive change. After the robbery, Morgan speaks to one of the revolutionaries who explains why Roberto killed Morgan's assistant Albert: "You see," the boy said, speaking quietly, "this man Roberto is bad. He is a good revolutionary but a bad man. He kills so much in the time of Machado he gets to like it. He thinks it is funny to kill. He kills in a good cause, of course. The best cause" (158). Later the boy says "You know he doesn't mean to do wrong. It's just what that phase of the revolution has done to him" (165).

Both thinkers articulate criticisms of the existing social, economic, and political institutions that are dominated by capitalism. And both share a blunt perspective on the limits of reform within the system. A characteristic that sets them apart from other critics of existing institutions and interactions, is their willingness to also extend harsh criticism to the Communist revolution, or any ideological revolution for transformative change. Yet through Adorno's philosophical writings and through Hemingway's novels, *To Have and Have Not* as one example of his broader oeuvre, there is space for fundamental change. While humanity has been lulled into acquiescence through dominant ideologies, either ideologies that support current regimes or ideologies that oppose them, Hemingway reminds us that certain experiences can shock you into liberated consciousness. This awakening brings the potential for individual self-realization and approaches solidarity rooted in liberation rather than ideology, and in spite of existing social, economic, and political systems. The next sections focus on Hemingway's novel, *To Have and Have Not* through Adorno's emphasis on autonomy, authenticity, and reflectivity as the ideal path to orient an individual's energies of opposition. A clear picture of ideals around the rebel, distinct from the revolutionary, emerges and raises questions about this type of change in the context of political democracy. A juxtaposition of the rebel and revolutionary in political democracy focuses the final section of analysis.

III. AUTONOMY

The success of a revolution depends upon collective action. Collective action is more likely when individuals are dependent upon each other but also when they rely on shared expectations for strategies and goals.

Shared ideology generates a set of similar expectations, and coordinated action is more likely and more efficient with this foundation of similar beliefs. Communication and compliance with shared standards also ensure greater certainties about behavior. In sharp contrast, the rebel exhibits much more autonomy—independent of others, independent of capitalist greed and power, and self-determining. The public world too easily devolves into manipulation, dependence, and power. "Given the importance that Adorno put on holding on to the last vestige of autonomy in the age of state capitalism, it is not surprising that, as Russell Berman puts it in "Adorno's Politics," the priority of private life over the manipulated public sphere corresponded to "the project of maintaining a personal autonomy" (Gibson and Rubin 2002 18).³ The rebel carves out personal autonomy, a private space, in order to feel, and ideally become, removed from systemic exploitations. Autonomy lays the foundation for the other ideal characteristics of the rebel: to experience authenticity and also meaningful reflectivity.

Harry Morgan personifies Adorno's claim about both the challenge to find autonomy and the struggle to retreat from emotional and transactional dependencies. Morgan pursues this type of ideal autonomy and through Morgan, Hemingway unpacks the meaning of autonomy for the rebel in the context of society. Like Adorno, Hemingway conveys the constant strains for individual autonomy especially when the public world necessarily means the capitalist world. While escape from material chains of exploitation appears impossible and materialism necessarily ties action to others' interests, Morgan tries to assert independence by limiting the influence of others. Hemingway conveys both the inevitability of exploitation in a capitalist world but then also Morgan's ability to carve some autonomy from the societal pressures. Certainly, some of his fears, his frustrations, and his judgments come from the social, economic, and political conditions around him. However, his decisions from this position of exploitation and relative powerlessness remain remarkably defined by himself and within himself. Through conscious effort, Morgan's decisions are untainted by public opinion and they evolve from reflecting on his own experiences much more than from any advice or conventional responsibilities. Morgan first decided not to transport three aliens and then dramatically changed his mind to bargain with Mr. Sing and transport twelve illegals into Florida. He refuses to discuss any of the plans with his wife or with his 'right hand' boat assistant Eddy; he makes these contradictory decisions on his own. Without consultation, he doesn't seem to need affirmation and he is better able to make an about face change to embrace the apparent contradiction without embarrassment or explanation or accountability.

Autonomy does not mean a self-imposed ostracism nor does it mean a life within a vacuum without meaningful human connection. People participate in Morgan's life and his actions certainly impact others, but he consciously refuses to let his own destiny be determined by those around him. He does not reach out for others' wisdom to determine action and there is little coordination of action. We see how the priority of autonomy can easily lead to decisions that are not in his interest. Morgan does not rely on camaraderie, solidarity, or advice for guidance. Camaraderie comes and solidarity evolves at several points in Morgan's life but they are not determinative. Rather than making decisions because of personal or ideological commitments, people and experiences become parts of the path to self-realization and opportunities for reflection. He recognizes the intimacies and accepts the connections without feeling burdened by them. After Morgan refuses to let Eddy come on the dangerous trip, Eddy sneaks into the hatch. As soon as Morgan discovers Eddy, their dialogue reflects Morgan's pity, melancholy, acknowledgement of their friendship, and recognition of its limits.

> "I knew you'd carry me, Harry," he said.
> "Carry you to hell," I said. "You aren't even on the crew list. I've got a good mind to make you jump overboard now."
> "You're an old joker, Harry," he said. "Us Conchs ought to stick together when we're in trouble."
> "You," I said, "with your mouth. Who's going to trust your mouth when you're hot?"
> "I'm a good man, Harry. You put me to the test and see what a good man I am."
> "Get me the two quarts," I told him. I was thinking of something else.
> He brought them out and I tood a drink from the open one and put them forward by the wheel. He stood there and I looked at him. I was sorry for him and for what I knew I'd have to do. Hell, I knew him when he was a good man (43).

At this point in the story, Morgan knows that likely rummy-Eddy will ruin his plan. Rather than perceived as constraints for future action, these self-defined moments of camaraderie and denial become part of his capabilities and identity. While a subtle distinction it is also an important one in terms of intentions. Certain characteristics associated with autonomy include solitariness at times and contradictory behavior. Even more, the 'rebel' framework contrasts sharply with other types of opposition where discernible dependencies and commitments allow for predictable calculations through a more narrow range of potential behavior. However, autonomy can drive an individual to consider seemingly riskier behavior, and often much less predictable behavior. Cues come from the individual perception of needs and interests at the moment, independent of dependencies on others and independent of past behavior. Morgan's decisions emerge from the wrestle within, or spontaneously from the primitive emotions surging through him. Primarily, his decisions are oriented around his own sense of place and identity in the moment.

Part of Morgan's autonomy is an adamant, often violent, response to others' efforts to possess or direct his behavior. One particular outburst reveals his active rebellion against human connection that is most obviously about dominance and possession. Attracted to him, a woman dares to suggest that she would like to have Harry Morgan 'purchased'. His excoriating and unrefined response reveals strong virulence for the presumption that he can be bought and sold. In another scene, he meditates on the need to provide for his family but it is about him and how he considers himself, much more than a sympathy or empathy for them. Rather than family bonds it appears like his stubborn determination to perform as the provider for his family. Similarly, surrender to the economic forces that have placed him in a position of material 'desperation' is never an option. Again the difference is subtle but important. If motivated by family affection and their dependence upon him it is likely he would consider more of the risks associated with the crimes. If it is about well being he might be more inclined to share the decision with his wife. Instead, Harry Morgan draws strength from inward reflection and maintains autonomy through challenges.

Typically, emotions emerging from relationships bind one to someone else's interest. Especially in times of crisis, the autonomy-seeking individual reduces the influence of those emotions that follow from dependencies. At the height of crisis on the boat, "[H]e had abandoned anger, hatred, and any dignity as luxuries, now, and had started to plan" (159). Relationships can be part of an autonomous life, but they cannot dictate intention or action. Emotions can be part of an autonomous life, and indeed emotions are very much a part of the ideal of autonomy, but they cannot be emotions binding and driving the individual to others in a way that manipulates behavior. Ultimately then, the reader experiences Morgan's intense camaraderie and marital intimacy but just as profoundly the reader experiences Morgan's withdrawal from these moments of connection.

Harry Morgan's steely disposition mirrors Adorno's claims that suggest "almost Manichaean division between a (false or forced) "collectivism" and an (authentic and free) individual autonomy" (Gibson and Rubin 2002, 18–19). It is not that the autonomous self is necessarily socially isolated but given the omnipresence of capitalism and concomitant relations of power it becomes much more likely for the autonomous seeking individual to gravitate toward more social isolationism. While not necessarily so, political, economic, and social conditions determine that the autonomous individual appears angry and disengaged. For Adorno, autonomy involves "the capacity for self-determination, but such autonomy (or, as Adorno also calls it, positive freedom) is currently denied to us. However, along with this idea of autonomy, Adorno takes from Kant a more limited conception of freedom, namely, negative freedom as independence from external determination" (Freyenhagen 2008, 110) Because we are caught in a capitalist world of transaction and power, full positive freedom may be impossible and so focus necessarily shifts to achieve more negative freedom instead.

In contrast to Harry Morgan and in contrast to Adorno's ideal, the other characters in *To Have and Have Not* are driven by the web of appearances and they accept identities and decisions that have seemingly been imposed upon them. Eddy and Albert assist Morgan during his smuggling runs and like Morgan, Eddy and Albert are caught in chains of capitalism that define them as part of the *have nots*. Whereas Morgan continues to fight against financial dependence and he refuses to ingratiate himself to others for assistance, Eddy and Albert appear more desperate and dependent. As characters representing the *have nots* they generate reader sympathy but their cloying pleas as well as Harry's depiction of Albert as a "poor hungry bastard" (160) present a sharp juxtaposition to Harry's own approach to the troubled circumstances. As one of the *haves* Helen Gordon reveals her husband's lack of autonomy through his ingratiating tendencies and similarly reveals her own nebulous identity within the marriage:

> I've seen you bitter, jealous, changing your politics to suit the fashion, sucking up to people's faces and talking about them behind their backs.... I've tried to take care of you and humor you and look after you and cook for you and keep quiet when you wanted and give you your little explosions and pretend it made me happy" (186).

Independence from others and removing chains of emotional dependence are critical aspects of autonomy. Also an important element of autonomy is Morgan's unwillingness to be defined by an ideology or a set of beliefs that are imposed upon him. Ideology invites ideals and hope that are entirely inappropriate for the rebel's decisions which are driven by the strongest emphasis on the here and now. Morgan's intentions and expectations are not postured by ideological claims of virtue. He is not energized by a righteous determination to implement the correct path for change. He acknowledges society with disdain but it is not a focus for retribution through the guise of ideology. When Harry's final plan to steal his own boat from customs starts to break down he seems to draw into himself and respond with matter of fact "I'll get a boat. I'll carry them to hell" (121). Later he announces "I got confidence. That's the only thing I have got" (126) and in the next scene with his family, his wife reflects: "She watched him go out of the house, tall, wide-shouldered, flat-backed his hips narrow, moving, still, she thought, like some kind of animal" (128). During the final boat trip with the revolutionaries Hemingway described Morgan as the autonomous man: "He had abandoned anger, hatred and any dignity as luxuries, now, and had started to plan"(159). Action comes from some other place that feels to him and conveys to the reader as much more internally oriented rather than externally derived.

In contrast, ideology offers certainty and consistency where individuals are incapable of realizing any collective outcome with certainty. "If moral worth lies in intentions, then there is the grave danger that people may behave self-righteously and irresponsibly by simply aiming at morality without any sense for the havoc they might cause in doing so" (Cook 2008, 105). In *To have and Have Not* the revolutionaries justify their armed robbery and murders by the ideological goals of the revolutions. Although associated with the leftist revolution, Adorno rejected all ideological motivations and all types of Kantian ethics that focused on intentions rather than behavior oriented around actual outcomes. Adorno uses *The Wild Duck* Ibsen play to show that striving for the good can cause bad (Adorno 1963 in 2000, 157–166). One of Hemingway's characters explains the revolutionaries' goals to Morgan

> "You know how they've been financing this revolution with kidnapping and the rest of it."
> "I know."
> "This is the same sort of thing. They're doing it for a good cause" (109)

In this novel, Hemingway's revolutionaries present their ideology as the justification for the most heinous crimes: "'We are the only true revolutionary party' and then 'We just raise money now for the fight,' the boy said. 'To do that we have to use means that later we would never use. Also we have to use people we would not employ later. But the end is worth the means'" (166). Rather than bringing citizens together, blind adherence to ideology undermines the protection and value of relationships. Rather than the solidarity associated with revolutionary movements both Adorno and Hemingway reveal the disconnections between individuals especially those oriented around a particular formalistic philosophy or ideology.

Also, for the revolutionary, ideology defines and confines choice. "'I regret the necessity for the present phase very much. I hate terrorism. I also feel very badly about the methods for raising the necessary money. But there is no choice. You do not know how bad things are in Cuba'" (167). For the revolutionary, it is ideology rather than the here and now, or interpersonal relationships that justify behavior. Instead, the rebel is free from objectifying beliefs and a hierarchy that subsumes relationships for some loftier cause. Morgan presents the contrast of rebel and revolutionary:

> I want a drink, Harry was thinking. What the hell do I care about his revolution. F- his revolution. To help the working man he robs a bank and kills a fellow works with him and then kills that poor damned Albert that never did any harm. That's a working man he kills. He never thinks of that. With a family . . . They get what they deserve. The hell with their revolutions. All I got to do is make a living for my family and I can't do that. Then he tells me about his revolution. The hell with his revolution (168).

For the rebel, there may be less consistency and obviously less attention to one's role and responsibilities within collective goals. For the rebel, ideology is sacrificed for vigilant attention to individual interpretation and meaning around here and now. Of course, this can lead to profound moments of solidarity with friends and sacrifice. The rebel is not necessarily selfish in his or her self-centeredness. It is an emphasis on here and now rather than lofty goals for the future and it is an emphasis on here and now which can include moments of intimacy. The key distinction between rebel and revolutionary is that the rebel approaches these relationships without dependencies.

A final point about autonomy is the extent to which it can challenge conventional morality. Harry Morgan violates so many socially defined standards and while he has moments of intimacy and evidences of loyalty it is his belligerence, and apparent selfishness, that dominates the portrayal of his character. The reader may not *like* Harry at all. At the very least, it becomes very clear that Morgan lives by his personal code of acceptable and unacceptable behavior. And perhaps it is only in the contrast with the other characters that he can be redeemed in some sense for the reader. In the final pages of the novel, Hemingway provides brief glimpses behind the wealthy lives of those on the yachts in port. Capturing the moments and exchanges on many of the yachts reveals conversations and the deceptions around blackmail, thoughts of suicide, alcoholism, drug addiction, fraud, vanity, adultery. Through these vignettes Hemingway invites the reader to juxtapose the multitude of individuals who also violate society's expected standards with Morgan who sticks to his own unique code without compromise. Morgan's morality does not conform to society's conventional standards and Hemingway doesn't suggest a higher standard for Morgan's behavior by his contrast. After all, Morgan commits murder outright. However, while the *haves* dance around 'murderous' deceptions, they don't actually murder anyone, but nor are they held accountable to those around them or in any court of law. Rather, Hemingway accentuates Morgan's honesty and transparency compared to those who appear to live within society's standards but then harbor secrets and deceptions from the reality of their hypocrisy, crimes, and desperations. Morgan's willingness to murder cannot be part of a higher standard of morality but the decisions and actions that led to the murder and include the murder are compatible with the preservation of Morgan's autonomy.

IV. AUTHENTICITY

With autonomy it is possible to develop an authentic identity. Relationships and emotions can lead to exploitation and domination. However, relationships and emotions, perhaps even especially with exploitation and domination, when experienced with preservation of autonomy facilitate authenticity. Again, it is not social connections that determine the difference between the autonomous and non-autonomous individual. The key to an authentic life is that the identity formation takes place without reliance on relationships or dependencies around society's judgments. Then in order to move toward liberation and authentic identity formation within social, economic, and political systems, one needs an awakening to all forms of insipid and ubiquitous power.

> Adorno's account amounts to a psychoanalytic foundation for a possible political education, which would have to address several components: the claustrophobia in administered society which leads to a sense of rage against civilization; the lack of autonomy and attractions of collective identity formation; masochism and sadism; a festishism of technical means without regard to ends; and, especially, coldness as a preponderant characteristic" (Berman 2002, 126).

Within this context of consciousness, Adorno advocates experience and opposition, but not necessarily protest. This is an interesting point of clarification for understanding Adorno's distinct voice within the Frankfurt school. Adorno's critique of capitalism and institutions of power aligned him with 'new left' intellectuals and Adorno became associated with the more radical leftist student protests in France. However, according to Rubin and Gibson

> Adorno's student said: "Adorno was incapable of transforming his private compassion toward the 'damned of the earth' into an organized partisanship of theory engaged in the liberation of the oppressed.... He found the student's "actionism" akin to Nazi anti-intellectualism. For him the student's "praxis" was an unreflective, regressive, collective, knee-jerk activity that sacrified independent thinking for immediate goals (2002, 18).

On the one hand, Adorno's central focus on overcoming oppression and creating personal liberation, and on the other hand, his condemnation of the student protests as well as his unwillingness to publicly protest other current issues of the day like imperialism, sexism, and racism (Gibon and Rubin 2002, 23) seem to pose a contradiction. However, more recent studies of Adorno's philosophy maintain his opposition to capitalism and all ideological rigidity, but also opposition to blind protest as the momentum for change or catalyst for self-fulfillment. Adorno opposed action that appeared to be opposition for the sake of opposition at the same time that he continued to call for the individual to struggle against existing institutions of power. The key element that makes sense of these apparent incongruent positions is his emphasis on subjective autonomy driving subjective identity. Adorno's emphasis on authenticity is much more compatible with Hemingway's characters than Adorno's association with others with the Frankfurt school. From this perspective, the individual may move forward in solidarity or just as reasonably remove himself or herself from collective movements, but an adherence to one or other as an objective truth for the individual is abhorrent to Adorno's understanding of cultivating identity. When driven by ideology or action for action's sake

> The feeling of new security is purchased with the sacrifice of autonomous thinking" (Adorno 1978, 68) Yet succumbing to the temptation to belong merely in order to overcome the isolation of the thinker, opting just "to do it", without any prospect of success, is nothing else than resignation, as Adorno turns his critics' complaints back at them." (Adorno 1978, 68 quoted in Berman 2002, 130)

Adorno presents authenticity as more complex and often more subtle than opposition, action, or ideology, and more individually constructed than any ideology can permit.

Harry Morgan personifies Adorno's ideal. He experiences solidarity in terms of class identification and he recognizes a part of himself by these terms but Morgan's self-identity includes values that are distinct and potentially in conflict with an overarching and determinative class consciousness. Repeatedly he insults his boat assistant Eddy as much as he helps him. While friendly, he continues to call the boat assistant Wesley a "nigger" and in a moment of harsh tenderness when Wesley apologizes for not following through on the boat during crisis, Morgan says "ain't no nigger any good when he's shot. You're a all right nigger, Wesley"(87). And in a brutal scene he kills the Chinese trafficker and then leaves the twelve individuals who paid their money to be transported to Miami stranded in knee-deep water. Repeatedly, Morgan's behavior is determined by the connection between his autonomous self and the surroundings and people of the moment.

The juxtaposition of Morgan with descriptions of the yachtsmen in the novel provides the sharpest distinction between authenticity on the one hand, and increasingly apparent hypocrisy.

> Two wealthy gentlemen exchange statements: "You can't make up your mind. You don't know what you are even" (229).
> "I suppose when you're rich enough there isn't any difference" (230).

Then in another yacht of privilege the grain broker admits "twenty years of keeping up appearances" (235), of essentially ignoring his wife's, and he summarizes his character in terms of

> an ability to make people like him without ever liking or trusting them in return, while at the same time convincing them warmly and heartily of his friendship; not a disinterested friendship, but a friendship so interested in their success that it automatically made them accomplices;

and an incapacity for either remorse or pity, had carried him to where has was now (236).

As victims of the liberal democratic capitalist world they are representative insofar as they have lost their curiosity, their passion, and the process of authentic self-realization. Relationships crumble without drama, suicides take place without second thoughts, families seem to separate without emotion. When Richard and Helen Gordon realize the insurmountable barrier created by their infidelities Helen punctuates their previous world: "This isn't just an ordinary row. It's over. I don't hate you. It isn't violent. I just dislike you. I dislike you thoroughly and I'm through with you" (184). Pretense surrounded their marriage until the awakening to consciousness which is so comprehensive and alarming that repair seems untenable. The tragic unfolding of their relationship is an intense commentary of the day to day interactions and crimes of hypocrisy within a transactional society. Professor MacWalsey, guilty of luring Helen Gordon from her marriage, describes a moment of angst following from his disloyalty. There is modern irony in his statement that he refuses to fight Richard Gordon and yet he has willingly participated in the destruction of Richard's delusory life through the undoing of his marriage. Bourgeois crimes keep one's hands clean and often carry worse internal consequences simply because there is no remedy. A straight, clean fight might offer an honest resolution but the *'haves'* wallow in misdirected aggression and seething insecurities. Instead, webs of deceit, emotional sabotage, and betrayal wreak insipid consequences beyond the individual and violate the collective.

In a pithy scene, Hemingway contrasts Morgan's wife with Richard Gordon. Gordon sees an unknown woman walking down a lonely road (Morgan's wife). Gordon doesn't realize that she has just learned about Morgan's imminent death and she is returning home. Previously, the reader has enjoyed glimpses of the raw emotions that connect Morgan and his wife. A primary bond is sexual and untarnished by other's perceptions or expectations. Their primitive but nourishing interactions seem to draw a space away from the public sphere. Adorno describes the ideal interaction in terms that are fitting to describe Morgan and his wife as she realizes that he is in a dangerous situation: "What is at issue here is not a rationalized form of pity, motivated by thoughts of reciprocity or reward, since such thoughts would undermine identification-based solidarity. At issue, rather, is natural compassion—a "physical impulse" (Adorno 1973, 285) of which other animals are allegedly capable (though perhaps only in exceptional circumstances, as in the rare instances of an animal raising young of a different species)" (quoted in Freyenhagen 2008, 108) There is no doubt that Morgan and his wife share a relationship that is rich with emotion and connection—but there is also no doubt that dependencies and dominance remain outside the private space of their marriage. Inevitably then, their connections while profound can be transitory, fleeting, and without comprehensive or articulated commitments.

Gordon sees Morgan's wife in mourning; he perceives her as the unkempt woman skulking on the road and imagines that he has captured her essence: "He had seen, in a flash of perception, the whole inner life of that type of woman. Her early indifference to her husband's caresses. Her desire for children and security. Her lack of sympathy with her husband's aims. Her sad attempts to simulate an interest in the sexual act that had become actually repugnant to her" (177). In this image, Richard Gordon could not have been more incorrect in his assessment of her. Instead, Gordon very much reveals his own identity in his hollow, disconnected life. Hemingway guides us to understand that Gordon is so lost in self-delusion that he cannot see that this commentary describes himself. Shortly after, Hemingway places Gordon on the same lonely road weaving from drunkenness and collapsing under the revelation of his wife's adultery. Here, Gordon is similarly observed and pitied by an onlooker, but in this instance the reader acknowledges how Gordon's emptiness is defined by his own character, not the loss of a loved one or a tragic event.

Finally, an important aspect of authenticity comes from the attention to our place in nature. Authenticity embraces the diversity of life paths; each individual forges his or her unique formation. However, if there is a shared component of identity it is this association of every individual to Nature and connection with our life cycle. Inevitably, the life cycle includes death. Whereas most individuals neglect and revile against the looming inevitability of death, Hemingway's characters embrace this opportunity to probe their most authentic selves. It is in these moments of wrestling with Nature that we learn our greatest capabilities and frailties and so cultivate critical aspects of our individual and authentic identity.

Harry Morgan is always conscious of his potential death particularly since he makes a living from smuggling and then trafficking. However, it is at the moment when he heightens the risk and accepts the likelihood of his death that he begins to feel vital: "Harry stood there, never having felt so tall, never having felt so wide, feeling the sweat trickle from under his armpits, feeling it go down his flanks" (161). As readers, we experience his heightened sensitivities and euphoria from a confrontation that he knows will conclude with death: "All the cold was gone from around his heart now and he had the old hollow, singing feeling and he crouched low down" (171). Amidst the tragic drama, the clutter of life's baggage dissolves and Morgan has an opportunity to be his very best self—defying the power relations that want to ruin him and not denying or fighting Nature but writhing with it. Emotions are raw and real and transparent and invigorated by truth of death.

Given the driving motivations that are emotional much more than calculated and strategic, there is potential to locate Hemingway within a romantic perspective of a return to nature. Similarly, with an emphasis on opposition and continued critical analysis, there is potential to locate both Adorno and Hemingway as nihilists. However, a key characteristic that saves Hemingway from comprehensive primitivism and saves Adorno from nihilism is their shared attention to self-reflection and responsibility.

V. REFLECTION

For Adorno, the ideal rebel is driven by reflection and experience, conscience and responsibility (Adorno Lecture Seventeen 1963, in 2000, 169). He or she does not blindly confront bourgeois values only but perceives and confronts the power structure underlying them. This process cannot be excessively formalistic and dependent upon a rigid ideology.

> The rescue of the idea of consciousness from its Hegelian and Marxist limitations is an important move. The consciousness in question is that of individuals, not of groups or classes. An emphasis upon consciousness as *perception*, and awareness of detail, presents it as the property of the individual. A good man is truthful, loving, brave, concerned for others, he has overcome the barriers of egoism, he sees clearly, he perceives details (and so on). If we try to describe him we are led also to reflect upon his states of consciousness, his capacity for recollection, for reflection, for *attention*, for the deep intuitive syntheses of moral vision. 'The layer of unpremeditatedness, freedom from intentions, on which alone intentions flourish.' (Minima Moralia 150) Such ideas may be *placed* by philosophy though they cannot be systematized or set up as a clear definition" (Murdoch 1992, 378).

History matters and locates an individual in a time and place where the process of autonomy, authenticity, and rebellion varies. As mentioned above in the discussion of autonomy from ideology, at some times and in some places there is a call for opposition and destruction but so too there can be situations which call for solidarity and constructive energy. Protest in particular must be unencumbered by ideology and Adorno spent a significant part of his teaching career confronting his students who wanted to be part of ongoing protests in the streets.

> Existentialist ethics appears to many of you to be advanced. Motivated by its protest against the administered world, it made an absolute of spontaneity and of the human subject in so far as it has not been co-opted. That is the error of this ethics since precisely because this spontaneity lacks reflexivity and is separated from objective reality, objectivity re-enters it, just as Sartre has ended up placing himself at the service of Communist ideology (Adorno Lecture Seventeen 1963, in 2000, 176).

This flexibility is a defining difference between the types of formalized philosophies, like a categorical imperative or nihilism for example, and

Adorno's perspective. He argued that flexibility and the "contingent aspects of the world which are lost in the Idealist totality" (Murdoch 1992, 376), was the natural outcome of reflection. The evolving authentic individual needs experience, impulsiveness, and thought without the dominance of one over the other. Reflection of conditions, process, and consequences in terms of the individual but also the impact on social, economic and political systems is the key characteristic to guide this balance between experience and thought.

Part of Morgan's autonomy is his willingness to bear the weight of each situation and his refusal to entangle anyone else into his crises. Prior to accepting the deal to carry three outlaws aboard his boat he recognizes that he has selected a path with more dangerous criminal activities. On the one hand he acknowledges his feeling that he has no choice: "I don't want to fool with it but what choice have I got? They don't give you any choice now" (105). The government has seized his boat and so he needs to find a big deal to bring in a significant amount of money. However, he then accepts his decision without blame, without consultation, and without complaint. In recognizing and preserving his autonomy, he limits relationships and constructs independence as much as possible. Rather than a responsibility to protect his loved ones from worry and his absence, Morgan's claims are strong assertions about independence. They reinforce the perspective of the autonomous individual but also importantly, he consciously and actively cultivates his autonomy: "It would be better alone, anything is better alone" (105). Good or bad, risky or not, he chooses to seek the solitary path. The solitary path means taking responsibility for the here and now regardless of the particularities that could place blame or suggest Fate. Rather than slipping into the pattern of blaming others for his problems and predicaments he embraces each situation as a transitory experience for his wrestle within himself. In the first glimpse of Harry Morgan, he has been cheated by a client who spent over two weeks on his boat fishing. Mr. Johnson leaves the hotel without paying for eighteen days of Morgan's fishing charter. Rather than curse the injustice, he assumes responsibility for trusting Mr. Johnson and accepts the outcome as a fairly reasonable consequence of his own decision. Rather than feeling like he has been manipulated, he can absorb the experience into himself. It may be more painful but it is more authentic.

In a similarly reflective scene, during the final moments of his life, Morgan contemplates whether he went far enough with his pursuit of autonomy and an independent life. Whereas those who *have* in the novel longed for affirmation, more money, and greater power over others, Morgan longs for more simplicity and more autonomy. As Harry heaves in pain on the deck of the boat, he contemplates the 'better' life running a filling station. For him, and in retrospect, a filling station wouldn't bring the unlucky business of smuggling. For Harry, the predicament comes because of his own poor judgment. His meditation focuses on the path of life not taken and the missed possibility of an even more autonomous simple life without so many dependencies and contingencies.

Harry's reflectivity contrasts with the delusion of the *haves* depicted in the vignettes at the end of the novel.

> "The grain broker concludes his meditation: "He would not need to worry about what he had done to other people, nor what had happened to them due to him, nor how they'd ended . . . Somebody had to lose and only suckers worried. No he would not have to think of them nor of the by-products of successful speculation. You win; somebody's got to lose, and only suckers worry" (237–238)

The final vignette captures Dorothy Hollis in her self-justification for adultery and hypocrisy as she concludes her meditation by reminding herself how lovely she is: "I don't care. What difference does it make? It isn't wrong if I don't feel badly. And I don't" (246).

Hemingway and Adorno express the importance of feeling the range of emotions in reflectivity, perhaps most especially pain, as a necessary part of the human condition.

> Adorno chided everybody, and his positive and passionately held view is not easy to formulate. He expounds what may be called a new philosophy of consciousness. His philosophy lives, dangerously but also fruitfully, in proximity to an ascetic puritanical moral rage, an attachment to some items in the structure and vocabulary of Marxism, and a feeling that human suffering is the only important thing and makes nonsense of everything else" (Murdoch 1992, 373).

The descriptions of Morgan's consciousness unfolding are not met with warmth and joyful resolution. Liberation does not remove sadness or pain, nor does it necessarily bring peace. Reflectivity is not about letting go of pain but bringing that pain into our identities. Pain in particular affirms our very unique individual identities: "to consider suffering is to consider what is individual, private, unintelligible and contingent" (Murdoch 1992, 374). If we become autonomous, authentic, and reflective selves we are able to admit all of our potentialities[4] and we are able to accept all of our past struggles as necessary pieces of our uniqueness. While Hemingway's vignettes show those who hide from their pains, Morgan's accepts it all—at least for the reader.

IV   THE REBEL IN TODAY'S DEMOCRACY

Critics have recognized the adaptability of democratic capitalism in terms of absorbing diverse opposition and competing ideologies. There are many contemporary empirical examples of revolutionary ideologies directly opposed to democratic capitalism being successfully incorporated into the institutionalized competitive structure of democracy. From Clause Offe's theoretical analysis of collective mobilization in industrial relations, to Adorno's own criticisms of nationalist liberation movements in the 1960s (Adorno and Horkheimer 1999 [1972] in Rubin 2002, 183), to more recent empirical commentary on post-Communist societies it is clear that transformative ideologies may be more likely to transform into the current institutional system rather than fundamentally transforming the system.

Even if revolutionary movements remain apart from the existing power structure, Hemingway and Adorno guide us to recognize the likelihood of parallel institutions within a revolutionary movement and institutions with the similar contamination of power and corruption. Ultimately, if there can be change it will be individual and not likely to emerge within the public or political sphere. Hemingway reveals the individual process of liberation, which often depends upon oppression as grist for transformation. In this way, politics can be a source for individual change but cannot be the manifestation of liberation. Adorno focuses attention on literature and art as both the likely catalyst for individual transformation and the likely solace for the liberated individual:

> the model of aesthetic education, inherited from Kant and Schiller, which located opportunities for social progress in the aesthetic rather than in the political sphere . . . Against this background, the strategy of maintaining an autonomous theoretical discourse about the possibility of resistance, while focusing on emancipator moments in philosophy and art, appears less as a political failing than as a much more plausible stance than the direct political action of the student movement and the terrorism in which it quickly collapsed (Berman 2002, 114).

As art, Hemingway's oeuvre presents a vision of humanity struggling within institutionalized power and transactional values. The central characters are trapped and emblematic of the more general societal malaise. Many of them emerge as rebels, often raging against a system that brings meaningless interactions and perpetual angst. Their actions are unpredictable but they share the effort to find autonomy and authenticity amidst the hypocrisy. They are not political insofar as they often turn away from the political system as a solution.

However, thinking about Hemingway through the lens of Adorno reminds us that the consequences of their actions remain very political—sometimes within the novel but more importantly, beyond the novel and for the reader. Amidst the web of institutional seduction, political change must come necessarily from far outside the political realm.

For Said, politics and literature were related through an Adornian paradox: "In itself, the investigation of literature will certainly neither determine an election nor end exploitation and cruelty. But it might encourage the deeper tension and irreconcilability between the search for knowledge and political oppression and injustice ..." (Rubin 2002, 185).

If the collective did engage in these individual transformations it is not clear what the political manifestation could be. Neither writer revealed the particularities or potentialities of politics defined by liberated selves. For Adorno (and Hemingway), liberation was an individual exercise that meant continually carving personal space away from the public realm (Berman 2002). An individual in search of autonomy and authenticity often benefitted from confronting the injustices of the political world but not through formalized channels of participation. Institutionalized opposition manipulated motivation toward a new but parallel power structure and revolutionary ideologies similarly crushed individual autonomy.

As theorist and novelist, their creative arts do not call for a particular political change and they do not call on individuals to follow a particular path of rebellion. Instead both authors invoke like-minded subjectivity (Huhn 2004, 6) from their readers. Neither wrote a manifesto and both offered evidences of empathy for very contrasting political systems and both were taken up by sharply contrasting ideologies. It is only in the context of their overwhelming advocacy for the individual to confront and push away from the formalized politics of power, but also the everyday politics of power, that the apparent inconsistencies cohere into a shared perspective of politics and the place of the individual in political systems. Hemingway's hero rebels are aware of the ubiquitous inequalities and competitions, and like Harry Morgan, they self-consciously push to the realms outside of politics and the legal system. Morgan exhibits Adorno's ideal characteristics of the liberated self—the rebel—through his autonomy, authenticity, and reflectivity continually grinding against politicism, but finding liberation necessarily apart from the public sphere of formal political participation.

NOTES

1. When I was graduate student Norman Schofield directed my readings and our conversations included Theodor Adorno as well as many of the Frankfurt thinkers. He remains an inspiration as a 'rebel' academic—autonomous, authentic, and always reflective.
2. "According to document released under the Freedom of Information Act, as early as 1935 the Institute for Social Research (or the Frankfurt School as it has come to be known) was the object of a widespread surveillance operation by the Federal Bureau of Investigation. Almost without exception nearly every member of the Frankfurt School in exile—Theodor Adorno, Max Horkheimer, Herbert Marcuse, Henryk Grossman, Leo Lowenthal, Karl Wittfogel, Frederick Pollock, Franz Neumann, and several others—were policed and investigated; their mail and telegrams were opened and

read; their telephones were wiretapped, their apartment burgled; their private affairs scrutinized; their income taxes audited, all for the slightest sign of any radical left-wing political activity" (Rubin 2002, 173).
3. According to Berman "Adorno's political agenda . . . insists on maintaining that autonomy: of art, of theory, and the individual, for only the autonomous subject has the capacity to resist the violent collective" (2002, 123).
4. "Here mimesis in Adorno becomes the name for the projection and reprojection of subjectivity, of an unfolding of aspects. Mimesis is not then the copying or imitation of what has been but the continuity from reflection to reflection, of the multiple aspects and movements of subjective possibility" (Huhn 2004, 7).

WORKS CITED

Adorno, Theodor. "Lecture Sixteen 23 July 1963." In *Problems of Moral Philosophy*, edited by Thomas Schroder, 157–166. Translated by Rodney Livingstone. Stanford: Stanford University Press, 2000.

———. "Lecture Seventeen 25 July 1963." In *Problems of Moral Philosophy*, edited by Thomas Schroder 167–176. Translated by Rodney Livingstone. Stanford: Stanford University Press, 2000.

———. *Negative Dialectics*. Translated by E. B. Ashon. London: Routledge, 1973 [Originally published as *Jargon der Eigentlichkiet: Zur Keutsche Ideologie* (Frankfurt: Suhrkamp, 1964).

———. "Society." Translated by Fredric Jameson. *Salmagundi* 3 (10–11) (1969–1970): (Fall-Winter). Originally published as "Stichwort Gesellschaft", *Evangelisches Staaatslexikon* (Stuttgart: publisher unknown, 1967).

———. "Resignation." Translated by Wes Blomster. In *Telos*, 35 (1978): 165–169.
Adorno, Theodor and Max Horkheimer. *Dialectic of Enlightenment*. Translated by John Cumming. New York: Continuum, 1999 [1972].

———. Adorno, Theodor. *Minima Moralia Reflections from Damaged Life*. London: Verso, 1974 [1951].

Berman, Russell. "Adorno's Politics." In *Adorno: A Critical Reader*, edited by Nigel Gibson and Andrew Rubin, 110–131. Oxford: Blackwell Publishers, 2002.

Bowie, Andrew. "Adorno, Heidegger, and the Meaning of Music." In *The Cambridge Companion to Adorno*, edited by Tom Huhn, 248–278. Cambridge: Cambridge University Press, 2004.

Cook, Deborah. "Theodor W. Adorno: An introduction." In *Theodor Adorno Key Concepts*, edited by Deborah Cook, 3–20. Scarborough, North Yorkshire: Acumen, 2008.

Claussen, Detlev. *Theodor Adorno: One Last Genius*. Translated by Rodney Livingstone. Cambridge, MA: Harvard University Press, 2008.

Freyenhagen, Fabian. "Moral philosophy." In *Theodor Adorno: Key Concepts*, edited by Deborah Cook, 99–114. Scarborough, North Yorkshire: Acumen, 2008.

Gibson, Nigel and Andrew Rubin. "Introduction: Adorno and the Autonomous Intellectual." In *Adorno: A Critical Reader*, edited by Nigel Gibson and Andrew Rubin, 1–26. Oxford: Blackwell Publishers, 2002.

Hemingway, Ernest. *To Have and Have Not*. New York: Scribner, 2003.

Huhn, Tom. " Introduction: Thoughts Beside Themselves." In *The Cambridge Companion to Adorno*, edited by Tom Huhn, 1–18. Cambridge: Cambridge University Press, 2004.

Kraushaar, Wolfgang, ed. *Frankfurter Schule and Studentenbewegung. Von der Flaschenpost zum Molotowcocktail* 1946 bis 1995. 3 vols. Hamburg: Rogner and Bernhard, 1998.

Murdoch, Iris. *Metaphysics as a Guide to Morals.* New York: Penguin Books, 1992.

O'Connor, Brian. *Adorno's Negative Dialectic Philosophy and the Possibility of Critical Rationality.* Cambridge, MA: MIT Press, 2004.

Rubin, Andrew. "The Adorno Files." In *Adorno: A Critical Reader*, edited by Nigel Gibson and Andrew Rubin, 172–190. Oxford: Blackwell Publishers, 2002.

Said, Edward W. *Representations of the Intellectual.* New York: Vintage, 1994.

Tettlebaum, Marianne. "Political Philosophy." In *Theodor Adorno Key Concepts*, edited by Deborah Cook, 131–146. Scarborough, North Yorkshire: Acumen, 2008.

Contributors

Conklin, David Winston (Ph.D. MIT) is Professor at the University of Western Ontario, Richard Ivey School of Business where he teaches courses in the Environment of Business and Business in a Political World. Professor Conklin has taught in many countries, in Economics and Political Science Departments as well as in Business Schools. His ten books focus on the interface between corporations and public policies and include Soviet Profit Reforms, and Comparative Economic Systems.

Curtis, William (Ph.D. Duke University) is Assistant Professor at The University of Portland. His research interests lie in contemporary liberal theory, modern political philosophy, constitutional law and theory. He is currently working on a book about Richard Rorty's political philosophy and literary criticism. His publications include "Members Only? Critical Response to Herr's 'Defense of Nonliberal Nationalism,'" *Political Theory* 35, 3 (June 2007) and "Liberals and Pluralists: Charles Taylor vs. John Gray," *Contemporary Political Theory* (February 2007).

Frederking, Lauretta Conklin (Ph.D. Washington University) is Associate Professor at The University of Portland. Her research interests include politics and literature, as well as comparative immigration policy. Currently she is writing a book on comparative institutional responses to terrorism. Her recent publications include *Economic and Political Integration in Immigrant Neighbourhoods: Trajectories of Virtuous and Vicious Cycles* (2007). Her recent publications within politics and literature include "Demystifying Social Capital through Zola's Germinal" and an article on Irish Murdoch's The Bell: "*The Bell: Our Symbols as Bridges between Sacred and Secular.*"

Hamann, Kerstin (Ph.D. Washington University) is Professor of Political Science at the University of Central Florida. Her research interests lie in Spanish politics, comparative political economy (Western Europe), and the Scholarship of Teaching and Learning. Her recent books include *Parties, Elections, and Policy Reforms in Western Europe: Voting for*

Social Pacts (with John Kelly), *Assessment in Political Science* (co-edited with Michelle Deardorff and John Ishiyama), and *Democracy and Institutional Development: Spain in Comparative Theoretical Perspective* (co-edited with Bonnie Field). Her articles have appeared in journals such as *Comparative Political Studies, British Journal of Industrial Relations, Industrial and Labor Relations Review, European Journal of Industrial Relations, South European Society and Politics, Journal of Political Science Education*, and *PS: Political Science & Politics*.

Mansfield, Harvey (Ph.D. Harvard University) is William R. Kenan, Jr. Professor of Government, Harvard University. He is the author or translator of many books, including Tocqueville's *Democracy in America* and Machiavelli's *The Prince*, and a frequent contributor to *The Wall Street Journal, The Weekly Standard,* and *Times Literary Supplement.*

Prud'Homme, Joseph (Ph.D. Princeton University) is Assistant Professor of Political Science at Washington College and Director of the Institute for Religion, Politics, and Culture of the Goldstein Program in Public Affairs. He has published numerous articles in the areas of political theory, public law, religion and politics, and literature.

Rudy, Sayres (Ph.D. Columbia University) is Visiting Professor of Politics at Hampshire College. His research interests include political theory and revolution from a comparative perspective. His publications include "Pros and Cons: Americanism against Islamism in the War on Terror," *Muslim World*, 97:1 (Jan 2007) and "Global Books and Local Stories: Theory and Anti-Theory in Social Research," in *Identities* [Institute for Human Sciences (Vienna) 1998].

Zuckert, Catherine (Ph.D. University of Chicago) Catherine Zuckert is Nancy Reeves Dreux Professor of Political Science and Editor-in-Chief of *The Review of Politics* at the University of Notre Dame. Her books include *Natural Right and the American Imagination: Political Philosophy in Novel Form, Postmodern Platos: Nietzsche, Heidegger, Gadamer, Strauss, Derrida* and, most recently, *Plato's Philosophers: The Coherence of the Dialogues.*

Index

A

Achilles, 11, 91, 95, 96, 97, 99, 100, 101, 102
Across the River and Into the Trees, 5, 16, 28, 43, 46, 48, 81, 156, 167, 169
Adorno, 6, 7, 12, 13, 15, 16, 171–195
aggression, 63, 91, 99, 100, 101, 187; aggressive, 86, 91, 99
Anselmo, 60, 108, 139, 141, 144, 168
apolitical, 7, 14, 15, 59, 173
Aristotle, 4, 101, 102
Authentic, 4–9, 11, 13, 14, 21, 37, 39, 46, 47, 53, 59, 68–9, 161, 172–181, 184–193
autonomous, 4, 7, 76, 181, 182, 184, 186, 190–194; autonomy, 13, 62, 79, 126, 137, 172, 173, 174, 177–194

B

Basque, 60, 135
"Big Two-hearted River," 30, 32, 33, 34, 35, 36, 45, 48
bullfight, 5, 22, 54, 62, 63, 64, 68, 93, 102, 152, 160, 162, 165, 166; bullfighter, 40, 61, 162, 163

C

Camus: Myth of Sisyphus, 8, 15, 111, 112, 125, 126, 128, 150
capitalism, 5, 9, 12, 13, 53, 154, 159, 170–175, 178, 179, 181, 182, 185, 187; democratic capitalism, 5, 154, 172, 174, 191, 192
Catholic, 11, 105–108, 115, 118, 119, 120–124, 127–129, 137, 140
Christ 11, 25, 94, 115, 118, 119, 120–125, 127, 128, 129

civil society, 4, 19, 20, 21, 23, 27, 29, 34, 36, 39, 55, 59
"Clean Well-Lighted Place, A," 46, 105
collective, 3, 12, 27, 87, 152, 162, 163, 166, 175, 182, 183, 185, 187, 193, 194; collective action, 156, 169, 178; collective conditions, 156; collective identity, 185; collective mobilization, 151, 192; collective movement, 186; collective political, 5, 139, 143, 146
communism, 5, 6, 7, 8, 9, 10, 13, 29, 30, 37, 52, 53, 63, 64, 133, 150, 152, 153, 154, 167; communism in *For Whom the Bell Tolls*, 134–150; communism in *To Have and Have Not*, 171–192; communist leadership, 139, 142, 143, 144, 148; communist revolution, 52, 154, 171, 178
contingency, 71, 81, 84, 172
corrupt, 6, 9, 10, 50, 52, 54, 57, 61, 62, 63, 64, 65, 66, 69, 77, 144; corruption, 6, 8, 13, 54, 58, 59, 60, 62, 63, 68, 173, 174, 175, 177, 192
Cuba, 8, 13, 52, 53, 54, 63, 93, 103, 115, 127, 129, 159, 177, 183

D

De Tocqueville, 155, 159, 160, 169
Death, 10, 20, 21, 23, 24, 27, 30, 31, 32, 33, 34, 35, 36, 37, 38, 39, 40, 41, 42, 43, 46, 47, 54, 57, 65, 75, 76, 77, 78, 79, 82, 87, 89, 96, 97, 108, 109, 110, 111, 113, 114, 120, 134, 137, 138, 141, 144, 146, 147, 148, 152, 155, 158, 161, 162, 163, 164,

165, 166, 167, 168, 171, 187, 188
Death in the Afternoon, 22, 34, 35, 40, 41, 44, 46, 48, 69, 71, 93, 102, 103, 136, 158, 162, 166, 169
Declaration of Independence, 19, 22
democracy, 6, 12, 13, 22, 29, 37, 51, 55, 87, 98, 135, 136, 137, 140, 149, 168, 169, 178, 191, 192, 198; democratic, 5, 37, 50, 51, 55, 79, 95, 133, 135, 140, 141, 144, 154, 171, 172, 173, 174, 187, 191, 192
disillusion, 9, 10, 12, 21, 24, 26, 30, 32, 37, 39, 46, 145, 156, 161

E

economy 5, 107, 171, 176, 197; economic determinism, 154, 157; economic forces, 154, 181; economic system, 13, 171, 172
education, 3, 24, 39, 45, 50, 51, 56, 59, 65, 72, 185, 192
Emerson, 6, 7, 15, 16
Enlightenment, 56, 59, 65, 174, 194
ethics, 55, 62, 64, 70, 105, 126, 158, 170, 183, 189; ethics and politics, 50, 51, 52, 87; ethics and *A Farewell to Arms*, 75–89
evil, 15, 40, 75, 89, 120, 122, 136, 145
equality, 20, 35, 50, 52, 55, 151;inequality 27, 57, 58, 72, 156, 174, 175
existentialism, 5, 9, 64, 104, 107, 110, 111, 112, 125, 126, 128; existentialist, 53, 68, 69, 70, 104, 105, 109, 110, 111, 112, 125, 126, 189
exploitation, 5, 47, 154, 174, 179, 184, 193

F

Farewell to Arms, A, 10, 16, 28, 42, 48, 54, 66, 71, 75–90
Fascism, 9, 38, 134, 135, 136, 137, 138, 139, 140, 142, 143, 146, 148, 167; Fascist, 9, 13, 30, 37, 38, 44, 154; Fascists in Spain, 8, 54, 54, 63, 64, 74, 108, 133, 134, 135, 137, 138, 139, 141, 143, 145, 148
feminism, 120; feminist, 4, 11, 90, 99, 100, 106, 125
For Whom the Bell Tolls, 5, 8, 11, 12, 16, 27, 42, 48, 54, 60, 63, 67, 71, 107, 108, 111, 119, 122, 125, 128, 133–150, 158, 161, 167, 169
Foucault, 51, 84, 90
Francis Macomber, 12, 153, 161, 163, 164, 165, 168, 169
Frankfurt school, 8, 173, 177, 185, 193,
Freedom, 3, 6, 50, 51, 55, 56, 58, 136, 140, 142, 148, 181, 189, 193
Friendship, 26, 38, 58, 78, 115, 145, 165, 180, 186

G

God, 10, 11, 22, 23, 28, 31, 43, 66, 75, 95, 96, 97, 102, 104, 105, 112, 119–128, 164
gods, 11, 80, 95, 96, 97, 99, 104, 125, 128
government, 5, 10, 13, 14, 19, 22, 30, 41, 43, 48, 52, 53, 55, 56, 100, 135, 136, 139, 140, 141, 142, 160; government in *To Have and Have Not*, 175, 176, 177, 190; government in U.S. 19, 29, 36
Green Hills of Africa, 8, 16, 53, 71
guerilla, 64

H

Habermas, 55, 71
happiness, 5, 19, 22, 27, 57, 58, 61, 65, 115, 126, 146, 165
Harry Morgan, 4, 13, 54, 63, 154, 155, 159, 171, 174, 175, 176, 178, 179, 180, 181, 182, 183, 184, 186, 187, 188, 190, 191, 193
Havana, 108, 171
Heidegger, 6, 16, 21, 36, 37, 38, 46, 47, 48, 49, 194, 198
hero, 6, 11, 20, 21, 28, 43, 53, 63, 65, 67, 68, 75, 76, 91, 94, 95, 96, 97, 102, 104, 111, 116, 126, 127, 128, 129, 144, 150, 175; Catholic hero, 106, 107, 108, 118, 119, 120, 121, 122, 123, 124, 125; hero in *A Farewell to Arms*, 85, 86, 87; hero as rebel, 154, 155, 158, 162, 163, 193; heroic, 6, 53, 63, 95, 97, 162, 175
Hobbes, 10, 19, 57
Homer, 91, 95, 96, 97, 101, 102
homosexuality, 60, 82
hopelessness, 10, 52, 53, 69, 70, 104

Horkheimer, 14, 173, 192, 193, 194

I

Identity, 4, 5, 8, 9, 10, 11, 64, 76, 77, 80, 81, 82, 83, 136, 138, 159, 171, 180, 182, 184, 185, 186, 188,
ideology, 5, 7, 8, 9, 11, 12, 13, 54, 64, 76, 78, 108, 133, 134, 139, 140, 143, 146, 148, 151, 154, 156, 159, 171, 178, 179, 182, 183, 184, 186, 189,
Iliad, 95, 96, 99, 100, 101, 102
In Our Time, 21, 22, 23, 28, 40, 41, 43, 44, 46, 48, 49, 54, 59, 66, 71, 89, 90, 156
instrumental rationalism, 158
intellectual, 66, 67, 83, 86, 88, 102, 103, 107, 150, 152, 160, 172, 173, 185, 194, 195; anti-intelletualism, 66, 88, 185

J

Jake, 60, 61, 62, 63, 65, 67, 69
Jesus, 22, 23, 28, 113, 114, 115, 119, 121, 122, 123, 127, 128
justice, 10, 22, 28, 30, 50, 51, 52, 54, 55, 56, 64, 68, 69, 100; injustice, 52, 64, 66, 69, 99, 100, 119, 168, 190, 193

K

kamikaze, 168

L

language, 37, 44, 57, 65, 66, 67, 68, 77, 79, 83, 84, 86, 151
law, 6, 19, 22, 24, 25, 26, 27, 31, 39, 41, 55, 63, 78, 87, 91, 100, 102, 142, 176, 184,
Lenin, 47, 140, 153, 157
liberalism, 5, 10, 21, 22, 29, 37, 41, 47, 48, 50, 51, 52, 55, 56, 59, 65, 66, 67, 68, 69, 70, 71, 72, 79, 80, 100, 111, 187
liberation, 3, 5, 6, 13, 178, 185, 191, 192, 193
liberty, 19, 20, 22, 27, 29, 35, 36, 52, 151
love, 12, 20, 23, 26, 28, 39, 41, 42, 45, 57, 58, 60, 62, 64, 65, 67, 93, 104, 108, 109, 118, 120, 167, 188, 190, 191; love in *A Farewell to Arms*, 75, 76, 77, 79, 80, 81, 83, 85, 86, 88; love *For Whom the Bell Tolls*, 134, 136, 137, 145, 146, 147, 148

M

macro, 12, 14, 151, 152, 153, 154, 156, 157, 176
manliness, 4, 5, 10, 11, 28, 91, 92, 93, 94, 95, 96, 97, 98, 99, 100, 102, 103, 106, 107, 120, 128
Marcuse, 173, 177, 193
marriage, 3, 5, 20, 26, 27, 34, 62, 79, 87, 141, 159, 165, 182, 187
Marx, 47, 139, 140, 153, 154, 156, 157, 169, 173, 189, 191
masculinity, 11, 106, 120, 121, 124, 125, 128, 129; masculine, 26, 104, 105, 106, 107, 120, 121, 123,
matadors, 126, 128, 153, 160, 165, 166, 168
metaphysics, 47, 48, 68, 76, 78, 89, 90. 109, 126, 127, 128, 195
micro, 12, 151, 152, 153, 154, 157, 159
moral, 25, 34, 50, 55, 56, 60, 62, 63, 65, 67, 68, 69, 106, 107, 108, 111, 136, 182, 189, 191, 194, 195; moral values, 110, 111, 112; amoral, 65, 84; morality, 6, 10, 11, 23, 34, 57, 58, 62, 69, 71, 75, 76, 77, 78, 81, 86, 87, 88, 90, 182, 184; immoral, 34, 69
Morgan, Harry, 4, 13, 54, 63, 154, 155, 159, 171, 174, 175, 176, 178, 179, 180, 181, 182, 183, 184, 186, 187, 188, 190, 191, 193
myth, 5, 13, 14, 112, 125, 128, 149, 171, 173, 174, 178

N

national, 3, 135, 149; nationalistic, 29, 31, 44; Nationalists, 12, 135, 136, 137, 138, 139, 141, 142, 148; nationalism, 9, 59, 151, 153, 169, 170; National socialism, 47, 177, 192
international, 15, 90, 126, 128, 135, 136, 137, 139, 142, 143, 145, 148, 149, 150
Nature, 27, 30, 36, 37, 38, 39, 40, 46, 47, 54, 56, 58, 60, 61, 62, 64,

65, 76, 77, 81, 82, 92, 115, 117, 127, 154, 166; human nature 4, 6, 20, 159, 177; man over nature 10, 93, 94, 159, 188; nature, back to nature, 4, 10, 21; nature and good life 10, 21; nature and Nick Adams 23, 32, 34, 35; nature and politics 4, 10, 24, 36, 59, 64, 78, 101; nature and religion 8, 11, 22; state of nature 19, 20, 21, 57, 59,
New left, 173, 185
Nick Adams, 4, 16, 19, 20, 21, 23, 24, 25, 26, 27, 28, 30, 31, 32, 33, 34, 35, 36, 39, 40, 42, 43, 45, 46, 48, 54, 59, 66, 69, 155, 156
Nietzsche, 23, 41, 43, 47, 48, 78, 88, 90, 126, 128, 173
nihilism, 5, 8, 9, 21, 38, 44, 45, 47, 48, 66, 70, 76, 77, 78, 79, 104, 107, 108, 109, 110, 112, 173, 189; nihilistic 46, 54, 76, 77, 78, 79, 87, 88, 105, 107, 108, 109, 111

O
Oak Park, 39, 111
Odysseus, 96, 97; Odyssey, 97, 103
Old Man and the Sea, The, 103, 107, 108, 115, 118, 126, 127, 128, 129, 166, 169
On writing, 34, 41

P
Pablo, 54, 61, 64, 137, 145, 147, 149, 153, 161, 168
participation, 4, 5, 6, 12, 14, 134, 139, 146, 168, 171, 172, 177, 193
Pilar, 60, 61, 64, 108, 119, 123, 138, 141, 145, 149, 161, 168
Plato, 43, 50, 102, 103
political institutions, 3, 5, 13, 21, 52, 133, 153, 178
political science, 12, 15, 126, 128, 133, 171, 172
power, 4, 5, 14, 58, 64, 70, 96, 100, 101, 119, 120, 123, 150, 170, 181, 185; power of individual, 11, 13, 91, 94, 114, 116, 120, 124, 160, 190; power politics, 6, 19, 35, 52, 55, 56, 98, 135, 137, 143, 148, 171, 172- 179, 188, 192, 193; power divine, 23, 28, 97, 115, 151
Promise Keepers, 11, 106, 121, 123, 124, 127, 128

propaganda, 59, 152, 156, 177

R
rational, 3, 12, 14, 52, 56, 68, 69, 79, 97, 99, 101, 157, 158, 159, 163; irrational, 56, 88, 99; rationality, 12, 68, 79, 97, 98, 101, 157, 158, 170, 195; rational choice, 3, 157, 158, 159, 160; rationalization, 68
rebel, 3, 4, 5, 6, 7, 8, 9, 10, 11, 12, 13, 15, 53, 69, 123, 134, 147, 148, 153, 154, 156, 157, 158, 159, 161, 162, 163, 169, 171, 172, 178, 179, 180, 182, 183, 184, 189, 191, 192, 193
rebellion, 3, 4, 5, 6, 7, 8, 9, 11, 12, 13, 14, 15, 19, 35, 38, 46, 68, 87, 133, 134, 135, 136, 138, 139, 143, 145, 146, 147, 148, 150, 151, 153, 154, 156, 157, 159, 160, 161, 163, 165, 172, 181, 189, 193
redemption, 54, 61, 65, 115, 116, 117, 122, 125, 129
reflection, 5, 66, 76, 109, 120, 127, 146, 173, 174, 180, 181, 189, 190, 194; reflective, 13, 34, 52, 67, 69, 79, 83, 93, 119, 119, 143, 172, 178, 179, 185, 190, 191, 193; unreflective, 57, 59
religion, 8, 30, 55, 56, 94, 98, 104, 105, 108, 125, 127, 128, 129, 135, 141, 151, 174
Republic, 12, 29, 59, 108, 133, 134, 135, 136, 139, 140, 141, 142, 143, 148, 148, 149; Republicans, 42, 52, 53, 134, 136, 138, 139, 141, 142, 143, 144, 145, 147, 148; Plato's Republic, 43, 50
revolution, 5, 12, 13, 30, 44, 55, 68, 100, 141, 149, 150, 160, 162, 163, 167, 168, 169, 170, 172, 177, 183; American Revolution, 151; revolution in Cuba, 13, 54, 63; revolution in Spain, 135, 140, revolution theories, 6, 12, 30, 44, 151, 153–158, 169, 178
Revolutionist, The, 12, 29, 30, 44, 151, 152, 153, 154, 156, 160, 166, 167, 169
revolutionary, 5, 12, 33, 35, 44, 52, 54, 63, 98, 154, 155, 158, 159, 160, 162, 167, 171, 172, 173, 177,

178, 182, 183, 184, 191, 192, 193; revolutionist, 12, 29, 44, 151, 153, 154, 155, 156, 157, 158, 159, 160, 161, 163, 165, 166, 167, 168
rights, 3, 10, 12, 16, 19, 20, 21, 22, 23, 24, 25, 26, 27, 29, 35, 37, 39, 49, 55, 87, 96, 97, 100, 141, 147, 148, 149, 169
righteous, 9, 54, 120, 174, 182
Robert Jordan, 54, 63, 65, 67, 108, 109, 110, 111, 112, 119, 120, 123, 133, 134, 137, 143, 150, 155, 167, 168
Robert Wilson, 163
Rorty, 6, 10, 50, 51, 52, 55, 56, 70, 71
Rousseau, 6, 10, 20, 52, 56, 57, 58, 59, 60, 61, 62, 63, 64, 65, 66, 69, 71, 72

S

Santiago, 11, 54, 61, 65, 92, 116, 117, 118, 155
self-reliance, 6, 7
"Short Happy Life of Francis Macomber, The," 12, 153, 163, 169
Sun Also Rises, The, 31, 44, 48, 54, 60, 61, 62, 67, 69, 71, 89
society, 5, 6, 7, 8, 10, 15, 27, 29, 31, 44, 50, 56, 57, 62, 70, 71, 91, 97, 98, 99, 100, 101, 102, 128, 133, 140, 141, 143, 144, 151, 154, 156, 169, 170, 175, 176, 179, 182, 184, 185, 187, 194; civil, 4, 19, 20, 21, 23, 27, 29, 34, 36, 39, 55, 59; liberal society, 51, 52, 55, 69, 100; modern society, 58, 59, 60, 64; solidarity, 9, 14, 71, 115, 150, 153, 156, 175, 176, 177, 178, 180, 183, 184, 186, 187, 189
Spain, 8, 53, 93, 108, 134, 135, 136, 137, 141, 142, 143, 144, 148, 149, 165, 167
spiritual, 76, 83, 105, 107, 113, 115, 117, 118, 141, 147
spirituality, 125, 127, 129
spiritually, 8, 57

suicide, 12, 25, 46, 111, 112, 160, 168, 169, 170, 184, 187

T

terrorism, 152, 169, 170, 183, 192, 197; terrorist, 12, 159, 160, 168, 169
theodicy, 11, 75, 76, 77, 78, 79, 87, 88, 90
To Have and Have Not, 4, 5, 8, 12, 13, 16, 53, 54, 63, 71, 154, 158, 159, 171, 172, 173, 174, 178, 182, 183, 194
"Today is Friday," 11, 107, 113, 115, 119, 121, 122, 125, 129
tragedy, 87, 88, 117, 149; tragic, 3, 33, 42, 49, 68, 69, 70, 75, 77, 87, 118, 119, 126, 128, 187, 188

V

violence, 26, 38, 54, 60, 64, 76, 79, 89, 116, 122, 145, 151, 152, 157, 158, 159

W

war, 3, 5, 9, 10, 12, 19, 20, 21, 22, 24, 27, 28, 29, 31, 32, 33, 35, 36, 37, 38, 39, 42, 43, 46, 48, 52, 59, 60, 64, 65, 66, 70, 75, 76, 77, 78, 79, 80, 81, 82, 84, 85, 86, 87, 88, 89, 95, 120, 122, 133, 134, 136, 137, 138, 139, 141, 142, 143, 144, 145, 146, 147, 148, 149, 150, 151, 153, 160, 165, 167, 168, 169, 170, 172, 176; civil war, 9, 12, 52, 108, 111, 133, 134, 135, 136, 137, 140, 143, 145, 147, 148, 149, 150, 153
warriors, 12, 95, 108, 152, 153, 157, 159, 160, 163, 164, 165, 166, 167, 168
Winner Take Nothing, 28, 43, 48

Z

Zeus, 95